Praise for *Your Place or Mine?*

'...wley uses an exciting, innovative approach to identify and
scribe the cultural transformations of contemporary Ireland.
Mixing personal memories with sociologically informed
debate, she provides an insightful and imaginative explanation
how Ireland has combined the local with the global.'

**Professor Tom Inglis, School of Sociology, University
College Dublin**

'This book makes a substantial contribution to understanding the
changing nature of Irish society. It provides a fresh and distinctive
approach to the subject by combining sociological perspectives and
personal reflections. The result is a unique insight on the interconnections between identity and place and a stimulating book that
deserves to be read by a wide audience.'

**Chris Curtin, Professor of Political Science and Sociology,
National University of Ireland, Galway**

Praise for Ethel Crowley's previous book, *Land Matters: Power
Struggles in Rural Ireland*

'A landmark study ... we could hardly ask for a better introduc-
to contemporary rural Ireland, with all of its subtleties and
...dictions.'

**Dr Chris Eipper, Department of Anthropology, LaTrobe
University, Australia**

'...his brave and significant book, Ethel Crowley investigates the
...l and psychological changes in rural Ireland since accession to
EEC. ... She brings a sociological scalpel to policies, structures
directives in a way that lays them open to the light: for sheer
...le information and reference, her book is invaluable. It is its
...ism, however, that makes it memorable.'

Michael Viney, *The Irish Times*

D1613138

Your Place or Mine?

Community and Belonging in 21st Century Ireland

Ethel Crowley

ORPEN PRESS

Orpen Press
Lonsdale House
Avoca Avenue
Blackrock
Co. Dublin
Ireland

e-mail: info@orpenpress.com
www.orpenpress.com

Paperback ISBN: 978-1-871305-98-2
ePub ISBN: 978-1-909518-44-5
Kindle ISBN: 978-1-909518-45-2

Printed in Ireland by Gemini International Ltd

Dedication

To the children and staff of the Hope Foundation, who expand and redefine the meaning of home, family and community.

Acknowledgements

Thanks to all at Orpen Press who helped with the production of this book: Elizabeth Brennan was the commissioning editor who initially accepted the manuscript, Eileen O'Brien looked after the cover design, and Jennifer Thompson edited and polished the text with both a very insightful mind and a meticulous eye. One is lucky indeed to be allowed the luxury of indulging one's whims and interests in print and to work with such professional publishers.

Thanks is also due to the Arts Faculty Research Fund at NUI Cork, which helped to defray some of the costs involved in the research for this book.

I also thank all of those friends and acquaintances in my life who have provided inspiration and encouragement of various kinds over the years. My sister Paula, my brother Michael and my mother, Kay, are always interested in and supportive of my work. My biggest supporter is 'himself' – Jim MacLaughlin – whose fabulously anarchic spirit ensures that there is never a dull moment in our life together and for whom debate and social critique is no less crucial to survival than oxygen itself.

Table of Contents

Table of Contents

Introduction

A very inebriated young male student was curled up in a foetal ball of Mammy-knit jumper and raggedy-arsed jeans on the footpath outside Cork's famous Lennox's chip shop. To test his lucidity, and to check whether I needed to call him an ambulance, I crouched down and asked him the question, 'Where are you from?' From his compromised position on the pavement, and from the depths of his drunken consciousness, he answered, 'Well, I'm from Clare originally, actually, but I'm staying with my friend on College Road.' Even in his half-dead state he felt the need to tell me his seed, breed and generation. This said a lot about this young man's umbilical sense of connection to his place of origin, the same region from which world-famous fiddler Martin Hayes absorbed what he calls 'the lonesome note'. I wonder if that dreamy student is in his beloved Clare now, with all that has passed in this little country since then.

'Where are you from?' This is usually the first question we are asked when we meet a new person in Ireland. It is not always easy to answer. My partner, with his lilting Donegal accent, is often asked how he is enjoying his holidays in Cork, despite his having lived there for over 25 years and knowing every back street in the city. When asked this question by a young shop assistant, for example, his favourite answer is that he has lived in Cork longer than they have been on this

earth. Cork is now his home, despite his still feeling a strong
connection to his treasured Inishowen peninsula. These kinds
of mixed-up, divided loyalties are at the heart of twenty-first
century social life.

Taking into account such complexities, this book is a set
of reflections on identity and finding one's place in the world.
Is there a place for the traditional forms of connection to
home, family, community and locality in the world as we now
know it, where people have a myriad of options for identity formation? What are the various ways that we relate to
these different social links? We all live with these issues in
our everyday lives, but I want to go beyond common-sense
perceptions and take a long, hard look at them instead.

A key idea I wish to employ here is that of 'comfort zone'.
This phrase, which has become a cliché in the business world,
is to be completely reformulated here in order to enable us
to think about our sense of belonging and our understanding of our place in the world. Our comfort zone is where
we feel happy, at ease, secure and unchallenged. It is also the
zone in which we feel a sense of connection with the place
we are in and/or the people we are among. The advantage
of this zone is that it makes life pleasant and easily liveable.
However, staying within the core of our comfort zone and not
pushing its boundaries may mean that we risk stagnation and
impeded growth. To push its boundaries means that we are
growing, learning and developing, even though we may experience discomfort, nervousness or even fear. In these days of
recession, numerous people are forced to do this by economic
circumstances when they lose their jobs and have difficulty
paying the mortgage. They may have to emigrate to a new
country, retrain and change jobs, or try to adapt to a lower
standard of living on social welfare.

People's attempts to negotiate the parameters of their comfort zones are determined by their personal and social resources, which they mobilise within the context of the society in which they live. The place in which we are born; the economic times into which we are born, both at global and national levels; the social class into which we are born; the education we receive; our personality; our physical bodily makeup; our role models; and our very particular loves and interests, all affect our ability to shape for ourselves the nature of our comfort zone. When it comes to examining the limits of our comfort zone we need to be cognisant, on the one hand, of the influence of social structures and broader social, economic and political life and, on the other hand, of the individual power that each person can exert over their own lives. The membrane that forms the outer limits of our comfort zone is very flexible, changing dramatically throughout the course of our lives. It is also permeable, with social, cultural, economic and political influences from the outside world seeping through. It is productive to think of our comfort zone not as having some essential 'natural' essence, but as the result of the choices we make and the series of ongoing processes of change we experience as we go through life.

Such choices can have a profound impact. For example, two people may grow up with the exact same life chances and opportunities presented to them. One person may be happy not to challenge themself too much, living a predictable life, whereas the other may constantly challenge themself, pushing at the edges of their comfort zone. Sometimes, perhaps, there might be just one thing that changes everything in our lives – a connection with a person, place, music, language or culture that is apparently inexplicable, but just *is*. Our perspective on where we belong may change dramatically throughout life, as we grow up and away, lose some loved ones and gain others along the way, leave some places and adopt others, forget old things and learn new things – all to help us gain a foothold in the world we are living in right now.

In exploring our sense of identity and belonging, the logical place to start in Chapter 1 is with the important anchoring idea of 'home'. For most people, home is completely synonymous with our comfort zone, where we are at our happiest. Even at the level of the language we use to discuss our sense of belonging, it is clear that one of the most emotionally powerful words in the English language is 'home'. However, the ideal and the reality often do not match. People may be forced from their homes – bullied, bulldozed or burnt out – or they may choose to go freely, feeling constrained by the limitations of domesticity.

Nothing, even an apparently obvious idea like 'home', makes sense without the set of meanings placed upon it by people in real social contexts. It seems obvious that 'home' and 'family', as the old song goes, 'go together like a horse and carriage'. It is not that cosy a picture for many people, though, such as those who suffer abuse in the home. Furthermore, the social meanings attached to 'family' also vary from one society to another. For example, it is common for grown-up, professional Indian men and women to have their marriages arranged for them by their well-meaning parents while, in the Western world, gay partnerships form the basis of millions of families. When it comes to the ties that bind, the results depend upon who does the binding. There is no such thing as a 'normal' family – everything is, indeed, relative.

Outside the family unit, the next level of connection we experience is that of community, as explored in Chapter 2. The language we use has a powerful impact on how we view it. There are at least two ways that people use the term 'community': to describe the place where they live or to refer to a wider sense of belonging to a particular social group. They might say, for example, 'we have a great sense of community where we live,' or they might say that they belong to a particular community, such as the Protestant community, the gay community or the Asian community. Each of these socially-constructed meanings has very different connotations, and Chapter 2 teases apart the threads of these meanings. Whether attached to a particular place or to a group of people, the word 'community' speaks to our need for a sense of connection with others, a feeling that we are not completely on our own in the world. It gives us a sense of belonging when we feel part of a community.

Sociological analysis of this key idea goes back many decades, as the means in which people form group associations has been a source of endless fascination for analysts of human behaviour in society. A major idea explored in this chapter is the distinction between people's reliance upon physical, place-based communities and the elective forms of community that are increasingly available to us now, because of either physical travelling or virtual travelling on the Internet. It is often assumed these days that community is dying in the Western world and that people are becoming more detached from each other. I suggest here that this is not the case, but that we just need to be more perceptive and analytical about the exact nature of the social changes around us in this regard. I view community more as a *process* created by active human agents, than as a static, idealised *state* that has been preserved in ideological aspic.

In Chapter 3 I explore how best to understand the process of globalisation that underpins so much of our social reality. It can affect how we view our localities, our own connection with them and, hence, our sense of identity in relation to those places. With all of the focus that there now is on the technological shrinking of the globe, to what extent do the places in which we live have an impact on our lives? Each place needs to be seen now in a global context, connected to other places economically, socially, culturally, politically and, above all, ecologically. Wherever our home is, it needs to be conceptualised as an open entity, shaped by forces that stretch well beyond its physical borders. Globalisation leads some people to feel alienated in contemporary society. The British-born, but extraordinarily multicultural, author Pico Iyer says:

> What is changing is the speed at which the world is turning, and sometimes I feel as if I'm going through the existential equivalent of that game I used to play as a child, in which I'd spin myself around and around where I stood, until I collapsed in a dizzy heap on the floor.[1]

Equally, globalisation facilitates human connection for those who revel in the global links facilitated by information technology, integrating it into the heart of their comfort zone.

Our communities and the places in which we live serve as the context for our development as humans, but the process of building our personal and sexual identities is addressed in Chapter 4. Analysis of the process of identity formation, or *identification*, goes to the heart of our relationship with our surrounding society. We identify, both consciously and subconsciously, with particular places, people and groups for social and cultural reasons. We 'perform' our identities, in that, whether consciously or not, we decide to look, dress, speak and behave in certain ways to build a picture that we think matches our chosen identity. When people produce a reasonable account of their 'true' identity, this is because of their success in persuading themselves and others of this 'truth' about themselves. Some people can exercise a lot of personal autonomy in this regard, and others cannot. The question of the amount of choice people have is an important one, and the concept of *individualisation* is integrated into the discussion. The major focus in this chapter is upon sexual identities, and people's attempts to create healthy sexual selves in the context of Irish society. Is secularisation having a major impact on Irish people's sexual lives? Are we now free to define our own comfort zone in this regard?

Chapter 5 discusses the effects of migration upon peoples' identities. Ireland is better known as a source of emigrants than as a destination for immigrants. However, both of these social functions have been visible in Ireland for some time now. There is a particular focus in this chapter upon the forms of cultural hybridity that arise from migration patterns. These are evident in cultural forms like music and literature, but also in the social geography of both urban and rural areas. The fascinating forms of mixing that have emerged from hybridisation have created exciting topics for further research. Narrow, exclusionary forms of national identity can no longer be deemed acceptable, as multiculturalism creates new opportunities for openness and inclusiveness. We all have both 'roots' and 'routes' as part of our identities, in one way or another. These are 'coexistent in culture, and both [are] subject to transformation in global modernity.'[2] And just because we integrate 'routes' into our comfort zones does not negate the need for 'roots', which are not, after all, only for vegetables.

Chapter 6 is an exploration of the idea of cosmopolitanism. This idea often has elitist undertones, with most people thinking, 'that's not for the likes of us!' However, I argue that to identify with the idea of being a citizen of the world is not necessarily the product of a formal education or a middle-class background. I develop a four-part typology of the idea that might help us to think through where we ourselves fit in today's cosmopolitan world. I also integrate short biographies of four very interesting people who embody, *par excellence*, in my opinion, the ideals and values of cosmopolitanism.

Overall, this book advocates that we take control over our own learning about our place in the world. The more we *think* about our own identity, the better, as this produces conscious, active human beings who can contribute positively to society. I begin this task here, from my own perspective, thereby hopefully encouraging others to do the same. The sense of belonging we experience is ultimately up to ourselves, as we can only take responsibility for our own actions and not those of others.

Following the adage 'you have to dig from where you stand', I feel it is important to come clean from the beginning about my perspective as author. The thoughts presented in this book are those of an Irish, female sociologist who grew up on a West Cork farm, who has lived and worked in cities in Ireland, the UK and the US during her adult life, who has liberally indulged her penchant for extended periods of travel and witnessing other global cultures, and who now lives in the Irish countryside again. Therefore, I personally know what it is like to have a deep familial attachment to a patch of land, to be challenged by and grow to love a big new city, to meander rootless, routeless and free on boats, buses and trains in India, the Middle East or Latin America, as well as being a 'blow-in' in a rural Irish village. These are all very different ways of being in the world that inform and challenge each other. The stories used to illustrate and add depth and colour to my discussion will be derived from my particular, random constellation of experiences and perceptions. These stories are thus very subjective and, no doubt, idiosyncratic, reflecting nobody else's life but mine. A professional training in sociology has afforded me thinking tools with which to attempt to make sense of these stories, so what follows is, I hope, an unpredictable and exciting journey where the rational tussles with the irrational, the analytical with the personal.

1

The Ties That Bind

The first word that comes to my mind when I think of my comfort zone is 'home'. This is where we feel completely unchallenged and deeply connected to our surroundings. When I think of the home in which I grew up, it conjures up a variety of sounds, sights and smells. I hear the twang of the country music my mother constantly played; I hear the rustling of autumn leaves as I shuffled through them on my way home from school; and I hear the trundling of tractors coming and going on the land, as my folks tried to cajole a living out of our few West Cork acres. In my mind's eye, I see the hateful bottle-green colour of my convent school uniform; I see the sleek seventies contours of our unconventional family car — a bright orange Opel Manta; I see Oscar the Grouch and Big Bird on *Sesame Street*; and I see my bedroom walls covered in posters of rock stars like Marc Bolan and Adam Ant, as well as pictures of some of the world's most exotic sights, such as Japanese Shinto shrines and the wild white horses of the French Camargue. These pictures had been carefully cut out of information packs that I had requested from various countries' embassies, in order to plan where to go when I grew up. When I think back to those days, I smell the tempting aroma of apple tarts in the oven; I smell my brother's sweaty socks; and I smell the sharp farmyard tang of fresh slurry and the rich, frothy fragrance of milk straight from the cows' udders. To think of any of these things takes me right back to my childhood in the 1970s – they form some of the rings on my tree. I have been around many corners since – working, studying, travelling, living and loving – but this was where my story began, whence the narrative of my life unfolded. It was that experiential package that defined what was normal, good and desirable. Of course, most of these young thoughts have since been unthought, reversed, revised and revoked, but this was the starting point, the launch pad, the well from which I was sprung.

Home

We associate the idea of 'home' with a comfortable place where we feel happy, relaxed and deeply familiar with our surroundings, a place where we know which ones are the creaky steps on the stairs. It is a place with which we feel naturally connected or *locked into* the place and its people, based on shared memories with family, friends and loved ones. It gives us a sense of wholeness and stability. The German word for home, *'heim'*, is derived from the Indo-European notion of *'kei'*, meaning 'something precious'.[1] Try using predictive text to type the word 'home' into your phone and, funnily enough, the first word to appear on-screen is 'good'. It is our own feelings about the place we call home that really matters, whether that home is located in a housing project in the Bronx, in a villa in the south of France, or in a *favela* in Rio de Janeiro. The evocative slogan used to advertise a certain brand of rashers and sausages is 'home is where you make it!' No physical place has inherent meaning until people attach meaning to it. No place is a home until it is actively made one, so 'home, then, is more the result of home-making than the effect of the place itself.'[2] Homemaking occurs when love for oneself and

2

one's family is expressed in the ways the house is managed. When a home is a happy one, it shows.

Our homes are where we can relax and let down our guard, unconcerned about what impression we create for others. We behave at home much as actors do when they go backstage, away from the glare of the lights and the eyes of the audience.[3] Even within our homes, there are frontstage and backstage areas. The sitting room and dining room are decorated with guests' perceptions and judgements in mind, whereas kitchens or utility areas may be plainer and purely practical, where work gets done. Frontstage is the zone of manners, smiles and politeness, while backstage is the zone of preparing food, cursing and topping up your lipstick before facing your guests.

The Home in History

Historically in Ireland, the idea of home has not been one to be taken for granted. As Fintan O' Toole says, 'domesticity in the Irish context isn't banal or cosy. It is a struggle for dignity and survival.'[4] When we examine a painting like James Brenan's *News From America* (1875), for example, it reminds us of our past, still somehow speaking to our souls. In this painting, a peasant family in a nineteenth-century one-roomed cottage gathers around a young girl reading a letter, clearly from emigrant kin in America. She is the only one in the family who can read, so she is the cultural conduit from the outside world, the most powerful person in the room – at that moment, at least. The emigration to which this painting refers has remained a constant theme in Irish society, creating social, cultural and economic links between many thousands of Irish homes and other parts of the world. This is a theme to which I will return in Chapter 5.

The separation of home and work is a relatively recent historical phenomenon. It is only since the emergence of factory production during the Industrial Revolution in the late eighteenth and early nineteenth centuries that we designate two separate areas for work and relaxation in the Western world. This was the first time that people actually left their homes to go out to the workplace.[5] Before this, all labour was performed by men, women and children at home on the farmstead. The Industrial Revolution introduced the new idea that factory work was for men, while women were more suited to staying at home. Men thus became associated with the public sphere of paid work, while women became attached to the domestic sphere of the home.[6] So women have been cooking, cleaning, washing, scrubbing, painting and decorating ever since!

Décor and Social Status

How we present and decorate our homes has become an important means of defining our social class and level of social status in society. When we choose one type of décor over another, it is a way of publicising our aesthetic taste, our priorities and our very identities. What one person thinks is old-fashioned, another will think is classy and understated. One person's idea of beautiful is another's idea of gaudy. For example, 'threadbare, shabby rugs and mismatched antique furniture are clear signifiers of upper-middle and upper class homes, for the truly aristocratic inherit their belongings.'[7] We usually place significant items on the mantelpiece in the sitting room, giving pride of place to items we want guests to notice. We might want them to see the hand-painted ornaments we got on holiday in Ibiza or a ceramic bowl from our trip up the Amazon, or we might want them to notice the framed pictures of our cute grandchildren or even our birthday cards to show off how popular we are! So our homes have become little personal museums that highlight significant moments in our lives. And we can never stop trying to 'improve' them as, for many of us, a visit to a DIY mega store has replaced a visit to church on a Sunday.

Home and Place

Of course, our home extends beyond the four walls of our house to the wider area in which we grew up and/or reside. When asked to write about her own home, travel writer Dervla Murphy mused:

> ... to me west Waterford, south Tipperary and east Cork are incomparably satisfying. Everything is congenial: every curve of the hills and valleys, every bend of the rivers and streams, every distinctive seasonal scent of fields and woods. This territory is my natural habitat, where I'm at ease in all weathers.[8]

Irish poet Nuala Ní Dhomhnaill, who is married to a Turkish man and who has lived abroad for many years, says of her native Kerry, 'We were always either going to it or coming from it.'[9] This denotes that it is the most significant place in the world for her in a psychological sense, and because of its early imprinting it surpasses all other places in its power over her. For others, it is not so simple. Writer Brian Keenan embarked upon an adventure to Alaska in recent years. A very thoughtful person who has endured unimaginable trauma in his life, he admitted that:

> ... a part of me has always been looking for a place of belonging, a spiritual homeland that has nothing to do with

ownership but a place where authenticity can be found and affirmed. Carl Jung called it a "psychic observation post" from where we might understand the deepest parts of ourselves and recalibrate the trajectory of our life.[10]

For some people, the sense of connection with their home is very strong, and they have no desire to move anywhere else. For others, who live more nomadic lifestyles, it is a case of, as the song goes, 'wherever I lay my hat, that's my home.' Irish travel writer Mary Russell says that her home is where her toothbrush is.[11] However, your home usually means most to you after you have been away from it. I never feel more at home than when making that first glorious cup of Barry's tea in my own kitchen after getting off a plane. As Canadian writer Michael Ignatieff says, 'home is the place we have to leave in order to grow up, to become ourselves.'[12] To return to your house, neighbourhood or region after an absence changes your perspective on it. Depending on where you have been, you might love being home or abhor it. It also depends on the circumstances of your leaving. If you have chosen to leave, the idea and reality of home is not as poignant and painful as if you have been forced to leave. For example, I have spoken to people in Palestinian refugee camps who still keep in their possession the keys to the homes they inhabited before being driven from them in 1948.

In my own life, I have found that where I feel at home depends on where I have just come from: everything is relative. If I have been travelling in India, for example, I feel at home when I touch down in London. If I have been in London, Dublin feels like home. And having been in Dublin, there is nothing quite like hearing the sing-song Cork accent for me. Once, many years ago, I arrived at the train station in Dublin, having been away travelling for the summer in South America. This was well before the Irish train experience was as polished as it is now. I asked the eccentric old conductor if this was the faster train to Cork. He replied, in his inimitable way, 'Ara, no, girl, 'tis the Wanderly Wagon one!' He would have given the same, shall we say, culturally-specific response whether I was from Tokyo or Timbuktu!

Cork, with its conviction that it is the centre of the civilised world, has its back to its Munster neighbours and its face towards the sunnier climes of northwest France. Walking through Cork's multicultural English Market, one experiences a strong sense of cultural disorientation, especially when there is a boatful of French or Italian people in town. Then, upon leaving Cork city, the sights, sounds and smells of the County Cork countryside are what resonate most of all for me. As a child of West Cork, I am heir to more cultural resources of songs and stories than to economic ones of pounds, shillings and pence. The county of Cork is almost like a microcosm of the whole country, in that, broadly speaking, the west of Ireland contains mostly ragged fields that have served as little more than a launch pad for those who have left on emigrant ships and planes, while the richer fields of the east of the country have served as a nursery of landed power that has passed from hand to hand throughout the generations.

Nostalgia

People often speak of being 'homesick' when abroad. They experience feelings of nostalgia and loneliness, missing what is familiar and comfortable, whether that is keeping up with the shenanigans on *Fair City* or a few pints in the local pub. In fact, in eighteenth- and nineteenth-century psychiatry, 'nostalgia' was defined as a psychological disorder, with the word derived from the Greek terms *nostos* (return home) and *algos* (pain). The term was first used in 1688. It was found to be a common complaint among soldiers, and the only effective treatment for it was to return the soldiers to their homes.[13] While no longer formally defined as a psychiatric problem per se, we all know what it feels like, just as we also know what it is like to have butterflies in our stomach or a broken heart.

One of the many old songs addressing the idea of home is 'The Homes of Donegal'. In it, the story is told from the perspective of a tramp who finds shelter and company in people's houses as he travels around County Donegal. He paints a scene of traditional domestic bliss of which De Valera would have been proud. The people are friendly, the fire is lit, a meal is prepared and, ultimately, there is a 'shake-down by the wall', a bed upon which he can lay his weary head. First sung by the recently deceased Bridie Gallagher, Paul Brady popularised this old song in more recent years, and in his extended live performance of it he adds to the romance and populism by mentioning by name, in a kind of dreamy rap, virtually every large town and tiny hamlet in the county. It is certainly evocative as a piece of social history, but it belongs firmly in the past. Imagine the scene in Ireland as we now know it. Firstly, tramps are no longer a well-known social category. Secondly, any door the man might knock on would be unlikely to be answered, as the house might either be a holiday home or simply empty all day because all the occupants are out working to pay off their huge mortgages. The financially independent woman of the twenty-first century is not usually available at home from nine to five, in Donegal or elsewhere. Thirdly, even if somebody did open the door, what are the chances of a 'weary wanderer' receiving anything like a welcome? He would be more likely to be greeted with suspicion, perhaps a euro thrust in his hand and the door shut in his face. Maybe life was never as pleasant a picture as that depicted in the song, but it provides us with a self-image that pleases us, and the song still gives us a rosy glow after a few pints. The image of home portrayed in this song is still very close to our hearts.

Contrary to this idealised image of home, the reality may be less pleasing for some. For many thousands in contemporary Ireland, their home is a huge financial millstone around their neck, as they are in negative equity, paying back more to banks than their home is actually worth. Many others cannot afford to pay back their mortgages at all since the recession has struck. Still others have no home at all, and all of our major cities and towns have too many people who have to sleep on the streets or in homeless shelters. For many thousands of women, their home is a place of crippling fear where they experience the soul-destroying horror of domestic violence. How we feel about our home thus depends upon our personal circumstances. On the one hand, people often see too little of it, particularly when they are forced to work long hours just to pay for the roof over their heads. On the other hand, some people can see too much of home, as when a person becomes unemployed or disabled and their home feels like a prison from which there is no escape.

Shelter from the Storm

Many people may also have several homes during their life-time, each satisfying different needs at different phases of their life. At a time when millions of people move from place to place every day, both voluntarily as travellers and invol-untarily as refugees, our home provides an anchor in the choppy seas of modernity. Now, perhaps more than ever, we are looking for a sense of security. It has been suggested that the 'revival of interest in basic institutions (such as family and community), and the search for historical roots are all signs of a search for more secure moorings and longer-lasting values in a shifting world.'[14]

There are times when all of the environmental disasters, ethnic conflicts and economic insecurity that we see around us make us want to stay at home and lock the door. Feeling safe and secure is not easy these days, with the evening news full of ominous threats of various kinds. These range from stealth taxes and E. coli in your salad to earthquakes, tsunamis, bombs on aeroplanes and people stealing your children. Some argue that this heralds a whole new era – a risk society – in which the risks are potentially global in reach and it is nearly impossible to attribute blame to any group or individual; the onus is always on the victim to prove the source of the hazard.[15] Another commentator says, 'at times I feel as if the whole planet is joyriding in someone else's Porsche, at ninety miles per hour, around blind curves.'[16] Living through the latest recession in Ireland these days, I know what he means.

There is a palpable sense of loss of control and helplessness, where our economy went from boom to bust apparently overnight, and ordinary citizens have to pay for the corruption and financial vandalism performed by those in charge. As writer Joseph O'Connor says:

> We are surrounded by advertisers, propagandists of the slick, chancers, salesmen, illusionists, liars. In Ireland we have banks with no money, apartment blocks nobody wanted, politicians we don't trust, an economy in ruins, a church so disgraced by child abuse and cover-up corruption that it must alter itself profoundly or die.[17]

My Home-Place

My home-place, where I took my first baby steps, was a small farm in rural West Cork. This matters. This fact remains central to who and what I am, focussing the lens through which I view the world around me. Irish country people use the term 'home-place' to refer to the farm where a person came from. This denotes that a person's home stretches beyond the walls of a mere house, encompassing the farmland that surrounds it. 'Home-place' is a very emotionally-loaded term, as it confers a visceral and almost spiritual sense of connection, the weight of tradition and a sense of duty to keep the farm going. For country people, it might be termed their emotional headquarters. The fact that the farmstead is likely to have been passed down through the generations means that the farmer has a responsibility to respect the memory of his forebears as well as to look after his/her own family. The priority of farming people is keeping the family name on the land, making sure that 'ancestral territory, deeply imbued with memory and work and sweat and pain, survives intact.'[18] Some recent amateur historical sleuthing on my behalf found that my family's land had been in the possession of a colonial landlord called Zachariah Hawkes until the late nineteenth century. His family had been given huge plots of land all over County Cork from the late 1600s. This historical knowledge makes the connection to the land all the more powerful and poignant.

Learning

My home-place is the context within which I learned various skills, formed values, developed coping strategies and had some of my earliest and most enduring memories etched on my childish brain. The place where we are raised is, after all, the primary foundation upon which our later experiences are built. Growing up in the countryside, for example, imbued me with a certain resourcefulness and toughness that has stood me in good stead throughout my life. As a child, for example, entertainment was not laid on, and I had to go find some fun wherever I could. My siblings and I were also trusted with jobs that would only be the preserve of adults now, such as milking cows, tending to small calves, or stacking bales of hay at harvest time. There was a sense of teamwork – if a job needed to be done, it was all hands on deck, no matter how old you were. This is not to suggest that a Dickensian child-labour regime was in place! On the contrary, it was actually educational and empowering to be trusted to help out with some small part of the daily workings of the farm.

Emotional Connection

This emotion-laden link with the soil, so familiar to me, at least partly explains why farmers are so slow to sell up in times of need. Urban dwellers often do not believe that farmers can really be poor, because they own land and, there-fore, can potentially sell it. They do not always understand, or perhaps do not want to understand, that the land itself is the very foundation upon which farmers can earn an income, a blank canvas on which to paint the colours of their futures. Without it, farmers feel they have nothing, either in terms of income or of social status. It may be that 'it's imprinted on our psychology or on our soul that unless you have land, you won't survive.'[19] It is with a heavy, guilt-laden heart that a farmer will sell a farm, or even a portion of it, that has been in the family name for generations. They will go into debt, take a second job and/or lease the land to a neighbour before cutting the umbilical cord tying them to their home-place.

One elderly farmer in an Irish TV documentary likened being separated from his farm to cutting off his own hand and selling it. His son added, 'Once they buy the land, it's theirs; it's no longer yours. The history is finished.'[20] This

12

attitude has also been found in other countries. For example, a 2010 study of a Dutch village found that the survival of the farm for future generations was more important to farmers there than big profits, and that to stop farming would mean personal failure.[21] This points to a strong sense of connection to their home-place as well, so it is not unique to Ireland, by any means.

Having experienced this terminal severing from my own home-place in my late teens when our farm was sold, I can personally vouch for just how heart-wrenching it really is. Leaving the land was actually harder for me than leaving the farmhouse itself, probably because so much of my childhood was spent gadding about outdoors, usually with at least one dog or cat in tow. To think that you can never again walk through the fields that have sustained your family for several generations is very difficult indeed. While urban-dwellers can of course feel the same connection to the streets in which they grew up, the difference is that they can at least still walk through the streets of their old neighbourhood. When a private farm is sold, it belongs to someone else, and you are no longer free to roam it. The sense of loss is therefore much more permanent, as it's all off limits.

The other difference is the connection a country person fosters with the world of nature. All kinds of memories radiate from every laneway, hill and stream: right here is where I saw the bloody reality of my first calf being born; over there I found the nest where my cat had given birth to five kittens; that was where we always picked huge, scrumptious field mushrooms; in that field I drove a tractor for the first time at the age of 10; in that bog I found pink wildflowers that I later identified as ragged robins; there I watched a JCB demolish a ditch that had been bursting with foxglove purple; up there I had a close encounter with a rat that has fuelled a lifelong phobia; and in that high field my father collapsed with a heart attack from which he later died.

Privacy

In my experience of growing up in the countryside, there was a strong emphasis placed upon privacy by country people. I get the impression that this is not as trenchant now as it was then, that people are perhaps a bit more open now; however, I am open to correction on that. Nevertheless, thirty or forty years ago, in my experience, it was crucial not to let other people know your business. If farmers were in financial trouble, they might put every available penny into buying a shiny new car to keep the bright side out and put the gossipers off the scent. If poverty existed, it was of a discreet variety. Good dinners could be made from cheap cuts of meat, children's clothes handed down to the younger ones, elbows darned, knees patched, collars turned. Anything that was bought had to be of good quality, built to last. Nothing was thrown out, as some new use could always be found for things. They call that 'upcycling' these days. I still patch holes in the knees of jeans, even though I could buy a new pair for €20! The satisfaction you get from doing it has absolutely nothing to do with saving money, but more about being thrifty and not wasting resources. Coincidentally, and only coincidentally, this is concurrent with contemporary ecological philosophy. In my childhood, this was just normal behaviour, completely unexceptional in my social milieu. These habits can remain with you long after the financial need for them has passed.

This concern with privacy extended beyond financial secrecy into personal life more generally. Family matters were kept within the family. Asking direct questions was taboo, and to be 'nosy' was labelled one of the worst sins. Funnily enough, later in life, I conducted doctoral research that involved a large number of in-depth interviews with West Cork farmers. It helped enormously that I came from the same cultural world myself, and could therefore gauge when it was okay to ask certain questions. This highly individualised culture of privacy hints at the idea that there was not really a very strong sense of community among neighbours where I grew up. You more or less kept yourself to yourself. This is very different to the intimacy of social life in country villages, which is discussed in Chapter 2. Farming men usually only came into contact for contractual reasons or in times of crisis, whereas the women were somewhat more linked by their children. If women were unmarried and/or did not have any children, it was difficult for them to integrate in their communities, perhaps being seen as a little bit strange. True friendships among neighbours were very rare. It was considered unhealthy, even dangerous, to talk too much about anything important. Your popularity hinged instead on your entertainment skills and your ability to spin a good yarn. This interaction style kept the mood light.

The 'Stations'

About every four years, we had the 'stations', which was, and still is, when the local priest said Mass in the house in order to collect the parish dues to support themselves, to hear confessions and to bring the sacraments to the more unreliable of their parishioners. It is also commonly held that the Catholic Church introduced this custom in order to instil in the Irish peasantry a sense of pride in their homes. This was part of their mission to 'civilise' country people. In the nineteenth century, 'the individual could not evade surveillance: the priest came to his or her locality and all householder names were publicly called; their dues and "duties" commingled, conflated and publicly noticed; and absentees given "a good scolding".[22] The stations were a means of exerting power over the local people. While the religious and surveillance functions retreated somewhat over the years and the social function came more to the fore, it still put pressure on householders to toe the line and submit to the Church's power. It also usually involved redecorating the house, and my mother told me that when one of my sisters was born in the early 1960s, she had to come straight home after giving birth to paint the house for the station, with the local hospital keeping the baby for her for a few days to enable her to do it. Even a momentous event like childbirth could not get in the way of conformity to the Church's diktats.

I remember my mother removing and painstakingly painting all the sash windows on the summer days preceding each station. It also involved cooking a meal for all the neighbours and friends. Afterwards, drinks were provided and songs were inevitably sung. The family, and particularly the 'bean an tí' (the woman of the house), was judged according to how lavish the party was, as opposed to the piety of the occasion. Each farmer's wife did her utmost to host as good a station as she and her family could afford, and derived great pleasure from a job well done. It was a very meaningful indicator of wealth and/or generosity in the rural community. It was, and still is, a popular social occasion where friends, family and neighbours gathered, but it unfortunately also had a very strong competitive element, which is hardly a characteristic of Christianity. Nowadays, it is usually a simpler affair, without as many bells and whistles attached. Local priests are glad if anybody agrees to host them now, as the powerful grip they had on people's hearts and minds gradually loosens.

Appreciating Nature

As a child from the country, I developed a relationship with nature and the animal world that became the basis of a life-long love. Growing up on a farm, I never really needed, and nor did I receive, a talk on the birds and the bees, as I was surrounded with nature's natural cycles all the time. It was perfectly normal to see the cows calving, the dog having pups, the cat having kittens or chickens hatching from eggs. Just how valuable such experiences were has really only dawned on me in recent years. Farm life had its little glories, like training a calf to drink milk from a bucket by holding your fingers under the surface for it to suck, and its traumas, like watching the vet stab the engorged stomach of a bull who was suffering from bloat or, on another day, watching him castrate a batch of young bulls. The gory sight of a bucket overflowing with bull's testicles tends to stay in your memory for life!

As the youngest of six much older children, I spent many a solitary hour wandering through the countryside discovering nature for myself, relishing the kind of freedom that few children experience nowadays. We had a 'nature table' at school, for which we would bring in wildflowers to identify, or frogspawn to watch develop into those little commas that were juvenile frogs, or unusual types of rocks, or a bunch of daffodils from the garden. I still surprise myself sometimes by dredging up from the depths of my memory the name of an obscure wildflower or plant. Lesser celandine, herb robert, wood anemone – where did those words come from? I recently found one of those old magic viewfinders with a slide of my little tomboy self in it. It was strangely revelatory, a periscope into the past.

Growing Vegetables

This connection with the soil that forms part of my rural identity has been resurrected in me in recent years, as I have started to grow some vegetables. It is difficult to express just how good this feels, as it helps me to reconnect with my past growing up in the countryside. Like a new convert to a religion, I have to restrain myself from preaching to others as they stock up at supermarket vegetable counters. Litanies about carcinogenic carrots, horsemeat burgers, food miles, fragile ecosystems, labour exploitation, oil consumption and poisonous pesticides want to spew forth from my mouth. But is there anything more off-putting than such preaching? Just a few years ago, I would have told such a person to buzz off and leave me alone. However! (Briefly) When you have planted a seed in soil, watered it, watched it show its first little tentative, pale green shoots that gradually get stronger, taller, deeper, until it becomes actual food to nourish your body, then you get it. It feels good. It feels better than (almost) anything else you will have done in your life. To sit down to a dinner where the vegetables on the plate have come no further than the few metres from the garden gives you a very, very deep sense of satisfaction. Also, instead of working to earn money to buy food, you are working directly to grow food, without having to leave the house or even change out of your purple pyjamas!

American author Barbara Kingsolver describes that population's relationship with food as 'alimentary alienation'. By this she means that, following Marx's analysis of capitalism, people feel alienated from the products of their labour by the factory system of production. When they only perform one small job in the overall process, they cannot feel connected to the final product. She says that, 'in the case of modern food, our single-bolt job has become the boring act of poking the thing in our mouths, with no feeling for any other stage in the process.'[23] For me, it is about being self-sufficient and in control of what I eat. The ephemera of globalisation processes, economic jargon, the secret machinations of power elites, the billions owed by governments, the skittish vicissitudes of stock exchanges, the corruption of banks – most of us can do absolutely nothing about these. Listening to how the wealth generated in our economies has been sold up the river by a small handful of politicians, property developers and bankers makes us feel very, very angry and, above all, very insecure. We cannot be too sure of anything, really. People are asking themselves – how long will this recession last? Can we come out the other side? Should I emigrate? Where could I go? Will I ever work again? How will I pay next month's mortgage? Are my savings safe in my bank account? Where will my children find work?

When faced with such massive insecurity, is it any wonder that adopting the simple practice of growing some vegetables has become so popular? It brings out the inner survivalist in all of us. The act of pulling a big carrot out of the ground or digging up a stalk of potatoes speaks to the inner core of our selves. There is a deep sense that even if it all goes to hell in a hay basket, I can still feed myself. I am connected to the ground on which I am standing. I can make it work for me. And, as well as that, to swap some vegetables and growing tips with your neighbours is a great opportunity to get together when you might not have otherwise.

'Culchies'

Such skills are far from universally valued, however. The bias against country people and country life is perhaps close to universal. In the US, common terms for country people include 'hayseeds, hillbillies, rednecks, yokels and white trash',[24] while in Ireland more common terms are 'culchies' and 'mucksavages'. Country people are often seen almost as an early human prototype that will inevitably become urbanised over time. Countryside culture has been laughed at and debased, despite the fact that farmers are the ones who actually feed and sustain the urban population. Many new demands are being placed upon a dwindling number of farmers, and there is a plurality of new visions for rural space and its inhabitants. The urbanisation of Irish society means that the previously dominant construction of rural areas as remote and backward is now being overtaken by a vision of them as potential scenic, peaceful retreats from the hectic pace of urban life. These newer constructions are not solely abstract metaphors, but have a very concrete impact upon the present and future of real places like the West Cork of my childhood. Farmland now often exists cheek by jowl with suburban housing estates, holiday cottages, theme parks or wind turbines.

Popular images of country people often have a Janus-faced character. On the one hand, they are romanticised as honest, simple and hardworking. This romantic perspective is exemplified in Alice Taylor's nostalgic *To School Through the Fields*, which is, to date, the biggest-selling book ever in Ireland. On the other hand, this very simplicity can be denoted pejoratively as backward, ignorant and superstitious, leading to the emergence of a hostile relationship with the urbanised population. This latter attitude was very evident in the advice given to farmers by the Irish state in the 1970s and 1980s. They were to cast off the yoke of small-scale, so-called backward farming methods and embrace 'modern' fertilisers and pesticides in order to produce higher and higher yields every year. The JCB digger (or JC Buí as they call them in Connacht!) was the new god. Where I grew up, ditches were regularly knocked in an effort to transform the intimate, hilly patchwork of West

Cork fields into the vast, flat pastures of Norfolk or Illinois. This was in accordance with the zeitgeist of the modernising era. Of course, it is only in retrospect that we can see the error of our ways back then. The whole package – bigger fields, bigger machinery, more chemicals and, ultimately, more debt – led to the economic and environmental disaster in Irish and wider European farming that became apparent in the early 1980s. We have been paying for the huge mistakes associated with that modernisation drive ever since, propping up an economically-unsustainable and environmentally-destructive agricultural system. It has, however, prompted some debate and policy changes that have attempted to both maintain farmers' incomes and protect the environment.[25] I suppose things had to get worse before they got better.

'Townies'

Journalist John Waters grew up in Castlerea, County Roscommon, which most urban-based analysts would agree belongs firmly within rural Ireland. However, he never felt himself to be a country person when he was younger. *Au contraire.* The leather-clad urbane 'townies' of Castlerea called their country cousins 'culchies'. They were avidly listening to the revolutionary riffs of the Horslips or Thin Lizzy, rather than the country and Irish strains of Hugo Duncan or Big Tom and the Mainliners. Even though he could see green fields from his back window, Waters and his friends scorned everything associated with the country. He says, 'plugged in as we were to the Universal City, the country represented backwardness, thick accents and the past.' They saw themselves as 'part of the thrusting, modern, forward-looking Ireland, which we had tasted on the wind.'[26] Having grown up in the urban metropolis of Macroom, County Cork, renowned vegetarian chef Denis Cotter muses on the same topic. He reckons that the proximity of the countryside was a 'constant reminder of how close we were to what we snobbishly saw as the poverty, savagery and endless toil that our ancestors had only recently escaped.' He goes on to say, 'the country was the past; and in our fantastic future we wanted to work indoors in nice shirts and soft shoes.'[27]

Having attended secondary school not far from there, in Bandon, County Cork, I can verify that the same biased attitude was very much in evidence. The contrast with the country primary school I had attended was marked. There, nearly everybody came from a farm or at least lived in the countryside. The smell of slurry would have been very familiar to all of them! I remember when I was about 9 years old, about fifteen of our calves escaped from our fields and went missing. We had to assemble a search party until they eventually were found over two days later, 8 miles away. Everyone was very concerned, and I had to miss a couple of days of school. On my return, my teachers and classmates were very sympathetic. Everybody understood very well what a big loss this would have been for a farming family like ours.

Later on, at secondary school in Bandon Convent, the country girls and the townies tended to stick with their own. At that time I learned that it is really only when we are involuntarily defined by others that we begin to think about defining ourselves. If you were not quite sure what you were in terms of class or status, mixing with children from different backgrounds to your own tended to make you realise the strengths and weaknesses of your own class position and status group.

A Country Girl

To call yourself a 'country girl' or a 'farmer's daughter' in Ireland dredges up a particular set of associations and images in people's minds. The heroines of Edna O'Brien's 1960 trilogy *The Country Girls* and Maeve Binchy's *The Lilac Bus* struggled with patriarchal power and traditional familial and community expectations. They had the mark of their wellington boots on their thick calves, wild hair and had to learn how to speak properly for their jobs in the shops and offices of the 'big city'. These rural Eliza Doolittles were good girls who never let their boyfriends get too far, preserving their most prized asset for their wedding night.

A generation or three on, things are a bit different. Since I grew up in the countryside, us girls have had much more freedom in deciding our own fates. We earned our own money, learned to drive on the day of our seventeenth birthdays, chose our own course of study in college, learned even more during our J1 summers in New York and Boston, picked our own clothes, boyfriends and careers. The enforced innocence of the past gave way to exceedingly dodgy eighties 'rock-chick' hairstyles, too-tight jeans, driving a bit too fast to the pounding rhythms of Bruce Springsteen, Prince or Billy Idol and, inevitably, the occasional teenage shotgun wedding. Some things do not change very much, however, and very few young women trump their brothers to actually inherit their family farms. But they might still settle back in the country after their wandering is done, building a house on a site they got from their Ma and Da as a wedding present.

Even if families are not actually making their total income from the land any more, there is still a common idea that it is better to raise children in the country, that it is a healthy outdoor nursery for the next generation. Perhaps partly because of this, we have seen a gradual process of suburbanisation over recent decades, where it is hard to know where towns stop and the countryside begins. Urban and rural cultures are merging. Farmers can record the weather forecast using Sky Plus and talk to their sons and daughters in Australia on Skype. Upper middle-class town dwellers can buy free-range eggs directly from one of their farming neighbours and take little Jack and Emma for nice country walks on a Sunday, to boost their Vitamin D levels and to promote appropriate play behaviour and healthy muscle development!

Farmers' Markets

One of the results of this cultural merging has been the growth of the phenomenon of 'farmers' markets' in towns and cities all over the country. Suddenly, growing your own vegetables, doing your own baking and getting yourself a Casual Traders License to set up a market stall is not considered embarrassing or old-fashioned, but is instead the height of cool. This trend, which I like to term the rediscovery of the rustic, appears to reverse the age-old denigration of country ways. As David McWilliams has said, 'if Patrick Kavanagh did groceries, he'd do farmers' markets.'[28]

How did this come about? The sight of First Lady Michelle Obama digging up a patch of the White House lawn was a turning point in the US. She tried to turn the sod on a new movement, to combat the enormification of the US population and to cut the cost of this trend to the health sector. In the UK and Ireland, the trend has been led by certain media figures like Jamie Oliver and Darina Allen who advocate healthy eating and staying out of McDonalds. One of those shortlisted for the 2010 Irish Social Entrepreneur of the Year Awards was Michael Kelly, who has started the Grow It Yourself (GIY) movement in Ireland. The goal of this movement is to enable almost everyone to grow at least some of their own food, in order to challenge and circumvent the hugely wasteful and exploitative global food system. This idea is certainly spreading. Lots of schools now have their own vegetable patches and bookshops have burgeoning sections on growing vegetables and keeping hens. Who would have believed it? My own bookshelves are populated with quite a few books from this new genre that I have christened 'mucklit'. From the US, Barbara Kingsolver's *Animal, Vegetable, Miracle* is a shining example; from the UK, Rosie Boycott's *Spotted Pigs and Green Tomatoes*; and from Ireland, Michael Kelly's *Tales From Home Farm* is both entertaining and educational. Books in this genre will have some soul-searching about the global food system and the evils of supermarkets on one page, a recipe for cauliflower soup on the next, and tips on keeping slugs off the cabbage on the one after that.

When I was growing up on a farm thirty or forty years ago, surrounded by what I thought were smelly old hens, I would never have thought that city people would ever be interested in keeping these creatures in their pristine gardens, complete with very cool plastic igloos for them to sleep in! Where I came from in West Cork, to have dirt under your fingernails was an indicator of 'culchiedom', whereas now it is a badge of honour in polite circles. And country people would never have worn their wellington boots into town; you had to wash the smell of the country off yourself before hitting the pavements. Wellies come in all sorts of bright patterns and colours now – not just plain old green or black. I nearly bought some with lovely colourful chillies on them recently. I didn't though. I thought the ghosts of my forebears might come back and haunt me.

In Bandon, as in many other towns, these new farmers' markets have existed for the past few years, but the town's *country* market has predated it by several decades. The two types of market could hardly be more different. Firstly, the farmers' markets usually have very few actual bona fide farmers in them, selling more *crêpes suzettes*, red onion tartlets and fairtrade arabica coffee beans than actual home-grown produce. They are play markets that sell mostly luxury goods, not particularly cheaply, attracting a middle-class clientèle. There is a party atmosphere where children can get their faces painted, the mums chat over lattes and the dads network with their golfing buddies. It is an outdoor event that is most successful in good weather. On the other hand, the country market operates out of a basic indoor premises every week, come rain or shine. It is full of real farming women and men. You have to queue up to buy the beautiful plants and vegetables they grow and the eggs and great brown bread and cakes that they bring to the market. It is full of good food sold at good prices. There is a no-nonsense, down-to-earth atmosphere, and there is nothing remotely trendy about it. These people were organic long before the word ever entered our contemporary lexicon. It is run co-operatively and, no doubt, will outlast the farmers' markets for eons to come, because it is literally organic, coming from the heart of the community and providing real food that people like to eat.

Having discussed our connection to home and my particular experience of my home-place, it is now time to move on to the important realm of family life and its link to the definition of our comfort zone.

Families

In our childhood years, our families form the heart of our comfort zone and are synonymous with 'home' because they are our first point of contact with the world. It is through this lens that we have our first – our primary – experiences, and our memories thereof stay with us for life. Our memory constitutes the essence of what and who we are. People who lose their memory, perhaps due to a brain injury, for example, are left bereft of emotion, connection and a sense of their place in the world. Everybody is born with a biological mother and father, and everybody is born in a particular place. We cannot generalise any further than this, because every single human being's experiences and memories of their parents, families and homes are different.

Even two siblings growing up in the same house can have completely different experiences and, hence, perhaps, divergent life-paths. This is especially heightened when the family is large, with perhaps fifteen or twenty years between the eldest and the youngest sibling. The memories they have when they grow up can be fractured too: lives lived in bits and pieces like shards of a broken mirror. This might even mean that one sibling feels that he/she grew up in a happy, stable home, while another might feel alienated and excluded. This may be because one was female, the other male; one was educated, the other not; one was loved, the other not so much. The list of potential differences is endless, and that refers to just *two* people! If a brother and sister from one family were asked to put together a scrapbook of their childhoods, each would probably be completely different – different events, different interpretations of events, different role-models, different sources of happiness and sadness.

My Family

I grew up as the youngest of six children, with the others much older than me. Statistically speaking, I was apparently doomed from the start. Psychologists say that 'offspring of families with five or more children are significantly more likely to be delinquent and to suffer mental illness.'[29] If this is truly the case, most Irish people are rendered incurably bad or mad just by their demographic profile! This subject would certainly make for an interesting interchange between a psychologist and a sociologist. In any case, the majority of my most enduring memories date from times long after nearly all of my siblings had left home. Emigration has loomed large in my family – an important subject to which I shall return in Chapter 5.

My father died when I was 4 years old. My older siblings were aged from about 10 to 19 when this happened, so they feel a sense of grief or loss at his early death, whereas this is not a strong emotion for me at all. They speak fondly of him, and the stories they tell serve to remind me of where I came from and create a sense of continuity with the past, even though I cannot personally remember it. My only real memory relating to my father is of his funeral, and even that is very faint. My eldest sister tells me that I cut a lonely little figure carrying a wreath, walking behind his coffin. It seems that it was more painful to watch that little child than to actually be her. Psychologists would probably say that my primary socialisation was complete by the time he died. That is to say that I had had enough bonding with him by then to give me a sense of identity in later life. Later on, my eldest brother, fifteen years my senior, became something like a father figure to me as a growing child. I was often his little companion as he went about his farming work, herding cows or perched in the cab of a tractor.

One emotional legacy of this aspect of my family history is to be intensely aware that accidents and illnesses can happen at any time, to the extent that I am hardly even surprised when I hear tragic tales of people who have died suddenly. I almost expect it. But perhaps this dark side of my character has more to do with the fact that I was born on All Soul's Day, termed *Día de los Muertos* in Latin America. My experience, however, is probably very different to not ever knowing who your father was in the first place. Family issues like this inevitably loom large in the minds of adoptees, who often want to find out about their biological origins: who their birth parents were, if they look like them and – the biggest question of all – why they gave them away. That sense of rejection may stay with them for life, undermining their sense of personal security. Such family issues are also sensitive for orphans, refugees and the displaced, as they try to weave a tapestry of identity from the frayed or broken threads of their lives.

My mother was widowed in her early forties. Her life was grounded in a small, local context and filtered through her family and immediate neighbourhood. The aspects of life from which she received fulfilment were the same as those experienced by country people everywhere: the satisfaction derived from reaping a good harvest, producing healthy livestock or eating a good dinner around the kitchen table with your young family or, in other words, producing and reproducing life itself. In the latter half of her life, my mother has functioned in an extremely independent manner, without a man by her side. After the death of my father she had to adapt to very difficult circumstances, and I, as the youngest, was the one who witnessed her strength most closely as the years passed. She went from being a busy young mother and farmer's wife who milked cows every day to an elderly woman living alone in suburbia after our farm was sold. She now enjoys witnessing the progress of her children and grandchildren, almost experiencing their joys and woes by proxy. So, in contrast with feminist principles, her life has been lived basically for and through others.

In reality, however, she has derived, and continues to derive, pleasure from it. However, she regrets that the many skills she possesses are not commonly socially valued. She says, 'my generation of women can do everything, and yet nothing.' I interpret this to mean that all the things she can do well are associated with homemaking and childrearing, which are skills that are viewed as 'natural' and therefore unpaid. For example, she can knit Aran jumpers like an angel. She learned new skills, and perhaps forgot many others, in order to adapt to her new life away from the farm and among her suburban neighbours. They know little or nothing of country life, which is so dear to her heart, yet they are very kind to her indeed. The advantages of convenient, urbanised life probably outweigh any disadvantages for her. To be able to pop down the street to the doctor, chemist, shop or pub is a godsend for an elderly lady, especially one who cannot drive a car. To live on our old farm now would be hard for her, a place 'blessed by nature [but] cursed by peripherality'.[30]

Thinking About Families

The family context into which we are born makes a huge difference to the shape of our life ahead. This realm of bonding, caring and love is usually deemed the core institution of society but, unfortunately, it often fails to meet such high expectations. In *Anna Karenina* Tolstoy famously wrote, 'all happy families resemble one another, each unhappy family is unhappy in its own way.'[31] Our families are often the source of our most profound happiness, but also our most profound sorrow. Poet Philip Larkin expressed a poor opinion of family life when he wrote in 'This Be The Verse':

They fuck you up, your mum and dad.
They may not mean to, but they do.
They fill you with the faults they had
And add some extra just for you.

Whether or not one shares Larkin's unequivocally bleak outlook, decisions made by different family members throughout their lives are not made in a vacuum. They are made in cultural, economic and social contexts. Even our most apparently private thoughts emerge out of our relationships with the social structures that surround us. This is a two-way street, because the thoughts of individuals can have a strong impact on society too, depending upon the amount and type of power they possess. Our families are also a major source of personal identity and status, which can have positive or negative effects on our life paths. Our family reputation precedes us, whatever it may be. This may or may not be very important, depending upon how strongly integrated we are within our families and, in turn, within our communities. The family is, of course, also still the major means of passing on inherited wealth, reproducing forever the gaps between rich and poor.

Social conservatives have a strong attachment to an ideal, *'The Waltons'* version of the nuclear family. For those too young to remember this TV show, it was about an Appalachian country family with eight children, where everybody loved each other and there was never any serious conflict. It is seen as crucial in this rose-tinted idealised view that each parent, both Ma and Pa, fulfils his or her particular social and psychological role. Conservatives all over the world view the absence of a father figure in many modern families as detrimental to children's development. They have attributed increased levels of crime to the breakdown of 'family values'. However, such picture-perfect views of family life fail to see the major problems that can exist within the traditional family structure, where abuse and violence often destroy the lives of so many people.

Author Caitlin Moran remembers her angst-ridden teenage years, during which she says she had no friends, 'unless you count family, which obviously you don't, because they just come free with your life, wanted or not, like the six-page Curry's brochure that falls out of the local paper.'[32] Conservatives also fail to register the amazing diversity of family forms that exist throughout the world, formed as they are out of people's coping strategies in a harsh, unequal world. The traditional Western norm of the nuclear family – bread-winning father, stay-at-home mother and children – is by no means the norm universally, and arguably not even in the Western world itself. Female-headed families, divorced families, blended families, gay families and polygamous families are all significant actors on the world stage, whether the conservatives like it or not. You cannot, after all, put the toothpaste back in the tube: the liberalisation of family structures may be a challenge to some, but there is no going back now.

The Irish Mother

Such conservative thinking has been very obvious on the part of the state since Independence. The 1937 Constitution of Ireland enshrined a very constrained and pre-determined role for Irish women. Witness Article 41 – 'The Family':[33]

1.1. The State recognises the Family as the natural, primary and fundamental unit group of Society, and as a moral institution possessing inalienable … rights antecedent and superior to all positive law …
2.1. In particular, the State recognises that by her life within the home, woman gives to the State a support without which the common good cannot be achieved.
2.2. The State shall, therefore, endeavour to ensure that mothers shall not be obliged by economic necessity to engage in labour to the neglect of their duties in the home.

While this wording now looks almost laughably archaic, it is still the basis of family law in this country and the huge boulder that blocks the way for progressive legislative change. This wording was unpopular even in 1937. Hanna Sheehy-Skeffington, the veteran of the nationalist movement, organised a campaign against it, and all of the women's organisations opposed it. It was narrowly approved by the electorate, even with 31 per cent of them abstaining from the vote.[34] Moves are currently afoot to have this regressive legislative wording changed to reflect twenty-first century reality.

Fianna Fáil advocated a strong familial ideology after the foundation of the Irish state. It is worth reminding ourselves of De Valera's famous St. Patrick's Day speech from 1943 as an illustration of this ideology:

That Ireland which we dreamed of would be the home of a people who valued material wealth only as the basis of right living, of a people who were satisfied with frugal comfort and devoted their leisure to things of the spirit – a land whose countryside would be bright with cosy homesteads, whose fields and villages would be joyous with the sound of industry, with the romping of sturdy children, the contests of athletic youths and the laughter of comely maidens, whose firesides would be forums for the wisdom of serene old age. It would in a word, be the home of a people living the life that God desires man should live.[35]

Underlying this ideology was a very strong cultural and symbolic strength attached to mothers and motherhood in Irish society and culture. The underlying goal of this ideology is the strict control of female sexuality. This is largely derived from Catholic teaching, where the mother is at once

virginal and nurturing, pure and long-suffering. The relationship between the Irish mother and her sons, particularly, has
traditionally been very strong. New research would be needed
on this topic to determine if this relationship still looms as
large in Irish men's lives.

Family Problems

Irish popular culture is suffused with family issues and
dysfunctional mothers and fathers. For example, the one play-
wright whose work is guaranteed to put bums on seats in the
theatres is, of course, John B. Keane. Funnily enough, it is that
very accessibility that has led to the patronising, snobbish attitude towards him that has been evident among many theatre
critics. All of his plays are based on family struggles of some
kind, and despite the fact that the works are usually set in the
1950s and 1960s, the themes still resonate with a twenty-first-
century audience. For example, his character of Big Maggie
in the eponymous play can be seen either as a 'protofeminist
who has survived institutionalised oppression' or as a 'spirit-
crushing psychopath'.[36] She is in truth probably a little of both,
but her feminist credentials are cast-iron, as her personal goals
are independence and freedom from men's abuse and exploitation. She will do whatever is necessary to achieve these
goals, both for herself and her daughters. The scene where she
seduces the travelling salesman in order to show her daughter
his true nature is memorable and thought-provoking.

In Keane's *The Field*, the main character, Bull McCabe, is
a cruel man who has terrorised his family to the point that
his wife is actually mute. His patriarchal persona renders
him a figure of fear and admiration in equal measure in his
community. A similar patriarchal figure is seen also in John
McGahern's *Amongst Women*. The father in this story exhibits

the same emotional coldness, breeding a climate of fear in his family. A more contemporary family story was told in the 1990s in Roddy Doyle's TV series *Family*. This was a dark tale of poverty, violence and abuse, but written with Doyle's characteristic empathy and warmth. The scene where Charlo, the father in the family, was bashed around the head by his wife with the frying pan is unforgettable! Anne Enright's Booker Prize-winning novel *The Gathering* brings us into the world of a very contemporary family – fractured, divided, in pain and in denial. The family here only come together because of the suicide of one of the brothers – an all too topical subject. The relationship between father and son in Belinda McKeon's recent novel, *Solace*, is also a troubled one, which the pair have to try to manage in the face of adversity and trauma. This brief tiptoe through a very random selection of some Irish literary works points us to the idea that there are many unresolved problems in Irish families, providing an abundant crop to be harvested by our national bards.

If we look closely enough, we can often find in our own family histories the kinds of stories that have inspired these fictional accounts. The family stories unearthed in the popular TV series *Who Do You Think You Are?* can be amazing tales of bigamy, migration and murder. And we cannot get enough of them! There has also been a huge interest in the 1901 and 1911 Census since it went online. In rural Ireland, survival was often, and indeed continues to be, a major challenge. Children were frequently farmed out to live with grandparents or other extended family as a coping mechanism when families got too large. When there were a lot of children, the relationships between older and younger siblings were often more parental than those of brothers and sisters. This fractured picture serves as a strong contrast to the idealised image of family life presented by De Valera above.

Parents Under Pressure

The traditionalist type of thinking, which associates mothering with life-long devotion to your children to the neglect of all else, has been partly responsible for Irish women's relatively low participation in the workplace and public life in general. This attitude is still reflected in the lack of availability of affordable childcare for women who work outside the home. Working couples now speak of having expenses equivalent to two mortgages, one for their house and the other for their childcare. I know of several couples where, when they have had their third child, the woman had to give up work, as it did not make financial sense for her to stay on. It is still the norm for working mothers to experience employers that are very inflexible towards their childcare considerations and who view a woman's child-rearing problems as her own business – a problem to be solved outside the workplace. So, while women, and especially married women, have been entering the workforce in their droves since the 1980s, it is still the case that childcare problems and expenses create a 'glass ceiling', a barrier to women's higher achievement in public life.

In the exceptionally consumerist society that Ireland has become, couples are under enormous pressure to juggle all aspects of their lives – both their jobs, child-rearing, an ever-increasing standard of living and the spiralling costs associated with that. Parents, especially mothers, are under increasing scrutiny too, to make sure that their children are afforded every opportunity to achieve their highest potential. The number of extra-curricular activities in which children are now involved can be mind-boggling, and it takes very level-headed parents to resist the US-style competitive ethos that has begun to pervade their lives.

Furthermore, while one might say that Catholic teaching no longer influences Irish people's lives, I would argue that it is still there in the background. After all, most newborns are still baptised, most 7-year-olds still make their Holy Communion, and most 12-year-olds still get confirmed. The fact that the clothes, presents and parties are probably the primary motivation is beside the point. The old Catholic ethos has merged with newer standards of parenting to make parents, especially mothers, feel eternally guilty about trying to 'have it all'. 'Experts' preach to us from our TV screens about little Josh or Kylie's psychological development, and Heaven help us if we are not doing it right! This mind-bending cocktail of old and new expectations makes parenting a major challenge, especially in the context of economic recession.

More Choices

The pace of change in family trends in Ireland in recent times has been quite astounding. The major point is that the family as an institution is not declining or in 'crisis' per se, but is undergoing profound transformation and diversification that present some challenges for the future.[37] Because of the many progressive changes for women in recent decades and the introduction of divorce in the late 1990s, people have more *choices* as to how they want to live their personal lives and express their sexualities. Women and men now have a choice as to whether and when they want to commit to a relationship, have children, get married, stay married or re-marry. Social researchers now find that there are more single people living happily in society; people are deferring marriage and first births until their late twenties and early thirties; most couples live together before marriage, and it is often the birth of a child that precipitates their walking up the aisle; about one-third of births are outside the bounds of marriage, and it has almost completely lost its stigma; divorce is now available, and people are less likely to stay in unhappy and/or abusive marriages; people are now free to legally re-marry; blended families are not now uncommon, with two sets of children sharing a home; more people are getting married in civil ceremonies rather than church ceremonies; there are more open gay relationships, and a version of a civil partnership agreement is now possible for gay couples.[38]

Male dominance is no longer socially acceptable in families, as women's power within the home has increased parallel to their incomes. Gender roles within families are usually negotiated now rather than taken for granted and may even be completely reversed in some cases. All of this does not necessarily happen smoothly and without incident. Family conflict and violence is an ever-present feature of our societies. It can still be very difficult for women to escape from abusive partners, and state funding for women's refuges and rape crisis centres is still pathetically low.

The end result of the increased number of choices currently open to us is that men, women and children may now experience major changes throughout their lives. Family forms are no longer always homogenous and stable, but instead can be incredibly mixed up and diverse. Both men and women now live fragmented, individualistic lives, and it can be a challenge to find a compatible sexual partner who wants the same things out of life at the same time. When you think about it objectively, to find someone to whom you are emotionally drawn, sexually attracted, as well as socially compatible in terms of class, education and income, and to expect all of that to last a lifetime – a tall order indeed! Everything has to be negotiated, life can sometimes seem to be overly complex and 'love is becoming a blank that lovers must fill in themselves across the widening trenches of biography.'[39]

The choices faced can be mind-boggling, especially when people are also under pressure to have brilliant careers. This is the territory of TV shows like *Sex and the City*, but it is apparently not solely relevant to skinny white women who wear designer shoes and live in Manhattan. All this freedom has to be managed now by the individual; we can no longer rely on a time-worn set of rules passed down through families and religious institutions. Our sexualities and the lifestyles that result from them are now flexible, elastic and reversible, and there are very serious consequences to the plethora of choices that we have. This brings its own problems: after all, one person's source of oppression is another's stabilising anchor. These contradictions are summarised nicely by Spanish sociologist Manuel Castells:

> Liberation from the family confronts the self with its own inflicted oppression. The escape to freedom in the open, networked society will lead to individual anxiety and social violence, until new forms of coexistence and shared responsibility are found that bring together women, men and children in a reconstructed, egalitarian family better suited to free women, informed children and uncertain men.[40]

An aspect of this freedom and flexibility that I have found useful in my own life so far is to throw open the windows of the traditional unbending idea of family by adopting a less restricted approach to who you want to belong to it. Why not challenge the old adages 'you can choose your friends but not your family' or 'blood is thicker than water'? It is perfectly normal to develop different types of love for different types of people that may be ultimately far more fulfilling and enduring than those with your actual blood relations. One can have friends who are brothers and sisters in everything but DNA. These connections are as real and meaningful as any with genetic siblings. One might also have temporary 'microwave' families, where circumstances create a quick blast of bonding and connection that may not last long but is nevertheless very intense, meaningful and memorable. For instance, when I was younger, I worked in a pub in London for a few months, during which the Christmas holidays occurred. It was a very unconventional and, therefore, very memorable experience. We were a very disparate group of people who were determined not to let the expectations of having a 'normal' family Christmas get in the way of having a very good time indeed. This might also be experienced, for example, by a group of NGO volunteers when they are far away from home in a hostile environment.

Ultimately, the core of our family is made up of those people whom we shape our life around: those with whom we feel adequately connected by ties of love and/or duty that we modify our own life-paths in order to take their needs and desires into account. Decisions about what jobs to apply for and accept, where to live or what house to buy are determined in part by some combination of partners, children, parents and siblings. Dreams of trekking in the Himalayas, riding down Route 66 on a purple Harley Davidson or owning your own vineyard may have to be put on hold, or go unfulfilled altogether, for the sake of others.

Families in the Countryside

Social life in country villages and small towns often revolves around families. Family reputation is all-important.

Anthropologist Alwyn D. Rees also found in his study of a Welsh village that this preceded all else in the assessment of an individual, epitomised by the proverb: 'the nature of the chick is in the broth.'[41] One of the most important factors shaping our place in the community is whether we have children attending the local school. If so, we have immediate access to a wide group of playmates for our children and to fellow parents for ourselves to befriend. Mums and dads can meet at least at the school gate, and perhaps at parent–teacher meetings, fundraising events, sports days, birthday parties, play dates (even though we do not yet commonly use this term in Ireland, it is only a matter of time), coffee mornings or cake sales. Aside from formal events, parents (usually mums) will probably meet to help each other out, share information and do everything in their power to keep little Kylie and Jack happy in their nappies. If, however, you are childless by accident or indeed child-free by design, you are excluded firstly from this slew of activities that are centred around the children and, secondly, from the sense of social legitimacy accrued to one for contributing new little bums for the seats of the local school.

The village is a direct extension of the family in rural areas. Even if people are not directly related, they often might as well be. There is a very blurred line in rural communities between blood relations, friends and neighbours. For example, everybody feels alarmed on hearing an ambulance pass by: it is likely that they will know the person involved, to a greater or lesser extent. The ideology of neighbourliness is crucially important, and people are expected to take care of each other. To be called a good neighbour is to be paid a high compliment. Locals are often swathed in a blanket of caring but, of course, the other side of that equation is social control and surveillance, whether we realise it or not. Anecdotally, it seems to me that people often self-censor their behaviour, because of what the neighbours might think. You cannot get up to too much without somebody knowing about it. If you want to have a heart-racingly passionate affair, you had better do it somewhere else. Even exposing a little cleavage on a Saturday night will probably get noticed!

In these little republics of neighbours, which are dotted throughout Ireland, there is a fairly strict moral code in such matters. This might seem oppressive to city-dwellers, but this aspect of village life has been explained elsewhere as 'an essentially different relationship between individuality and the overall collectivity.'[42] The maintenance of harmonious relationships between families, neighbours and friends is much more important than the indulgence of any one individual's personal fantasies. There is an old Irish proverb that says, 'ar scáth a chéile a mhaireann na daoine,' meaning 'people live in each other's shadow.' In rural Ireland, this idea is taken very seriously indeed.

Conclusion

To conclude, we can say that the definition of home and family is, for many people, much more flexible than it used to be. Neither concept stands alone and is completely dependent upon our subjective construction of it. For some individuals, these ideas elicit unquestionably positive responses, whereas for others, they are meaningless or perhaps the subject of a lifelong quest. In this arena, there is an intimate connection between one's 'personal troubles' and 'the public issues of social structure'.[43] The actions we take in our personal lives are heavily circumscribed by the options presented to us by the surrounding society. The next chapter will consider the impact of the broader community on our lives.

2

Community Is Not Dying

As well as the home and the family into which we are born, the next feature of our comfort zone to address is that of the wider community to which we feel connected. There are, in fact, a number of parallels between how we can understand the bonds of family and community. There is no essential quality or authentic version of either of these aspects of life, as each person's experience of family and community is different. Also, individuals within both families and communities can have a major impact on our lives by being role models who provide leadership. At a wider level, both family and community dynamics are dependent upon global socio-economic relations, which structure their overall impact on our lives.

It has been said by conservatives that both the family and community are dying in contemporary society. This is not true per se, but major changes are indeed occurring. In fact, Canadian author Michael Ignatieff argues that so much has changed with regard to community and social solidarity that we no longer possess adequate language to express our need for connection. The old words used to describe community are soaked with 'nostalgia and utopianism' and, with the changes in modern life, 'our language stumbles behind like an overburdened porter with a mountain of old cases.'[1] Let us see if we can acquire some efficient new luggage that suits our new, more variable and mobile needs.

Do We Choose Our Community?

Whether or not we attach ourselves to, or buy into, a particular community in a conscious way can become a major aspect of our personal identity. Membership of a community can occur in two ways. On the one hand, it can be ascribed by others in the community, i.e. we are born into it and our status is thus unquestioned. On the other hand, it can be achieved, in that we earn our stripes by working for our status within the community throughout our lifetime, rather than relying upon family reputation or connections. In reality, it is more likely to be a complex mix of the two.

The manner in which people choose to live their everyday lives is at least as important as how others see them, or ascribe a position to them in society. While some people may have to jump over the hurdles of social bias or cultural stereotyping in order to fit in, the sense of community we experience *largely depends on ourselves*. It depends on how much we put into getting to know our neighbours, and that shapes what we receive from them in return. We can never underestimate the significance of an individual's personality and intelligence in evaluating how they fit into their communities.

There are different social forums in both rural and urban settings that offer opportunities for social integration, perhaps in cultural activities or sporting organisations like the GAA. Some people choose to get involved in these, while others do not. In other words, some are active and some are passive. It is ultimately a matter of choice. There are people who, no matter where they live, will be loners. Conversely, there are others who are joiners and innovators, who will always add an extra spark to the area they live in.

There is also a spectrum of belonging within communities, from the isolated bachelor or widow to the self-appointed local cultural guardian who is 'stuck in everything', to use local parlance. The former hardly ever sees anyone from one end of the week to the next, while the latter is out at a different meeting every night, moving and shaking his/her way up the social ladder.

Romanticising Community

The term 'community' summons the idea of an imaginary romantic society 'in which horizons were local, the meaning of life was relatively consensual, co-operation prevailed, everyone knew everyone else and "knew their place".'[2] It is an intensely loaded term that can be used by different types of people to different ends. It can be placed at either end of the left–right spectrum, and also at either end of the spectrum of inclusion and exclusion. It can be used to keep some people out of a particular place or to get others together to achieve a particular goal. It can also be used to develop a sense of camaraderie among people who may never have physically met, or, more commonly, as a social policy cliché. Taking a cynical perspective, it could be argued that 'the term "community" is often applied to a group in order to divert attention from the deep divisions within it and thereby serve the interests of its dominant class.'[3] It is above all a cultural construction that changes over space and time. If, for example, a potentially polluting factory is about to move into an area of high unemployment, some will say that job creation is what the 'community' needs, another will prioritise maintaining the environment, also in the interest of the 'community'. 'Community' is a powerful word in public discourse and, like 'sustainability', it can mean just about anything to anyone. But if you are 'for' the 'community', it has to be good, right?

In today's globalised world, it seems like a contradiction that people still even feel the need for the connective tissue of community. The culture that we inhabit in the Western world is an intensely consumerist one, in which spending money on the goods produced by capitalism is justified and celebrated. Through the medium of advertising our tastes are created and even new identities forged. We are bombarded with media imagery whose primary goal is to make sure we keep shopping. In order to feed this habit, we also need to work harder, hence perhaps leaving less time for family and community life. The speed at which we experience daily life may leave us with a somewhat empty feeling after a while, a need for contact with others. Why do we feel this?

Defining Community

At this point, let me outline some of the ways that sociologists have conceptualised community, a topic that has fascinated them for decades. This is no surprise, considering that the major *raison d'être* of sociology is analysing social life and group behaviour. The main distinction that is made in the definition of community is between viewing it as *fixed to a particular place or locality* on the one hand, and as *denoting a shared sense of identity* with an apparently disparate group of people on the other.

Community as Place

The former sociological perspective is associated with the 'modern' era of social theory, approximately between 1880 and

1980. Without going into detail on the classical sociological theories, they all share the basic idea that one can fundamentally differentiate between two types of society: traditional and modern.[4] The 'traditional' is associated with a simple way of life and a rural set of values. In this vision, people have close ties with one another, there is a strong sense of neighbourhood and everybody pulls together for the common good. The 'modern', presented as a simple opposite, is associated with urban life, where life is more selfish and individualised, and people have little or no ties with their neighbours. In this approach, then, modernisation and urbanisation are strongly linked with causing the demise of community ties.

There are major problems with the accuracy of the assumptions made in this traditional/modern dichotomy, which means that it is no longer deemed acceptable as a thinking tool by most sociologists. These problems can be divided into two broad categories: empirical and political.

Firstly, this approach is an over-simplified model of human life that is not based on empirical research in the real world, containing real people. Just because some people share a locality tells us nothing about how they actually interact with each other: a person may not see their neighbour from one end of the year to the next. It also underestimates the individuality and agency (or individual power) that people actually exercise in their everyday lives. The subtleties of human interaction demand detailed qualitative research that looks beyond schematic representations.

Secondly, the political bias of this traditional versus modern approach is a conservative one that presents a very nostalgic view of so-called 'traditional' life. In other words, proponents of this approach are quite happy to preserve a stratified and unequal society. They like this mythical world where everybody serves a particular function, fitting into social life like pieces in a jigsaw puzzle. There is no room here for conflict or social divisions based on class, race or gender.

Rural Communities

These so-called traditional values are usually most closely associated with rural areas. It is commonly assumed that country villages and rural regions in general necessarily have a strong sense of community. To the outsider, it looks like everybody knows each other. It is assumed that this sense of community could never be as strong in cities because they are composed of people who often originate from outside the area and are therefore not rooted in the place. I would argue that it is not that simple at all.

When arguing that rural areas have a stronger sense of community people often look at clear markers like the fact that country funerals are usually much bigger than town or city ones. They will probably infer from this that the sense of community is stronger in the country and that people are more cared for in the country than in the city. However, all that this indicates to me is that there is a strong culture of funeral attendance in rural communities, because the Catholic Church still has a firmer hold in the countryside, and people are more integrated in religious culture. Also, funerals are social occasions in the country where, perhaps, few others exist, especially for elderly people. These are times when people come together in a strong collective unit, when there is a ritual renewal of social bonds. Furthermore, a strong sense of social obligation dictates that it is important to be seen at funerals, whether you really want to be there or not. Any country TD can tell you that! They are very public displays of connection. As well as that, if we look at the overall culture of death rituals in Ireland, we are not squeamish here about seeing a dead body 'laid out', and one is expected to spend a little time with their loved ones, perhaps in the form of a wake.

If we look beneath the surface of such public displays of community spirit, however, it punches holes in the theory about strong community ties in the country. Think about the person whose funeral it was. Who was actively involved in caring for them if they were sick and/or elderly prior to death? Does the so-called strong rural sense of community mean that neighbours and friends were more than willing to get involved in the everyday hard work of their care? Even though there is no reliable sociological data available on such things, I have a strong suspicion that most of that work is still done by family members (and only certain family members at that), state carers or, if they can afford them, private nurses and carers. Organisations like the Carers Association, MS Ireland, the Alzheimer Society and the Cancer Society know a thing or two about that. This is not to say that some people in certain places don't have a more generous attitude towards their neighbours, but I would contend that this has little to do with how urban or rural the area is. Community is much less about the physical environment than about communicative relationships between people, whether urban or rural. In fact, social isolation is a massive problem in rural areas, and people can sometimes feel far more integrated in their communities in urban areas.

Urban Communities

A study of community in the East End of London in the 1950s was revolutionary in that it found very strong community ties among the urban working class there.[5] Also, when they knocked down the tenements in Dublin in the 1950s and moved the inhabitants out to newly-built suburbs, the people desperately missed the solidarity and camaraderie they had enjoyed in the inner city. The improved housing conditions came at the cost of intense loneliness and alienation. Anecdotally, friends who grew up on Cork City's north side speak of very close friendships with neighbours, where one was never stuck for help or company. Some friends who live in Dublin also have very good neighbours, based on the fact that they all have children of similar ages. So community is not necessarily lost in the process of urbanisation, which is commonly associated with 'modern' values.

Another important point here is that it is difficult to define just what is urban and rural in Ireland anymore because of the enormous amount of urban sprawl outside cities and ribbon development in the countryside. During the boom years of the Celtic Tiger, about twenty-five thousand new, one-off houses were being built in the countryside each year.[6] The proportion of the Irish population who live in the Greater Dublin Area rose from 25 per cent after Independence to around 40 per cent today, creating a planning nightmare in so many ways and commuter hell for many thousands of people.[7] This sprawl also exists around Galway, Limerick and Cork. There seems to be little political commitment to establishing more even regional development throughout the country, and this lethargy can only be exacerbated by the fact of the recession. Many thousands of Irish people now live in places that have the advantages of neither urban nor rural life. These places are under-serviced, soulless and their inhabitants prone to social isolation. It has even been suggested in recent years that suicide rates are higher in these in-between places.[8] The most extreme version of this type of suburban development is, of course, the archetypal spawn of the Celtic Tiger era, the unfinished 'ghost estate', hundreds of which are unfortunately dotted around the country.

Researching the Urban and Rural

The conclusions we arrive at are determined by the kinds of questions we ask. It is a common misperception to *define* rural areas solely in terms of community and traditional values and urban areas solely in terms of economic relationships. People only look at the realm of cosy culture in the country and the realm of bald economics in the city. How about if we do the opposite? If we analyse the economic composition of many rural areas now, we will probably find the decline of the importance of agriculture and most farmers and/or their spouses working away from their farms, a lot of social isolation, a lot of commuting by local workers within the region, a lot of migration to towns and cities, and emigration abroad. None of these trends bode well for the maintenance of local culture and community ties. The cultural connections and community ties in urban Irish life have yet, to my knowledge, to find their sociological analyst. However, one social historian, Kevin C. Kearns, has done Trojan work over the years in recording Dublin stories, told especially by its women.[9]

Analysing local communities without reference to their socio-economic connections with the outside world is a major mistake. No place exists in isolation. A second big mistake is to refer primarily to the realm of culture and values, to the neglect of economic structures. American anthropologists Conrad M. Arensberg and Solon T. Kimball made both of these mistakes in the first and most famous community study in Ireland, *Family and Community in Ireland*, first published in 1940. This piece of research was carried out in a rural area of County Clare during the late 1930s. Coming from Harvard University, Arensberg and Kimball used the predominant theoretical approach in mid-twentieth-century anthropology and sociology, that of structural functionalism. This approach viewed society as being composed of various interrelated parts that form a complete system, much as biologists view the human body. Life was therefore regarded as one big jigsaw where everything and everyone fits together neatly. Local life was seen as equal and co-operative. There was no room for complexity and conflict. Anthropologists at that time really only studied rural areas, but that was to change from the 1950s onwards.

Arensberg and Kimball found a community that was governed by conservative values like 'keeping the name on the land' and collective solidarity between neighbours. It was a homogeneous society that was virtually isolated from outside influences, relatively undisturbed by market forces. Patriarchal control over the family was not seen as a problem, so the study was effectively gender blind. Arranged marriages and forced emigration were just seen as coping strategies to keep the community stable. The two basic institutions – the family and the community – governed life in the County Clare community they studied. The operation of the rule-bound strictures of the Catholic Church was not seen as problematic.

This was a very rosy, romantic picture that sat well with the ideological aspirations of De Valera's newly-independent state. It was no surprise that Arensberg and Kimball produced results like this, because they had to get clearance from both the state and the Catholic Church before embarking upon their community study.[10] A close official eye was probably kept on them.

The second major study of an Irish community – *Inishkillane: Change and Decline in the West of Ireland*, conducted by British anthropologist Hugh Brody and published in 1973 – was fundamentally shaped by the first. Brody revisited the same parish in County Clare in the 1970s to repeat Arensberg and Kimball's research, and the questions he asked were determined by those first asked by his predecessors. He found that there had been a significant loss of community in the intervening 40 years, especially because of emigration. He saw that more urbanisation (evidenced in the introduction of electricity, especially cinema, radio and television) had led to a sense of demoralisation and dissatisfaction with rural life.[11]

While these studies represent a particular set of analytical questions and answers that were shaped by structural functionalism, as explained above, there are many others that have gone unasked and unanswered in the study of Irish communities. One exception to this is Chris Eipper, an Australian anthropologist who conducted a less famous but more revealing piece of research in Bantry, County Cork in the 1970s and 1980s. He prioritised the analysis of power relations and social class in that locality.[12] This brilliant piece of work broke the mould, and nothing like it has been produced since. It is interesting that all of these major studies were conducted by non-Irish academics, outsiders to the field. Why is it that Irish academics shy away from this kind of work?

Another point to note about these studies is that they are all rural based. Rural areas were expected to be analysable in isolation, but not urban areas. This can now be seen to be a huge mistake, as there is nowhere today that is unaffected by global flows of ideas, culture, money and policies. In fact, since rural life is so governed by EU policy and global agricultural pricing mechanisms, one might argue that rural areas are even more globalised than cities. The effects of globalisation on community will be looked at in greater detail in Chapter 3. No anthropological study of a community in an Irish urban setting comes to mind. Certainly, aspects of social life in cities have been analysed, but these aspects are usually problem ones like poverty, violence and drug abuse that happen to occur in particular areas. These studies can be very useful contributions to our knowledge of our societies and in tackling social problems,[13] but it is still usually the poor who are studied, because middle-class and wealthy people have the cultural confidence and social power to block having their lives put under the microscope.

Community as Shared Identity

In contrast to the first approach, which sees community as attached to a geographical place, the second sociological perspective sees community as being linked to a shared sense of identity between groups of people. This has become the more popular approach since the 1980s. Since then, sociologists and anthropologists have generally become more interested in the ways in which people themselves actively construct their personal identities. It is now recognised that one can have multiple identities, feeling a sense of belonging in several different contexts and among different groups. This approach is connected with the focus upon social movements as a research topic. In relatively stable democracies, social movements articulate sets of interests in the public sphere and give members a sense of belonging, creating or reinforcing new identities. However, during periods of political crisis, they might form the constituency for new political parties, who might exert a strong influence on public life.

In the context of late modern society, there are a number of reasons why social movements might grow: the growth of the tertiary service sector, the division of the traditional working class, the expansion of cultural and leisure activities and, finally, the emergence of new types of social protest. An example in Ireland is the activism against cuts in the health sector in recent years, while a UK example is the pro- and anti-hunting political camps that emerged in the 1990s. The emphasis of this sociological approach is therefore on recognising social diversity rather than attempting to create unity where it does not really exist. In community studies, there is now a deeper concern with the particularities of local contexts and the cultural and symbolic aspects of people's feelings of belonging. It is now obsolete to distinguish between 'real' and 'perceived' community, because there is a general recognition that all social life is constructed and interpreted by humans, i.e. it is *all about perception.* Also, the newer, less-traditional forms of community can 'have a powerful capacity to define new situations and thereby construct social reality.'[14] For example, to say that we belong to the gay community or to the Traveller community has very real implications indeed, as we are setting ourselves apart from a perceived social or cultural opposite which we possibly view as a source of discrimination or oppression. The more choices we have regarding which community we would like to adhere to, the more conscious is the desire to make connections and express what we might call our 'we-feelings', or sense of belonging.

This type of approach to community studies, which connects community to a shared sense of identity rather than to a particular place, has become mainstream in recent years. Its single most influential exponent is British anthropologist Anthony P. Cohen. In his major theoretical work, *The Symbolic Construction of Community* (first published in 1985), he argues that there has been a massive upsurge in community consciousness in recent decades – for example, as expressed through ethnic and religious movements. People only consciously use the word 'community' to distinguish themselves from others, so he claims that it is used to denote the boundary between oneself and others, so it is a 'boundary-expressing symbol', but 'its meaning varies with its member's unique orientations to it.'[15] Community is primarily seen here as a mental construct, and the focus is very much on people's feelings about community, rather than any physical mapping of it – mental maps rather than cartographic ones. Cohen asserts that:

People construct community symbolically, making it a resource and repository of meaning, and a referent of their identity.[16]

In the following florid passage from his research on the island of Whalsay in the Shetlands, he details what he means by 'belonging':

'Belonging' implies very much more than merely having been born in the place. It suggests that one is an integral piece of the marvellously complicated fabric which constitutes the community; that one is a recipient of its proudly distinctive and consciously preserved culture – a repository of its traditions and values, a performer of its hallowed skills, an expert in its idioms and idiosyncrasies.[17]

However, while this analysis is hugely valuable, Cohen's specific focus on the boundaries seen to exist between communities has been questioned. Irish sociologist Gerard Delanty, for example, argues that belonging itself is a more important aspect of community than boundaries:

Especially today, as a result of multiculturalism, polynationality and transnationalism, the differences between groups are becoming more and more diffuse and overlapping. Community is more likely to be expressed in an active search to achieve belonging than in preserving boundaries.[18]

Community is analysed by Cohen as primarily being a cultural phenomenon, and while this approach has been a major contribution to the debate on community, it has less explanatory power when it comes to explaining conflict between different members of communities. Both place-bound communities and group communities are composed of different sets of actors vying for dominance in various arenas, so conflict will inevitably be inherent to them. To interpret all of the everyday life of communities as symbolic acts to delineate boundaries may not equip us very well to deal with the messiness of power relations. We also need to remember the ideological versatility of the term 'community', which can be used simultaneously by individuals and/or groups with very different political agendas. These might be business people, radical activists or church groups, so 'it always remains important to investigate *which* local people and local institutions are being included and which are being excluded, whenever "community" is evoked.'[19] This more critical approach can help us to differentiate between the ideology and the lived reality of community in particular contexts.

Overall, the distinction we referred to earlier between viewing community as *fixed to a particular locality* and as symbolising *a shared sense of identity*, is, in my opinion, a false dichotomy. I believe that these two views of community are not contradictory. Attachment to localities can be one of a chosen set of many identities. Indeed, we might speak of one's attachment to both residential and non-residential communities. A young person, for example, may play in the local GAA team, with all the ideological and sociocultural baggage that that entails, but they may also be globally connected via Facebook to various social networks, as well as perhaps being involved in a political party at national level. Contemporary analysts would be more interested in the active choices people make to connect with a particular group or groups rather than passively assuming that it means something or defines your personal identity if you were born in a particular place. It could mean little or nothing to some people who cannot wait to leave their place of birth, and absolutely everything to someone else. Human agency creates many possibilities. Two different people might live in parallel universes, even in a tiny place.

The Lived Reality of Rural Communities

It is productive to think of community more as a *process* rather than as a final *destination*, experienced in phases rather than continuously. Nobody is conscious *all the time* of their community ties or their lack of them, as we generally experience peaks and troughs of belonging throughout the year. Throughout the winter months, there may not be much contact between people, except perhaps at Christmas or to deal with weather-related crises. Community is often experienced through rituals or ceremonies that periodically reinforce feelings of connection and communion, like St. Patrick's Day parades in March and perhaps agricultural shows in late summer. These events punctuate the cycle of local life, marking the onset of spring and the end of summer. More important, they give everyone something to talk about when they meet.

The GAA

Community is heightened most of all, of course, when the locality is challenged by an outside force. Thus, a significant forum for peaks of togetherness in rural communities is provided by the Gaelic Athletic Association (GAA). Nationally, there are about three hundred thousand members of

GAA clubs, which is almost 10 per cent of the population.[20] This is a combination of Gaelic football and hurling, which might be termed 'the *Riverdance* of sport' because of its elegance and skill! The GAA has been a pillar of Irish identity since its foundation in 1884 and, amazingly, it has not been affected by globalisation, the availability of Sky Sports and the ubiquitous devotion to one or other English Premiership team. It seems that the average sports fan has enough love to go around. In fact, the showing of GAA matches on television has probably increased the popularity of this particularly Irish phenomenon.

The survival of the GAA is dependent upon a huge amount of voluntary work, as it operates on a completely amateur basis. Nobody makes a profit, and money only changes hands to keep the clubs running. Everybody plays a part, from the mammies who wash the team kits to the groundskeepers and the trainers. This strong sense of connection operates at county level as well as at local club level. Passions run high on All-Ireland Final days each September, but they can be just as high throughout the year in little places few people have even heard of.

Players on the local teams acquire a very high social status, and those who really excel are nothing short of local heroes. For a girl to date a good GAA player gets her great kudos among her friends. If a local boy or girl plays on the county team, his or her hometown or village will be festooned with handmade posters on match days. Later in life, this fame certainly does not hurt their career prospects, as, in the past, the top county players have had a much higher chance of success in their chosen fields than ordinary mortals. However, this is no longer a guarantee of success in this era of recession. There was an item on *The Late Late Show* during 2010 about the high level of unemployment among GAA players. A suggestion was aired that employers might consider a type of positive discrimination towards them in order to keep GAA culture alive.

Children get involved in local football and hurling teams from a very young age and some stay on as players into their thirties. Anecdotally, local teachers and parents in rural communities would say that those children who do not get involved in their local GAA club are far more likely to get in trouble later in life, and that the team feeling and community involvement fostered in local clubs has a stabilising psychological impact. Also, if a child engages in any kind of juvenile delinquency or anti-social behaviour, getting them involved in the football or hurling team is often the first attempt at a solution to their problems.

The players wear their team colours with pride, and the passion and commitment of the players has to be seen to be believed. The boys and girls train hard on the local pitch on miserable, wet winter nights and stay off alcohol for weeks before important matches. Pictures of winning teams from the past adorn the walls of the local pubs. For those who have not witnessed this culture first-hand, the series *Celebrity Bainisteoir* on RTÉ television is very instructive. The idea of 'the power of the "jersey"' (the club sweater), or the sense of responsibility to add to the honour or esteem of your local area, is a huge motivating factor to try to do well. In one pep talk by a coach on this show, players were reminded that they didn't own the jersey, but were only minding it for the next generation. The sense of being only carriers, receptacles of local culture, is very powerful. Sociologist Tom Inglis argues that, 'despite an incoming tide of American culture, consumerism, liberal-individualism and hedonism, there is still a very strong sense of identification with and belonging to the local and, from this, the national.'[21] The attachment to place still has

powerful meaning. This is a theme to which I shall return in
Chapter 3.

Social Class

When we try to understand the complexities of local life, we
might be tempted to turn to analysis of social class. However,
it is a blunt instrument with which to dissect social divisions
in the countryside, as the edges of class and status cleavages
are generally blurred, and there can be complex class trajectories even within the one family. Little things can say a lot,
however, like whether you eat 'the dinner' at 1 p.m. or 'dinner'
at 6 p.m.

Social life in rural villages is governed by what Anthony
P. Cohen terms equalitarianism, which is 'the intentional
masking or muting of social differentiation.'[22] This is different to egalitarianism, which is a belief in equality as a moral
principle. Everybody knows that social inequality exists, but
it is not seen as healthy to dwell on it too much. People are
only too aware that one's fortunes can change overnight, and
nobody is immune to financial problems, illness or tragedy.
As well as this, people have to deal with each other in many
and complex ways and, as I have alluded to before, maintaining harmony is the primary goal. This seems to be common
in country life everywhere and, as Dutch author Geert Mak
found in his recent research in a village in Holland, 'it takes
a great deal more courage to stick one's neck out in a village
than it does in the relatively anonymous world of the city.'[23]

Social life is more integrated at village level, and people must
try not to offend others, for the sake of the whole community. Cohen also says that life is far from simple in villages, as
people need far more sophisticated interaction and negotia-
tion skills than they would if they lived in the city. Managing

conflict, for example, is of paramount importance, because you cannot just walk away from the troublesome situation.[24] Furthermore, if two local businessmen were to have a disagreement over money, they must take into account that their wives may perhaps be friends, their children may go to school together and their sons and daughters might be dating. So it has to be resolved, as they cannot afford to fall out. Their lives wouldn't be worth living! At this point, it might be instructive to take a behind-the-scenes look at three of the main places where people meet in the intimate setting of the village – the church, the pub and the shop.

The Catholic Church

In a traditional Catholic society, Mass attendance is an important determinant of community belonging. However, in the early twenty-first century, this seems rather unconvincing, as Mass attendance is well down on previous decades. Between 1981 and 1998, the proportion of Catholics attending weekly Mass dropped from 87 per cent to 65 per cent, and all indicators would suggest that it has dropped much further again since then.[25] While this may be less true in small rural communities, it would appear to be accurate to suggest that Mass attendance has lost its resonance as a determinant of anything. To tick a box in a questionnaire is one thing, but to have a meaningful relationship with one's church is another. There has been a general process of secularisation in Ireland, as throughout the Western world. Church and state are more separate than ever before, and this process has been hastened by the numerous revelations of child sexual abuse by priests and the audacious cover-ups by senior figures in the Church hierarchy. Taoiseach Enda Kenny made a famous speech in July 2011 on the Vatican's response to the revelations of the

Cloyne Report into clerical abuse in that diocese. The following extract shows how far we have come in this regard:

> This is not Rome. Nor is it industrial school or Magdalene Ireland, where the swish of a soutane smothered conscience and humanity and the swing of a thurible ruled the Irish Catholic world. This is the Republic of Ireland, 2011 – a Republic of laws, of rights and responsibilities, of proper civic order, where the delinquency and arrogance of a particular version of a particular kind of morality will no longer be tolerated or ignored … The law – their law [victims of clerical abuse] – as citizens of this country, will always supersede canon laws that have neither legitimacy nor place in the affairs of this country.[26]

Relations with the Vatican have been chilly ever since, especially since the government closed down the Irish embassy there later in 2011, as a cost-cutting measure. Despite all of this, however, most people still view the Catholic Church as part of the furniture of public life, not feeling strongly enough to show either their love or hate for it. We might call them *submarine* Catholics, who surface at times of trouble or, indeed, celebration. Even if they do not attend Mass, most people do like all the bells and whistles of a traditional Catholic wedding ceremony; they will christen their children in church and have a big party afterwards; and they will bury their elders in a Catholic graveyard. In fact, I recently witnessed a two-for-one ceremony, where the couple were married, and had their 1-year-old christened at the same time. Mother and child wore matching dresses.

Even among those who do attend Mass weekly, it is generally a rather cursory affair, putting structure on their week.

They see and are seen by a few neighbours and buy the Sunday papers. The vast majority have no more involvement than that. The running of the parish is generally left to a small cadre of volunteers who help the priest in various ways, as church collectors, ministers of the Eucharist, flower arrangers or cleaners. Needless to say, this is mostly a voluntary female activity and delineates the outer limits of women's role in the Church. So to say that Mass attendance has a strong connection to one's status in an Irish community today appears misguided and redolent of lazy thinking.

The Local Pub

The other place where one can meet people is, of course, the local pub, which has enjoyed nothing less than iconic status in Irish society. It is one of the distinctive elements of Irish social life that is sought out by visitors who come from places where bars are no-go zones for all but a few hardened drinkers. It has to be said that excessive and problem drinking is a huge issue in Ireland, with a high level of tolerance for public drunken behaviour. We are among the highest consumers of alcohol in the EU, with each adult drinking on average 14 litres of pure alcohol every year.[27]

I want to stress here, however, the positive community-building function of pubs. The pub is a place where young people can learn how to behave properly after a few drinks, and it seems obvious to me that there is a close connection between the increase in uncontrolled home drinking, or indeed 'bush drinking', and alcohol-related public order problems. There are no measures and no limits. Conversely, the congenial, relatively orderly atmosphere of the local pub, where people get chatting after a few pints is crucially important in the socialisation of young people, as well as in the cementing of local friendships. It is 'where everybody knows your name'. It is a space where people can get out of the house, forget about work for a while and relax. This is where one can catch up on the local news – when men do it, they are exchanging information; when women do it, they are gossiping! The local gossip is a powerful tool for social bonding as well as social control. If you care about whether or not you are gossiped about in a negative way, it means you are socially integrated in the community, and will do your best to avoid it.[28] It seems to me that being talked about is a huge compliment, as it means one is part of others' lives, in one way or another.

There are, however, huge pressures on country pubs to survive now. The combined factors of the availability of very cheap alcohol in the supermarkets, the smoking ban, stricter drink-driving laws, and changing standards of living and life-styles have all led to challenging times for local landlords in country areas. In recent years, it has been estimated that pubs have been closing at the rate of one a day in Ireland, and mostly in rural areas. One writer said of pubs in 2006, 'we have money today, and the rarefied tastes that go with afflu-ence, and these are not likely to be satisfied in your local spit and sawdust emporium. It's last orders, if not last rites, for your humble offering.'[29]

While circumstances are straitened for many now, as the recession bites, there is more need than ever for a place where local people can meet, for just the price of a few drinks. For those who have lost their jobs and may be feeling low as a result, the local pub could be an important source of contact with the community. This is especially the case for men, who may not be part of the same communicative circles as women are. In many places, it is too late, and many or all of the local pubs have already been mown down by the scythe of fierce competition. Significant numbers of young people will probably have emigrated too, so the buzz might not the same on a Saturday night anymore. Stricter enforcement of drink-driving laws also means that it is very risky to drive the few miles home after a few drinks. One farmer I know recently said to me, with a glint in his eye and his tongue planted firmly in his cheek, 'sure, I have to bring herself out with me now, to drive me home!'

The pubs in country villages have to struggle to survive. Those who do survive have to lay on extras like food and entertainment just to entice people in the door. This is especially since pubs have become a bit more feminised and genteel than they were in the past. While there are, of course, advantages to having a drink in the comfort of one's own home, the social aspect of having a chat with neighbours and friends is missing. The real winners here are the off-licences and supermarkets that sell us our crates of beer and our cases of Chilean Merlot.

The pub, however, is an important and unique institution in Irish society, crucial to social interaction, especially where not many other venues exist. If you need to find something out in a country area, you can ask someone in the pub. If you want some company, you can get it, and if you want to be left alone, that is fine too. There is a tacit understanding between regulars. There are some who have their designated seat as well, of course.

The pub is also a great leveller, where one's social class position or status is parked outside the door. The unemployed, the business owners, the labourers, the farmers, the professionals and the housewives are all equal in the eyes of the bartender. Everybody knows that the class totem pole exists, but the democratic ideology of pub culture means that it is temporarily brushed under the carpet. All are subject to a certain code of behaviour and, for example, getting too loud after drinking gets you labelled a 'messer'. If you want to drink yourself into an early grave, that is perfectly okay, but you just have to be quiet about it. Any kind of aggressive behaviour is given short shrift. You are expected to be friendly and open, but this is circumscribed by the expectation of a certain modesty of behaviour. Congenial conversation about local events or current affairs is the order of the day. And, of course, it is very important to remember to buy your round when in company. Not obeying this rule is one of the few things for which you will be criticised.

Occasionally, in fact only very occasionally now, someone will start to sing a song, which may lead to a sing-song that might last all night. The ability to sing a song fairly well is very highly valued in this setting. However, you do not sing until you are asked, and it is preferable if you have to be cajoled a bit before you treat your companions to a few bars of 'Fiddler's Green' or 'Nancy Spain'! Some great memories are made in this way, and sometimes you see hidden sides to people's personalities. For example, a huge man with hands like shovels might unleash his vocal chords to sing a tender love song, or a diminutive young girl might sing a raucous old rebel song that could hardly be described as politically correct. A pub culture that does not allow spontaneous music sessions to erupt occasionally is a poor one indeed.

The Local Shop

The local shop is another source of connection with the community. A true test of whether one is part of a community is if you could still get your shopping done even if you have forgotten your wallet. Will the shopkeeper trust you to bring the money you owe the next day? It is all about trust. Everyone knows everyone else, and a well-run local shop can be a major hub for the community's social intercourse. In the best of them, there might be a notice board inside the door where you can find notices like 'hay for sale' or 'beautiful kittens free to a good home', tradesmen's adverts, holiday postcards from locals, or notices for local events in the nearby cinemas or theatres. It is a window on what is going on locally.

The shop is also a meeting point. If you are at home all day alone, you will undoubtedly meet someone to chat with when you go out to buy milk and bread. If something important has happened locally, you will hear about it. If you need the mobile phone number of a plumber, the shopkeepers will have it. If you need to find out the time of a local funeral, they will know it. If you missed the score of Sunday's match, they will know that too. They are guardians of the community spirit. You do not get that in Tesco!

The shopkeeper is at the core of local life, and his/her role in the community has a complexity that their urban counterparts do not have to worry about. He/she has to be all things to all people, and 'he is bound to his customers by a multiplicity of ties. He has perhaps a smaller choice of roles than he would in the town, and he has to play them all to the same audience.'[30] Nevertheless, local shops are finding it harder than ever to compete with the big chains who are invading most Irish towns. Local shops, whether in rural areas or in the centre of towns, cannot compete on price, which is increasingly becoming the bottom line for most people. Country towns are now experiencing the so-called 'doughnut effect' that has become the dominant pattern throughout the Western world. When people only shop in the suburbs, town centres begin to die. People are aware of this now, but perhaps it is too late. For example, in Macroom, County Cork, posters are currently up all over the town centre saying, 'Keep your business in town ... keep your town in business.'

There is also the issue of the public developing more cosmopolitan tastes, so local shops have to try to stock wine and pesto and paté and hummus to keep them happy. However, whenever one visits a village where the local shop has already succumbed to market forces, it leaves a void at its heart that is very noticeable. If people do not have a reason to stop in the village, its identity is very quickly reduced to a mere throughway for traffic, soulless and abandoned.

The problems experienced by rural shops are an indicator of bigger issues. Irish Rural Link, the national network representing rural communities, is very concerned about the overall decline of essential services in rural areas, especially on behalf of elderly people who live alone. The closure of rural Garda stations, for example, is part of an overall plan to reduce Garda numbers to 13,000 by 2014, under the EU–IMF agreement.[31] This has adversely affected, among others, the West Cork region. Speaking in late 2011, Michael Collins from the West Cork village of Goleen, and a member of the West Cork Rural Garda Station Retention Campaign, is annoyed that 'an area with the biggest drugs haul in the history of the state, one of the biggest open coast lines and the biggest unsolved murder [sic] would lose its station.'[32] The Minister for Justice was unrepentant in his response to this plea, however, responding that the number of stations 'hardly changed from the foundation of the state, despite the huge advances in transport, communications and technology in recent years.'[33] Cold comfort, then, for the elderly man or woman who hears a strange noise outside their house in the dead of night. Furthermore, the number of rural post offices has reduced from 1,900 to 1,100 within the past five years.[34] The loss of both of these institutions has a massively detrimental impact upon local life, especially for the most vulnerable inhabitants of isolated areas.

Engineering Community

There is a pervasive feeling in Irish public discourse that society is changing too fast, and many of the old certainties are gradually being eroded. The highs and lows of economic boom and bust have led to a general questioning of where we are at, socially and morally. This is a fertile ground for journalists and social commentators. The topic might be poverty, high unemployment, mortgage arrears, the preponderance of litter everywhere, the closing of rural pubs and post offices, the common use of cocaine and heroin among young people, the high number of deaths on the roads, young male suicide, drug gang wars, domestic violence, the experience of commuter hell, or homelessness in our cities. Some of these common problems may seem disparate and not remotely connected with each other, but there is a general sense in which they are all somehow part of one bigger problem of community decline in a relatively wealthy society. The increasingly individualised and consumerist lives led by many people have led them to experience problems of social isolation and the apparent decline of the communities in which they live.

Communitarianism

Problems like this exist throughout the Western world, or anywhere that unbridled capitalism has been allowed free rein. Many people appear to be losing their connection to traditional institutions like the family and community. While this has the advantage of increased personal freedoms, for some it might mean a sense of uncertainty regarding how best to live their lives in the absence of any set of rules.[35] The communitarian movement emerged in the early 1990s to attempt to solve the problems that they saw of community decline, excessive individualism and social dislocation. Amitai Etzioni, an eminent social scientist based in Washington DC in the US, is the founder of the movement. He defines communitarianism as follows:

> We are a social movement aimed at shoring up the moral, social and political environment. Part change of heart, part renewal of social bonds, part reform of public life.[36]

Etzioni has written extensively, energetically and passionately on the theme of rebuilding communities and restoring moral order, and continues his activism via the website www. communitariannetwork.org. He is a major figure in US academic life and exerts a strong influence upon public discourse on both sides of the Atlantic. Communitarians are advocates of so-called 'Third Way' politics, an attempt to forge a path between right and left, or between individualism and authoritarianism.[37] While it is tempting to try to classify Third Way politics in terms of left- and right-wing politics, this is rather futile, as it contains elements of both. Perhaps this partly explains its popularity. The approach has appealed over the years to politicians both left and right; for example, both to Bill Clinton and George Bush in the US and to Tony Blair's New Labour in the UK. Despite this, some argue that the approach is conservative, moralistic and authoritarian, as there is much more emphasis on people's duties and responsibilities rather than on rights and entitlements.[38]

Robert Putnam and Social Capital

This set of problems was also foregrounded by the Irish state in recent years. After all the years, indeed decades, of entrusting our economy to the vagaries of multinational investment, it dawned upon state representatives that all was not as well as it might be. In retrospect, of course, we can now see that the spotlight was turned in the wrong direction. However, that aside for the moment, such concerns led Bertie Ahern, head of the Fianna Fáil government that presided over the boom and bust of the Celtic Tiger years, to invite Robert Putnam, a distinguished Harvard political scientist, to Ireland. Putnam's major focus has been on community decline in the US. He published his influential book *Bowling Alone* in 2000, in which he presented an enormous amount of data to prove the following case:

> ... social networks have value. Just as a screwdriver (physical capital) or a college education (human capital) can increase productivity (both individual and collective), so too social contacts affect the productivity of individuals and groups. ... social capital refers to connections among individuals – social networks and the norms of reciprocity and trustworthiness that arise from them.[39]

His ultimate conclusion is that 'we Americans need to reconnect with each other.'[40] He therefore claims that social connections, like membership of neighbourhood groups and social clubs, are demonstrably good for the health and productivity of individuals and the broader society. He says we need more social capital, because these features of social life – networks, norms and trust – enable people to act together more effectively to pursue shared objectives and get things done in their communities. While he does not belong to the communitarian movement, he expresses similar concerns as Etzioni. He is also said to have influenced the thinking of both Bill Clinton and Tony Blair, and Irish politicians jumped on this particular bandwagon. In an interview in *The Irish Times* in November 2007, President Mary McAleese said that she wanted to 'inculcate people with a deep personal sense of responsibility.' When asked how one does that, she replied, 'I haven't a baldy clue.'[41] If she doesn't know, what hope is there for the rest of us? At least she was a bit more honest than the rest of the politicians who claimed to care about such issues.

Robert Putnam became a relatively frequent visitor to Ireland throughout Fianna Fáil's reign in the noughties, at the behest of Bertie Ahern. The National Economic and Social Forum (NESF) compiled a report entitled *The Policy Implications of Social Capital*. Ahern was so enamoured with Putnam's argument that he set up the Taskforce on Active Citizenship. This taskforce set up a public consultation process to assess people's needs and access their opinions on the state of their communities. Mary Davis, since a Presidential candidate, was appointed Chairperson. When I interviewed her in 2006, she said that Ahern wanted to 'start a national conversation'. She said that he:

> ... wanted to get people talking about the whole idea of active citizenship, who was participating and who wasn't, what were the gaps, and maybe what could be done to assist more people to take part and to get engaged, and then to make recommendations back to government that would influence policy in the future. That's the background to why he set up the Task Force.[42]

She went on to explain 'active citizenship' to me as follows:

> To create the vision, I would bring it down to a community or a village level, and say, what opportunities are there to ensure that nobody's left behind, nobody's marginalised, that the citizen can have a meaningful

involvement in the way the community is evolving, the infrastructure, how can you make it better?[43]

The situation the taskforce found throughout the country was a mixed one, with major social concerns expressed by various kinds of people. At the same time, however, they found a society in which many thousands of people regularly engage in voluntary activities to help the broader community. Davis evokes her own experience of bringing the Special Olympics to Ireland in 2003:

> Again, going back to the World Games, the success of 2003 was the fact that we got the corporate community working with the state, working with ourselves, the voluntary people and the wider volunteer community of thirty thousand people that got together, that's what made the Games successful, that it wasn't just one person or one group of people. It was everybody coming together that brought that will to do things.[44]

Through such discussions, the ideas of social capital and active citizenship have been mainstreamed, entering the official public discourse of Irish life. Social capital has become another catchphrase, like sustainable development did before it in the 1990s. I suspect that it may be so popular with politicians because it puts the focus on ordinary citizens' activities rather than on those in power whose job it is to formulate public policy and run public affairs in an honest and transparent fashion. It has an economistic ring to it, with something like a cost–benefit analysis in the background. There have been a myriad of similar bureaucratic attempts to 'build community' in the UK which 'has nothing to do with *real* community development but concerns social engineering: an instrumental approach to engagement strategies.'[45] This managerial approach uses community as a buzzword, as a moral absolute that is good by its very definition. Not all problems can be solved by closer social connections in communities, and there is still a strong role for the state in managing how society is run.

Also, in retrospect, we can see that Fianna Fáil gave free rein to banks and property developers to chase the fast buck, leading to the major financial disasters that almost terminally broke our economy and ended up with our going to the International Monetary Fund (IMF), cap in hand. They built huge housing estates and shopping malls where there are no other services available, exactly the kind of landscape that leads to demoralisation and the decline of community. They created the conditions for the recession in which we now find ourselves. Then, in true Celtic Tiger style, the government rowed in, hosted high-profile media events with high-fliers like Putnam and, using politically correct language, told people that they have to solve their own problems now.

Preaching to ordinary people about participating in their communities seems hypocritical and disingenuous when looked at in the context of these much bigger issues. In the absence of real democracy, when the shenanigans that occur behind the scenes are where it's really at, focussing on volunteerism and civic participation is inaccurate at best and deeply unjust at worst. This resonates particularly strongly since the 2012 Mahon Report confirmed our worst suspicions about Irish political culture. To bring it back to the level of a small rural community: if the state does not take charge of maintaining proper services, especially for the most disadvantaged who need food cooked for them or transport to hospital or nursing care at home, then no amount of voluntary neighbourliness will compensate for people's decreased standard of living and poorer quality of life.

Is Community Dying?

The idea that community is being lost cannot be trusted, in my opinion. This idea is usually conservative and oversimplified. It seeks to return to a mythical past in which everybody knew their neighbours and knew their place. This nostalgic view has no room for class conflict or differences in status in communities. It is a romantic perspective that does not acknowledge the backdrop of the machinations of capitalism. It also underestimates the amount of agency that can be exercised by individual members of communities. I do not think it is accurate or appropriate to talk of the death of communities. However, things are changing. For example, the activities people engage in are more organised, there are less random associations, and more temporary, yet strong, connections between people. So we might say that some old aspects of communities are loosening and other new ones are in fact tightening. Both of these trends are probably happening concurrently and vying for dominance.

In terms of life in the countryside, it is a myth that life there is simple, that it will inevitably follow a straight path to urbanisation, with an inevitable loss of community. It is very difficult to draw conclusions, as many conflicting trends are evident at once. The spontaneous aspects of community life, like dropping in on neighbours' houses unannounced or impromptu music sessions in the pub, may be in decline. However, as an alternative to these forms of social bonding, there are more organised initiatives, like community development groups, Active Retirement groups, book clubs, state-sponsored home help for the elderly, and scheduled recreational events like card games, concerts and farmers' markets, that enhance local life and did not exist in the past. The newest addition to this list of activities is 'Men's Sheds', an initiative to encourage men to get together in a friendly and non-threatening environment. Two examples of such contemporary initiatives that are already up and running are the Rural Transport Programme, which is a lifeline for the elderly living in isolated areas, and the Rural Social Scheme, which provides part-time employment for 2,600 people on infrastructural projects in their local communities.[46] Old and new cultural elements are waxing, waning and fusing, driven by the energy and creativity of local people.

While there may be a sense of disillusionment with formal politics, many people adopt a do-it-yourself approach to getting things done and building social networks. There is a lot of political action with a small 'p' where people compensate for gaps in state policy to address their needs and to change local social life in a positive way. There are thousands of hard-working people throughout Ireland, either in voluntary or paid positions, who make these schemes work well at the local level. These expressions of community are influenced by social policy nationally, as well as cultural trends globally, so ideas originating at the national and the international levels ultimately feed back into local life. The spectre of government cutbacks is a constant worry for those involved in such initiatives.

The term 'community', however, can have vastly different meanings, depending upon who is using it and why. Instead of assuming that communities have always had their own autonomy, we need to examine how they were formed out of interconnected space and social networks. There are different ways of engaging with community, depending on the context – from forming armed militias to protect it from attack, on the one hand, to the formation of Tidy Towns committees, on the other hand. The old assumptions that community is stronger in rural areas and that it is undermined by urbanisation can no longer be given credence. That community is even necessarily connected to a physical place can no longer be assumed, as people now form meaningful communities across the world, enhanced by telecommunications and the Internet. Communities of hearts and minds may or may not be place-based.

The connection of the idea of community to a specific locality cannot be assumed to be 'prior, primordial, more "real"', as 'local solidarities and imaginings may also be produced by global processes.'[47] This could refer to a group of foreign workers being imported into a locality, new mobile phone masts being erected, or a new motorway built to bypass a local town. To speak of attachment to a particular locality certainly is not passé but, overall, it is the symbolic attachments to places and people that are of primary interest to sociologists these days. With the secularisation of Irish society and the opening up of Irish culture to diverse social and cultural influences, all sorts of possibilities exist for cultural expression. However, the amount of freedom people feel they possess varies hugely, depending upon social and personal factors.

Conclusion

Community is a process of building and searching rather than a destination, and it may often include elements of conflict, as we have witnessed with the Shell to Sea campaign's struggle against big business and the state in County Mayo. It is also experienced more in moments than as a constant presence, with the inevitable highs and lows that result from any sort of emotional attachment to people or places. While there have been recommendations from the state on the benefits of maintaining social capital, community needs to grow organically because people feel the need for it rather than obeying an economistic edict from the state. One cannot engineer genuine social solidarity.[48] And, as we all know, faking it is never quite the same. There are no simple patterns, and the more we dig around in local life, the more complexities we find. We need to examine in detail how active social agents create communities from the raw materials of the interconnected space that already existed.

People will always feel the need for connection, but the conditions in which they operate and the types of communications they use change over time. A useful, open understanding of community is that it is an imaginative tool used by people as they go about their business of constructing an idea of a better society.[49] Community is also inherently random, as it is dependent upon the inputs of opinionated individuals, and famously prone to conflict and faction fighting. It appears to me that we need not fear this, but we should embrace the process through which people express their needs. People try to build communities 'as they grope for an understanding of the world, fallibly exchanging, adjusting and reconstructing their models as they harvest the experiences that ensue.'[50] In order for their experience to be meaningful, people should not feel a sense of duty around community, but participate in it with their hearts as well as their heads.

3

Globalisation and Place

Having discussed the various ways in which we identify with social groups like families and communities in Chapters 1 and 2, we can now address how people identify with particular physical locations and places. Some would say that the places where we come from or where we live no longer matter to our identities because of the extent of the reach of globalisation processes into our everyday lives. It is virtually impossible, at least in the West, to live one's life completely locally with no global influences. Places such as the aforementioned West Cork, where I grew up, cannot be written about in isolation, as decisions made in boardrooms in New York or Brussels – or perhaps increasingly, Shanghai or Beijing – have a very strong impact upon their futures. While local people muddle through and try to make the best of their circumstances, the extent of the globalisation of the Irish economy renders most of us relatively powerless in the face of global macro-scale decision-making.

Some go so far as to abandon connections between identity and places altogether. Spanish sociologist Manuel Castells argues:

Social meaning evaporates from places, and therefore from society, and becomes diluted and diffused in the reconstructed logic of a space of flows.[1]

Castells' argument that we now live in 'a space of flows' rather than places is untenable, in my opinion. In this argument, he implies that places are nothing more than locations through which money, people and ideas flow, and do not have strong emotional meaning in people's lives. There is a huge amount of evidence all around us that real geographical places still play a huge role in our lives. However, those places need to be recognised as open and globally connected, and their identities as socially constructed. They acquire meaning through the interventions of human meanings and actions. Global media also has an increasingly important role to play. In the era of YouTube, for example, while living in one part of the world we can watch major world events unfold in real-time halfway across the globe, as with the tsunami in December 2004 or the Arab Spring revolts of 2011.

This chapter looks at what is meant by globalisation and the effect it has upon how we see the places we live in and perhaps even love. It introduces some of the sociological literature on the topic and, hopefully, some thought-provoking ideas on how we identify with places throughout our lives.

Globalising Influences

'Where are you from?' Taking into account the many social complexities that we now know surround the idea of belonging and our attempts to define our comfort zone, English author Paul Gilroy's clever answer to the above question is, 'it ain't where you're from, it's where you're at.'[2] Think about it. This apparently simple reply encapsulates all of the discussions of the previous two chapters that focussed on our sense of belonging to families and communities. It resists stereotyping or pigeonholing us because of where we were born, the colour of our skin or the language we speak. It resists also the simplistic assumption that we will necessarily feel an uncomplicated sense of loyalty to our birthplace and acknowledges that our cultural origins can sometimes be problematic or painful. It speaks of our chosen social alliances and feelings of connection, instead of our ethnic origins. It prioritises a sense of personal power to connect with the places and people that mean something to us, as intelligent human beings. It reinforces a sense of openness and action, rather than exclusion and inertia. Those nine words certainly say a lot. So no matter where you were born, next time you are asked that question, you now know what to say!

However, when most of us are asked where we are from, we usually still answer with the name of a particular place. Depending upon to whom we are speaking, we will answer with the name of a country, a state, a region, a county, a town, a village or a townland. When travelling in faraway corners of the world, you might just answer Europe, as sometimes the other person may never have heard of Ireland. If they have had a little more education, on hearing 'Ireland' they might ask, 'north or south?' – the news of the bombs and bullets from our recent history has reached most parts of the world, gaining us a certain global notoriety. When back home, the other person may not be satisfied until they hear a street name or, the rural equivalent, the name of a townland. The conversation often ends up with finding someone whom you both know, thus making a new connection with that person. Irish people love that.

It is common to think of the ties to our birthplace as the most significant connection we can have, where we experience our strongest sense of community, though this is certainly not the case for everyone. The idea carries the following assumptions:

- *That where we were born remains our primary residence.* As already discussed, more people are moving around now than ever before, both voluntarily and involuntarily. We may develop much stronger ties to places in which we live later in life, whether in the same country or not. Seán Óg Ó'hAilpín, for example, was born in Rotuma, an island north of the main Fiji islands. He has since become one of the most iconic figures in Irish sporting history and a champion of the Irish language. Figures like Ó'hAilpín completely demolish essentialist notions of community and Irish identity. He broadens beautifully what it means to be Irish, with his Fijian features and skin tone and his *blas* (accent) when he speaks Munster Irish.
- *That our sense of community begins and ends with a particular locality.* As we saw in Chapter 2, we can develop community ties with disparate groups of people across the world by, for example, using networking sites on the Internet or becoming involved in a social movement of some kind. These ties may feel much stronger and more meaningful to us than the mere fact of where we were born. These multiple networks may also vary a lot throughout our lifetimes.
- *That one particular locality has fixed boundaries.* No locality can be viewed as simply as this when one considers the complexities brought about by globalisation. It is out of touch to look at communities as containers made up of only those who live within certain boundaries. This question will be explored in depth later in this chapter.

So what is the exact nature of our relationship with our localities in the light of processes of globalisation? Are they still important components of our comfort zones?

Place in Song and Story

Connections to places provide rich pickings for Irish writers of songs and stories. The 'sing-song' has always been the traditional culmination of parties in Ireland, where everybody is expected to sing, or at least to recite a poem if their singing voice doesn't bear too much scrutiny. The longevity of some of these songs is a frequent source of amazement to me. To hear a young person belt out 'Sean South from Garryowen' or 'Galway Bay' well into the twenty-first century really is surprising. These are the local songs that seem to have a foundational role in our culture, that remind us of home, of roots, of our often ballsy and defiant sense of self. The almost spiritual need for these stirring ballads has not diminished much, despite the plethora of cultural changes in Ireland. The highlight of any sing-song is still far more likely to be, perhaps, a soulful rendition of Luke Kelly's 'On Raglan Road' or Phil Coulter's 'The Town I Loved So Well' than somebody's version of a bland Abba or Beatles song.

Many thousands of these local songs exist, and, by definition, they vary from place to place. It is that variation, rootedness and connection with localities that makes them interesting. Even a younger artist like Damien Dempsey connects with this need for connection to places, with his songs on working-class life in contemporary Dublin portraying a very strong sense of place. The edgy social realism of songs like 'Factories, Trains and Houses' and 'Ghosts of Overdoses' updates and reinvents place-centred balladry for a new generation, making his work very different to the bland, sepia-toned old tunes like 'Dublin in the Rare Auld Times' that were preferred by an older generation.

Irish literary royalty like James Joyce, W.B. Yeats, Samuel Beckett, Seamus Heaney and John McGahern always remained imaginatively rooted to their places of origin, no matter where in the world they were writing. Whether Joyce was in Paris or Zurich, his material was derived from the streets and characters of his native Dublin. Whether Heaney was physically in Athens or New York, he was in rural County Derry in his head. We all have a sense of place of one kind or another, even if we cannot express it as well as the aforementioned giants of literature. This sense of place is 'part of the systems of meaning through which we make sense of the world', or, to put it another way, 'part of our cultural interpretation of the world around us.'[3] It might just be experienced as a feeling – of comfort, of familiarity, of orientation, of shared history, of home. It is, however, a great asset to have the ability to relay this system of meaning in a way that resonates with readers far and wide. Cork author Cónal Creedon evokes a marvellous sense of place in all of his writing, but most particularly, in the following excerpt from his play *The Cure*. In it, one of the characters recalls how his grandfather could walk from his home on the north side of Cork City into the city centre, recognising the smells emanating from the various small businesses along his route:

The first thing that would hit my Grandda and he leaving the house
Would be the thick country smell of cattle,
From the dealers' fields beyond the grotto in Blackpool.

Led on like a bull by the ring,
He'd close his eyes and follow his nose.
Past the stale stench of last night's stout and cigarette smoke
From the string of pubs along Dublin Street,
Past the Glen Hall – the full length of Thomas Davis Street.

And with the first hint of crusty bread coming from the
ovens of
Cuthbert's bakery over on Great William O'Brien Street,
He'd know he was at Blackpool Church.

Then that sweet smell of molten sugar –
The shawlies making toffee apples up on Gerald Griffin
Street,
Would carry him past the oak casks of the distillery
And onto the Watercourse Road.
[sniff] Ahhh pleasure…
A pleasure – cut short by the piercing, deathly, toxic,
foul cloud coming
From the slaughterhouse off Denny's Lane.

But then, just for a whiff of a second the subtle scent of
sherbet,
Drifting down from Linehan's Sweet Factory,
Would carry him past the putrid pelts of the tannery,
And on to the first taste of human waste at Poulraddy.

Turnin' right onto Leitrim Street and there'd be no
mistaking
The warmth of the moist malt of brewing stout –
Billowing from Murphy's Stack.
He knew then that he was on the right track.
So he'd put the hands into the pockets – and whistle.[4]

Many of the smells in this piece of romantic olfactory geography can no longer be smelt, so this piece is largely an ode
to times past. It is also written in the local idiomatic form of
speech, making it all the more evocative. It just has to be read
in a Cork accent! The forces of globalisation dictate that these

local idiosyncrasies ebb and flow as societies change, for better or worse. If this man tried to follow his nose now, he would sadly probably end up in the River Lee.

Another example of a piece of poetry that has a very strong sense of place is Van Morrison's track 'Coney Island' from his album *Avalon Sunset*. In this poem – Morrison does not sing, but recites the piece to sweeping dreamy background music – the author takes us on a road trip from his childhood home of Belfast to a favourite haunt on the Lecale Coast in County Down. I can well imagine how this route might have become a musical *camino* or pilgrimage route for Van fans. The track was apparently recorded in one take – what we hear on the album is actually a rehearsal.[5] It came to Morrison that naturally and spontaneously. The numerous place names on the route – Downpatrick, St. John's Point, Shrigley, Killyleagh, Ardglass – are recited with relish in his childhood Belfast accent, and he takes us there with his words, along 'the happily jumbled road map of one man's memories.'[6] He evokes such strong imagery that you share in his sense of happiness and can almost see, smell and taste what he describes. It is a strange coincidence that his favourite place, Coney Island, has the same name as the seaside resort close to New York where so many of his musical influences were based. There is a great sense of escape and pure love of the moment in this poem. The twice-mentioned 'autumn sunshine' reminds us that 'the harvest is in, the sun is setting, displaying a sense of the rhythm of the seasons, but also of time.'[7] He finishes with the magical line that resounds with a sense of nostalgia and his palpable longing for a simpler time before he was a rock star: 'wouldn't it be great if it was like this all the time?' But it cannot be like this all the time. Things change, for better or worse.

In another song, 'In the Days Before Rock and Roll', Van Morrison evokes the importance to him of the radio station

Radio Luxembourg in the 1950s. It was the only station to play young people's music and was responsible for expanding his mind, his music and his world beyond the back streets of East Belfast. He lists the musicians he discovered – Elvis, Fats Domino, Sonny Terry, Lightnin' Hopkins, Muddy Waters, John Lee Hooker – who spoke to his soul and influenced his music for the rest of his long career. In a clever literary tactic, he also lists the places he remembers that were on the dial of his old radio – Athlone, Budapest, Hilversum, Helvetia – as he made his personal voyage of discovery. This is a very evocative piece for those of us who can remember searching up and down the dials of those big old radios. I will always remember that it was on such a radio that I heard the news of Elvis Presley's death in 1977.

Analysing Globalisation

How are we to read the winds of change brought about by globalisation and their impact on small places and the localities in which we live, whether Cork or Coney Island? Globalisation can usefully be understood as 'complex connectivity', or 'the rapidly developing and ever-densening network of interconnections and interdependences that characterise modern social life.'[8] What effects do these complex manifestations of globalisation have on our everyday lives? One important question with respect to ordinary people's participation in public life is, for example, do national parliamentary politics matter much anymore? Should we tear up our voting cards? Michael Ignatieff argues:

> All the changes which impinge upon the politics of modern states are global in character: the market in which we trade, and in which our economic futures will

be shaped, is global: the ecology in which we live and breathe is global.[9]

He goes on to say that the political life of nation states has been 'emptied of relevance'. So, when analysing societies, social scientists can no longer look at individual states or countries in isolation, but must instead acknowledge the impact of wider global influences. Many contemporary economic, political and cultural developments are no longer dependent upon the state, as:

> ...the new pathways for the development of capital cut across national boundaries and intrude on national economic sovereignty, which renders irrelevant the notion of a national market or a national economic unit and undermines national sovereignty from within by fragmenting the national economy.[10]

When discussing the career of Irish businessman and CEO of Heinz Tony O' Reilly and his choice not to enter Irish politics, Fintan O'Toole argues:

> Given the choice between running a multinational company and running a small European country, he chose the former. He had seen that once Ireland had opened itself up to American multinationals, the idea of national sovereignty, of state control, had become untenable.[11]

Hence we can witness the increasing interpenetration from the global to the local levels. We have witnessed first-hand in Ireland recently how globalisation sometimes creates major political challenges to the power of nation states to formulate their own policies and decide their own futures. When welcoming transnational corporations (TNCs) to our shores, most recently in the information technology (IT) sector, like Google or PayPal, politicians will publicly congratulate themselves on maintaining the globalisation of the Irish economy. However, when waving goodbye to them, having left whole communities bereft of employment, they are not so sure. Such heavy reliance on just one type of employment is then exposed as the risky approach that it is. This scenario was familiar to 1,900 Limerick employees of Dell when they lost their jobs in 2009. Such workers in the IT sector often find that the skills they have learned are non-transferable to any other company.

Apart from TNCs, supranational institutions also affect policies and regulations at national level. These organisations include the World Trade Organisation (WTO) and the International Monetary Fund (IMF), which both regulate trade and finance; and organisations such as the North Atlantic Treaty Organisation (NATO) and the United Nations (UN), which are both concerned with peacekeeping and security. The UN also attempts to deal with another major concern: the environment. At the Earth Summits in 1992 and 2002, the UN sought to come to some international agreement on pollution and greenhouse gas emissions amongst Member States. However, the governments of some of the larger industrialised countries, especially the US, the biggest environmental offender and producer of CO_2 emissions worldwide, stoutly resisted these attempts. These supranational institutions often seem to disproportionately represent the interests of the richer countries. Some Member States like the US and Israel seem to be able to defend their interests easily, while others are left out in the cold.[12]

Anti-Globalisation Movement

Globalisation can be portrayed either as a good or a bad thing, depending on who is speaking. Some socialist and environmental campaigners define themselves as part of the broad church of the 'anti-globalisation movement'. Instead of seeing 'the global' as bringing economic wealth, prosperity and competitiveness, they see it as the source of all that is wrong and unjust in contemporary society. This is a rainbow term for a loose coalition of movements that address the problems caused by capitalist economics, aim to conserve the environment, and advocate the rights of women, ethnic minorities and indigenous peoples. These groups embody diverse goals and strategies, but 'anti-globalisation' is a keyword that forms part of all of their manifestos.

Some of the issues that are mobilising people to form movements in the early twenty-first century have been resistance to the austerity packages ordered by the IMF in various countries, including Ireland and Greece; the war in Iraq and Afghanistan; Third World debt; child labour and sweatshop labour; Fairtrade; global warming; genetic modification (GM) of food; immigration controls; and pharmaceutical patents for AIDS medications. These issues are indeed global and cannot be viewed solely within any national boundaries.[13] That said, they may, of course, have local resonance in particular places that are flashpoints for certain issues.

As these branches of the anti-globalisation movement show, globalisation makes caring, solidarity and agitation possible at a distance, even though the term 'anti-globalisation' paints such activism in very broad brushstrokes indeed. We can be passionate about a problem occurring in a country in which we have never set foot. With just a few clicks of a computer mouse, anyone can find out about almost anything under the

sun. The Internet has revolutionised political activity, facili-
tating the global gatherings that now happen all the time,
like the recent Occupy Wall Street movement in New York
which led to the 'occupations' of the financial districts of other
cities: the City in London and Dame Street in Dublin, among
others. So our friends and neighbours, those whom we are
concerned about, may now be across the world rather than
across the street.

Globalisation and Modernity

Debates about the social impacts of globalisation have been
lively indeed. Possibly the first author to address these issues
was Marshall McLuhan, who gave us the influential idea of
the 'global village' in the 1960s.[14] This work set the stage for
thinking that the world was shrinking and we were all, therefore, becoming more intimate.

I recently had the experience of calling my digital TV
provider with a query and finding that I was speaking to somebody in Bangalore, South India. This is certainly a globalised
experience, but I would contend that it has only a very superficial effect in the grand scheme of things: I still went back
to living the rest of my day where I was, and the telephone
operator went back to living his day where he was.

'Global village' has since been shown to be quite a glib idea
that does not bear up well in the face of rigorous analysis. It
was also replete with the zeitgeist of the early sixties: excite-
ment about the opening up and democratisation of culture,
especially by and for young people. Since then, sociological
perspectives on the social effects of globalisation have varied
widely. For sociologist Anthony Giddens globalisation is part
of modernity, of which the four key aspects are capitalism,
industrialism, relations between nations and militarism. These

are governed by three key aspects: *time-space distanciation*, where time and space are separated by modern communications, like sending an e-mail across the world; *disembedding*, where social relations are lifted out of local contexts and across national boundaries by financial exchanges or expert intervention; and *reflexivity*, where society and individuals are increasingly aware of each other, and mutual learning can thereby occur.[15] This optimism continues throughout Giddens' work, where globalisation is seen as ultimately empowering because more people can gain access to more information and knowledge-building blocks, thereby enhancing democratic participation. His argument is that 'the more societies are modernized, the more agents (subjects) acquire the ability to reflect on the social conditions of their existence and to change them in that way.'[16] This implies that the traditional left/right political axis is replaced by newer axes based on certain/uncertain, inside/outside and political/apolitical. When one reviews political life in this way, new trajectories are visible in how people make themselves seen and heard, and new alliances and divisions become possible. Environmental issues are especially important here, as no mere political boundary protects populations from pollution or nuclear radiation.

A More Critical Approach

World-systems theory provides a more critical macro-analysis of the dynamics of capitalist globalisation, which is viewed as perpetuating the exploitation of the poorer countries of the periphery by those of the core in Europe and the US. This theory argues that a transnational capitalist class governs the economic system, an entrepreneurial elite whose power far exceeds heads of state. These elites are composed of TNC executives and their local affiliates, globalising state bureaucrats, capitalist politicians and professionals, and consumerist elites.[17] The operations of this global elite are smoothened by the 'globalized spaces and connecting corridors which ease the flow of capital.'[18] These are the airline routes, the three-lane highways, the identikit hotels and secure corporate campuses that ensure that these executives can hop from Bangalore to Beijing to Bogotá without ever feeling challenged to adapt to a different cultural setting. These people probably never meet a local person who isn't serving their every need, dressed in a polyester uniform, speaking Berlitz English and sporting an anglicised nametag.

The core–periphery model that underpins this approach is no longer convincing, however, because of the emergence of new economic powers and the complex, overlapping, multi-way flows of money, people and ideas around the world. One of those new big economic players to emerge since the 1990s is India, whose annual economic growth rate currently stands at an average of 7–10 per cent per annum, which translates to about US$200 billion a year, exceeding the total GDP of Portugal or Norway.[19] This new economic strength means that India is now being taken seriously in world markets, as well as that other economic giant currently being courted by the Irish state: China. As sociologist Philip McMichael says:

There is no doubt that the phenomenon of 'Chindia' has the attention of the business community – whether as an investment opportunity or a threat to northern businesses or jobs.[20]

Nevertheless, the radicalism of the world-systems approach is welcome again, when we witness how a small cohort of bankers, businessmen and politicians can mortgage a whole country's economy. In Ireland, sociologist Kieran Allen is the most radical commentator on the globalisation of the Irish economy. Concern has been expressed at least since the early 1980s about the Irish economy's high level of dependence upon TNCs. We have known for many years now about TNCs' high rate of profit repatriation or 'capital flight' from Ireland. We also know about their ability to make or break local communities. In critical sociological and economic literature, a common critique of TNCs is that they are 'footloose', moving around the world at will in order to use what resources are locally available and to maximise their profits. Allen challenges this idea, stressing how embedded they are in local networks of power and how much it actually costs them to relocate. His argument is that this vulnerability actually adds greater weight to workers' resistance. He thus seeks to undermine what he terms 'the myth of invincibility', arguing that the economic giants actually have a rarely-acknowledged Achilles' heel. Allen attacks the sycophantic relationship between the Irish state and big business. He claims that this state has being willing to sacrifice human welfare and social justice to the needs and dictates of TNCs, with parliamentary rule being 'hollowed out from the inside by the rise of corporate power.' He goes on to say that what we have now is a '"managed-democracy" where periodic elections are used to legitimate decisions already made.'[21]

Globalisation as Homogenisation

It is common for people to think that everything is becoming the same all over the world now, and that everywhere has become Americanised. Homogenisation is thus usually equated with Americanisation or Westernisation. The transmission of a narrow range of Hollywood media images is often accused of being imperialist in its goals, where Western culture is aggressively promoted and assumed to be superior to others. If you wish to make this argument, there is indeed a plethora of evidence to support your case. American TV shows like *Dallas, Baywatch* and *Desperate Housewives* have been beamed all over the world for a few decades now.

As well as the TV shows people watch, the adverts that punctuate them are as large a part of the TV-watching experience as the shows themselves. Global capitalism is underpinned by the cultural ideology of consumerism. There is no end to the cleverness of the images used in TV adverts, with some of the most memorable ones intentionally bearing little or no relation to the product they are flogging. To get the viewers' attention, advertisers need to develop a very simple message that evokes an emotional response in the viewer, and in just a few seconds. For example, emigration has been a major theme in Irish adverts for as long as I can remember, and there is nothing more emotional than that subject in Ireland, short of death. This theme was memorably used in some fairly recent ads for Guinness, where an Irish emigrant living in New York has to do a lot of dodgy backstreet deals to get a ticket for the All-Ireland Final for his dad back home, or the one where one brother swims all the way across the Atlantic in order to say sorry to the other brother who is living in New York. The theme of emigration has also been used in ads for Barry's Tea, where an Irish emigrant living in New York is reading a letter from her sister at home; as well as in the famous 1970s advert for Harp lager, where the protagonist of the story writes home from a Middle Eastern desert saying, 'You could fry an egg on the stones here – if you had an egg,' and sharing with the viewer how he misses Sally O'Brien 'and the way she might look at you.' I guess the next generation of ads will be based in Australia and Canada.

These adverts want to ensure that we keep shopping to accumulate consumer goods. Shopping forms a large part of our leisure time, and Sunday has become one of the busiest shopping days in Ireland and elsewhere. Shopping malls in suburbia are cathedrals of consumption, where those who can afford it worship the fashion world's Holy Trinity: Hermés, Gucci and Prada. Shopping malls the world over now stock the same small range of over-priced goods. Even if we cannot afford the designer goods, we can buy the knock-offs in Penneys and perhaps aspire to being able to afford the real thing some day. This consumerist ideology is especially geared towards young people. Something like the 'global teenager' now exists, who probably wears some combination of Abercrombie & Fitch, Gap and Nike. It is impossible to tell where they come from – they are clones of some ideal created by North American ad executives. Individuality is not a value close to most teenagers' hearts, and looking like everyone else is much more bully-proof.

Advertising executives see themselves as 'meaning brokers' who create an association between a particular brand and a lifestyle that is usually youthful, carefree and based on the unspoken liberal use of Daddy's credit card.[22] Clothing manufacturers commonly branch out to make other products like homewares, perfume or shoes, extending the remit of their vision. Writer and activist Naomi Klein has highlighted the sweatshop injustices behind such banal vacuity. The aggressive promotion of Western culture, which implies the inferiority of other cultures, is imperialistic in its marketing approach. This creates the anomaly that poorer people who can barely afford to keep body and soul together still sometimes spend their meagre incomes on high-status Western goods like Coca Cola and Kentucky Fried Chicken.

Homogenisation Debunked

However, there is a major problem with stopping the analysis of the impact of consumerist global media imagery there. The more pressure that is exerted by hegemonic economic and cultural forces of globalisation, the more people may yearn for their local identity and seek to stress their difference to the homogeneity imposed from outside. People may need a human scale, to complement the global, a means of inserting their own experiences, feelings and opinions into a world that is often cold and alienating. Italian geographer Raimondo Strassoldo contends:

> Post-modern man/woman, just because he/she is so deeply embedded in global information flows, may feel the need to revive small enclaves of familiarity, intimacy, security, intelligibility, organic-sensuous interaction, in which to mirror him/herself, contrary to the process occuring in front of the subjectivity-effacing TV screen.[23]

We cannot assume that just because Westernised images exist on people's TV screens that they will resonate with local populations in non-Western countries and be interpreted in the same way. It is a huge mistake to think that people are just dupes who cannot make up their own minds about their likes and dislikes, and just because we indulge occasionally to watch some light-hearted, low-brow TV show does not mean that our whole identity is affected by it.

Many of the reality TV shows we watch now have the same appeal as a car crash: horrendous, yet we cannot take our eyes off them. Some interesting research was conducted on viewers from several different ethnic groups in Israel watching that great classic of materialist crassness from the eighties

– *Dallas*. The researchers found that each ethnic group viewed the show through their own particular cultural lens, mediating their reading of its messages. In fact, instead of being jealous of their wealth, most of the viewers actually felt sorry for the characters, saying that 'unhappiness is the greatest leveller.'[24] In other words, they were more concerned with developments in the characters' emotional lives and recognised that money could not buy happiness.

Two-Way Cultural Flows

As well as varied interpretations of TV programmes, media analysts have found that domestically-produced programmes still attract the highest audiences, with imported material being used to fill in off-peak hours. In this era of hybridity and cultural mixing, life is so complex that one cannot assume that the international broadcasting of a few TV shows equals global domination.[25] Media products are often also disseminated on a regional basis. An example here is the popular genre of *telenovelas*, the soap operas that emanate from Latin America, especially Mexico and Brazil. These are massively successful, as they are popular among the *émigré* Latino population in the US, and also in Spain and Portugal. These Latin American media products are popular in Spain and Portugal because they speak the same languages, as well as the fact that so many Latin American emigrants live there. So the flows of culture are not just one-way. This is an example of so-called 'Third World' countries actually exporting media products to Western countries and finding enthusiastic audiences.

Another example of a 'reverse' cultural flow from a post-colonial society is the massive movie industry based in the Indian city of Mumbai, which has now been nicknamed 'Bollywood'. Indians are so obsessed with the films made in their own country that they are barely concerned with what comes out of Los Angeles. Their own movie stars like Amitabh Bachchan, Shah Rukh Khan or Kareena Kapoor have raised far more temperatures in India and elsewhere than Brad Pitt or Angelina Jolie ever will. One Bollywood director, when asked if he wished to conquer the US market next, replied that the market there was far too small to bother with, at just 300 million! In fact, Bollywood-style movies have become more popular in the West now, with the music and dance scenes proving particularly infectious among Western audiences. This is one example of what Harvard political scientist Joseph Nye terms 'soft power', where nations can exert power in the world by attracting others to their cultural repertoires of, for example, film, food or sport.[26] This has real effects on economies. It has recently been pointed out that Indian curry houses in England currently employ more people there than the steel, coal and shipbuilding industries combined.[27]

In terms of the products sold on TV adverts worldwide, I would suggest that many of them are beyond the bounds of the purchasing power of most non-Western consumers. Again referring to India, the sheer size of the population there potentially makes it an enormous market for consumer goods like electronics and cars. Western companies slaver at the mouth when they imagine getting their hands on all those wads of rupees. The huge size of the economy is deceptive, however, considering that the purchasing power of the vast majority is extremely low. It is often quoted that the Indian middle class stands at about three hundred million. However, Western brands are still very expensive even for this middle class, and it appears that many of them prefer to stick to more familiar and cheaper Indian brands, of which there are plenty. Tata, for example, is an enormous Indian company that seems to make everything under the sun, including a new small type of car called the Nano that is sold for US$1,500. Can any US or Japanese company compete with that? Recent observations during visits to Kolkata's shopping malls would seem to suggest that the fancy shops selling Nike sportswear, Tommy Hilfiger sweaters and Swarovski crystals are treated more like entertaining museums than places to part with hard-earned cash. After all, professional salaries are still comparatively low in India, with a top executive in an IT firm perhaps earning €20,000 a year. So, to part with €150 for a pair of jeans would only be possible or desirable for a very small minority. However, many more can afford Indian-made clothes that fit better both culturally and financially.

'Glocalisation' and the Market for Local Products

Western firms have begun to grasp that they have to adapt their products to local markets. This has been termed 'glocalisation', where global products are tailored to suit the niche requirements of local markets.[28] For example, fast-food chain McDonald's sells beer in some European countries like Spain and France – imagine what would happen if they did that in Ireland! They also operate in India, but they do not sell beef burgers, the consumption of which is of course taboo to Hindus, but only lamb burgers. Also, Western cosmetic face creams that contain sun protection factor (SPF) are marketed as skin-whitening creams in India, because to be 'fair' is to be beautiful there, while to be dark-skinned is associated with poverty and working in the fields under the blazing sun. In the West, the same product is framed in terms of preventing skin cancer or premature aging, but in India, it is all about keeping fair-skinned in order to attract (and keep) a husband. These companies 'are taking advantage of a growing consumer market in a developing society that is already deeply divided along the axes of class, caste, creed, colour.'[29]

There is also evidence of a strong interest in localised products in various arenas, most particularly in food production. The more pressure that is exerted by hegemonic economic and cultural forces, the more people may yearn for their local identity and seek to stress their difference to the homogeneity imposed from outside. This new form of regionalism has been grasped by entrepreneurs in some regions of the Western world, and is especially visible in the realm of food and tourism marketing. A well-known example of this is Emilia-Romagna, the region of Italy from which Parmesan cheese, Parma ham and Balsamic vinegar are derived. We might also think of the French wine regions of Bordeaux, Champagne or Burgundy, or the Spanish wine region of Rioja. New concerns about food safety, food miles and the increasing sophistication of the taste buds of a large portion of the population of the West have created an international market for many varied new products. The desire for ethically and ecologically reliable, quality foods is inherently a product of globalisation because it is a reaction to the abysmally-low quality standards of mass-produced food, the manufacture and sale of which is increasingly controlled by just a few major global corporations.

Such demand for niche products is a significant phenomenon, whether it is associated with organics, animal welfare or local produce. In the arena of fashion, an interest in what they call 'tribal' prints and local craft styles from the non-Western world is sometimes evident. Fake copies of craft items can now be bought in high street chain stores. I once wore a hand-embroidered Mexican blouse to my local pub on a Saturday night. A woman came up to me, admired it and asked if I had gotten it in Penneys. I was torn between a sense of wry amusement and frustration. In fact, I had bought it straight from the hands of the tiny Mexican woman who had made it, on the dusty floor of a village street market in Chiapas, Southern Mexico. If the woman who had admired it had been there, she would have thought the market dirty and disgusting. However, I valued that blouse much, much more than if I had bought it at home from a chain store because it was a genuine craft item and 100 per cent of the money I paid for it went straight to its producer, in a respectful, mutually-appreciative, woman-to-woman trade of goods for money. The many transactions like this that I have made over the years have enhanced my life a little each time. The alternative, when wearing cheap mass-produced clothes, is to secretly suspect that one is wearing an item made in illegal, exploitative sweatshop conditions.[30] However, sometimes it suits us to think of our global connections, whereas at other times, it is the last thing we want to be reminded of, as when wearing such cheap clothes made by exploited children in a Chinese sweatshop or showing off one's new engagement ring made of blood diamonds from the Congo, or perhaps even snorting cocaine from Colombia.

Complexities of Globalisation

When discussing globalisation, it must be considered that its effects are very unevenly distributed throughout the world, both between regions and between different classes within those regions.[31] There are still huge parts of the world where people do not have access to electricity, never mind the satellite technology necessary for access to the Internet. There are also those within our midst in the West, like the poor and the elderly, who are excluded from globalisation processes because of lack of education and/or wealth. The world is extremely complex, divided and unequal, as Louis MacNiece put it so beautifully in his poem 'Snow', 'World is crazier and more of it than we think/Incorrigibly plural.'

This plurality can also take the form of cultural mixing to form new hybrid cultures. The aforementioned 'global teenager' may well wear a scarf to cover her hair, a *keffiyeh* to express solidarity with the Palestinians, a Maori tattoo on her shoulder or an intricate henna design on her hands and feet. The local and the global can blend, even on the one body. We therefore cannot assume that life is necessarily becoming more similar for everyone because of globalisation. As one author pithily put it, 'the assertion of global homogenisation of culture is a little like arriving by plane but never leaving the terminal, spending all one's time browsing amongst the global brands of the duty-free shops.'[32] If you walk outside the terminal and enter the city you will find difference, and plenty of it – maybe even more than you can stand – before you retreat to the Holiday Inn to get back to the heart of your comfort zone. This type of capitalist development 'has led to new forms and patterns of inequality, not simply to increasing similarity.'[33] The analytical framework discussed next can help us, I believe, to grasp the complexity of globalisation processes.

Types of Globalisation

It has become conventional within social scientific debates to argue the relative importance of three forms of globalisation: economic, cultural and political. However, it is difficult to separate them, as each profoundly affects the other. To divide social life up like this creates false divisions between discrete 'boxes'. Messy old everyday life does not lend itself to being artificially split up like this, and most sociologists do not like rigid models as much as economists do. While debates abound about all of this, the work of one author in particular helps us out of this trap. Arjun Appadurai provides a useful and very flexible framework for analysing globalisation processes. He argues that the contemporary world may be understood as a complex combination of five dimensions of global cultural flows, termed 'ethnoscapes', 'technoscapes', 'financescapes', 'mediascapes' and 'ideoscapes'. The use of the suffix 'scape' underlines dynamism, movement and the 'the fluid, irregular shape of these landscapes', and emphasises that they are the 'building blocks' of people's 'imagined worlds'.[34] He therefore stresses the power of individual agents and groups to interpret the world around them, despite powerful forces that may be aligned against them.

Ethnoscapes

The first of Appadurai's five dimensions of global cultural flows is ethnoscapes, 'the landscape of persons who constitute the shifting world in which we live.'[35] This refers to the enormously complex patterns formed by people moving around the world: tourists, migrants, refugees and exiles. When people migrate or travel it affects the society and politics of both their host countries and their home countries. There are stable communities all across the globe, composed of people who mostly stay put, apart from in major emergencies, perhaps, and whose usual experience of global modernity is the 'displacement' that the outside world brings to them.[36] However, to use a weaving metaphor, 'the warp of these stabilities is everywhere shot through with the woof of human motion.'[37] While stability is the norm for some people, movement is the norm for others. These tapestries of staying and going are evident within countries, communities and individual families.

Technoscapes

Technoscapes result from the global effects of all types of mechanical and informational technology. National boundaries couldn't possibly be more irrelevant when one considers the speed at which information can be transferred globally via the Internet and the instantaneous connections we can make across the globe using mobile phone technology. Information and communication technology now make it possible to maintain social relationships on the basis of direct interaction over any distance across the globe. Whether one wishes to organise a terrorist attack, start a new online company or just see a lover's face from across the world, global telecommunications now makes it possible. For many people, telecommunications also blur the boundaries between home and work; they find it difficult to completely switch off because they get addicted to networking. Apparently, a new trend in the elite hospitality sector is what is known as 'black-hole resorts', where you pay extra for *not* having Wi-Fi and a TV in your room.[38] This is techie rehab! This backlash against the Internet is a trend to watch. It is possible that people may begin to suffer from on-screen information overload and their interpersonal communication with others begin to suffer as a result.

So these technoscapes appear to be as complex as they are powerful. They do not follow any obvious, predictable patterns, as they 'are increasingly driven not by any economies of scale, of political control, or of market rationality, but of increasingly complex relationships between money flows, political possibilities and the availability of both low and highly-skilled labour.'[39]

Financescapes

Financescapes cover the world of global capital which 'is now a more mysterious, rapid and difficult landscape to follow than ever before.'[40] The mysterious workings of currency markets and stock exchanges can make or break whole economies and, hence, the opportunities offered to their populations. Financescapes are deeply connected to other scapes. They are visible both in the realms of production and consumption. The actors here are many and varied, including investors, brokers, workers and consumers, but they share the idea that time is money, where 'a loss of minutes can translate into a loss of millions.'[41] TNCs, for example, fragment their production processes so that they can benefit maximally from the availability of resources (like a good physical infrastructure or cheap labour) in different places.

Another invaluable resource for them is the endless generosity shown to them by some countries like Ireland. This has taken the form in Ireland of building Shannon Free Zone (the world's first free trade zone), grants, tax relief, advance factories, guarantees of un-unionised labour and lax environmental laws. States can choose whether to offer these incentives, hence the spread of TNCs is very uneven. Places are routinely viewed by the capitalist business elite, or agents of economic globalisation, in the entrepreneurial terms of opportunities for investment, infrastructural pluses and minuses, linkages, networks and flows of goods and information.[42] The favoured locations of US-owned TNCs are Ireland, Singapore, Canada, the UK, Honduras, Costa Rica, the Netherlands, Malaysia and Australia.[43] A simple model of economic globalisation is thus inaccurate, as states and groups of states in the form of trading blocs like the EU and the North American Free Trade Association (NAFTA) can and do negotiate with TNCs. Very uneven economic development is the result.

Of course, this whole system is underpinned by the more or less secret workings of international finance, where the only commodity traded is money itself. As we have seen in these recessionary times, skittish financial markets can tumble based on nothing more than rumours and lack of consumer confidence. In Ireland these days we are entreated to spend our money as beseechingly as citizens are enticed to sign up for the army in times of war. Instead of brandishing a gun, they just want us to brandish our wallets. Instead of the famous US Army recruiting poster of 'Uncle Sam Needs You!', one could easily imagine a new one saying 'Mother Ireland Needs Your Euros!'.

Mediascapes

Mediascapes refer to both 'the distribution of the electronic capabilities to produce and disseminate information ... and to the images of the world created by these media.'[44] So they cover that increasingly important aspect of cultural life, the distribution networks of media images and the interests of those behind them – connected to selling products and distributing news. This is the imagined world where image rules over reality, style over substance. In terms of people's cultural identity, globalisation has afforded people more choices in the ways they choose to express themselves: what music they listen to, where they go on holidays and what clothes they wear. However, all of this is ultimately about buying and selling things.

Ideoscapes

The fifth set of global cultural flows is ideoscapes, which are 'collections of directly political terms, images and ideas which drive political discourses.' They provide 'a loosely structured synopticon of politics, in which different nation-states ... have organised their political culture around different keywords.'[45] Ideas like democracy, rights and sovereignty originated in the European Enlightenment, but their meanings have loosened since they have been dispersed around the world. Three more contemporary examples of political buzzwords are *development, sustainability* and *social capital.* There is, of course, often disagreement between states and social movements about particular issues. Disjunctures between different interpretations of ideas like democracy form what Appadurai terms 'terminological kaleidoscopes', meaning different things in diverse societies. As we know, real democracy is difficult to achieve, and lots of states that claim to practice it are, in fact, nowhere near the realisation of this ideal.

Socioscapes

Another author, Martin Albrow, added an additional 'scape' to Appadurai's cultural flows. 'Socioscape' refers to the social formations 'which are more than the people who occupy them at any one time.'[46] Socioscapes are composed of the varying lifestyles and social networks of individuals, what Albrow terms each person's 'sociosphere'. Each of these separate worlds intersects with the others to form a socioscape. In many places, perhaps especially urban areas, inhabitants have regular but superficial interactions, more or less happily co-existing. People might be more connected to virtual neighbours in Australia or Jamaica than they are to their physical neighbours because of advances in information technology. They can be part of 'networks of social relations of very different intensity, spanning widely different territorial extents, from a few to many thousands of miles.'[47] As a result of all these varied networks, inhabitants of neighbourhoods 'live stratified existences, just as airliners operate in different air spaces according to the length of their journeys and cross each other's paths at different heights in co-ordinated but unconcerned ways.'[48] The sum total of all of these connections forms the socioscapes of the places where people live.

Crimescapes

To the above list I feel the need to add my own new set of flows: 'crimescapes'. The regular economy of which we are all a part constitutes only the public face of global economic activity. There is a whole alternative, illicit economy staffed by global criminal networks that usually evade the law, using ingenious methods. These networks run what author Misha Glenny terms the 'shadow economy', which, at a conservative estimate, is responsible for 15–20 per cent of global trade. In his comprehensive study of these networks, *McMafia: Crime Without Frontiers*, Glenny highlights the fall of the Soviet Union as a turning point for the emergence of criminal gangs. He focuses upon the geographical area from the former Balkan states up to the Caucasus, the 'stans' of Soviet Central Asia to the west of China, down to the north-west of Pakistan. This 'New Silk Route' sees flows of trafficked people, drugs, weapons, money, endangered species and hardwoods to consumers in Europe and the US.[49]

The trafficking of women and children is one of the most distressing realities of globalisation. It is currently the third largest illegal trade in existence, behind drug smuggling and gun running. Human trafficking is estimated by the UN to generate US$7 billion every year.[50] Eastern Europe is a major source area for girls to be trafficked for exploitation in the sex trade. Veteran journalist Alexander Cockburn found that:

… any bar owner in Greece can send someone up to southern Bulgaria to buy women for cash. The cost of a girl in that area is $1,000, or, if you negotiate, you might be able to get two for $1,000. Best to try on a Monday for cheap prices, because most trafficking happens at weekends. Mondays are slow, so you can get the leftovers.[51]

As reprehensible as this is, in India, Pakistan and Bangladesh the price of a girl is much, much lower – perhaps as low as US$30. Child trafficking is a particular problem in this region of Asia. It is thought to be of a magnitude ten times larger than the transatlantic slave trade was at its peak in the late eighteenth century.[52]

It is difficult to draw a dividing line between the issues of child labour, trafficking, bonded labour, gender discrimination, prostitution and slavery. They all intersect in mind-boggling ways and are closely linked by poverty, powerlessness and misogyny.[53] It would be empirically naïve as well as morally wrong to exclude this crimescape from the overall picture of globalisation presented here, as it generates so much revenue for the criminals who profit from it, as well as the costs it imposes upon states – and ultimately taxpayers – to attempt to regulate it.

Arjun Appadurai's complex model of global cultural flows is adequately open-ended to capture the multiple realities of globalised everyday life. It incorporates the actions of individual social actors, as well as those who represent the powerful worlds of politics, crime, finance, media and technology in different places and contexts. All of these networks are related in complex ways, and for every discernable process or trend there is a countervailing force or resistance group. To leave these out of the picture would be unrealistic. Let us now turn to the effects of these many and varied debates on globalisation upon real places.

Understanding Places

The Irish Times ran a competition in 2012, asking readers to nominate the best place to live in Ireland. In order to launch it, some writers and journalists argued for their own places.[54] Musician and producer Philip King loves the landscape and the musical heritage of Dingle. He says that 'there is something in the spirit of this place that is very empowering in this age of clamour.' Veteran journalist and naturalist Michael Viney reckons that he is a millionaire to live where he does on the west coast of Mayo, where outside his door he gets 'birdsong and the small talk of commuting ravens, the swish of leaves, the distant rumble of surf and lungfuls of the cleanest air in Ireland.' Journalist Carl O' Brien quotes Seán Ó Faoláin when he argues for Cork city, admiring its 'quiet sense of self-possession … it's something that one can only speak of as an air or a tradition, indigenous, time-established, as old as Shandon's bells.' Journalist Fionola Meredith likes the fact that Belfast is 'weird and complicated and truculently charming.' So it is each to his or her own. *À chacun son gout.* The ultimate winner of the competition was Westport, County Mayo, of which there is further discussion later in this chapter. *Irish Times* journalist Kathy Sheridan described the town thus:

Westport is still a living, breathing, working town with a proper, old-fashioned ironmonger's shop and others that look as if the displays haven't changed since the 1950s; shops selling tweeds and near-designer boutiques; a Super Valu that has lobsters floating in a tank; a salon offering fish pedicures; fast-food outlets as well as a superb seafood delicatessen and restaurants.[55]

But what is a 'place', like Westport or anywhere else, when one takes into account the profoundly complex effects of globalisation processes just discussed? How are we to understand the role of place in the lives of groups of people? In what ways can the sociologist use geographical concepts and categories in order to better understand the dynamics of social life? The physical reality of a place is affected by the interaction and relationships between the actors who live in it. Power relations between social actors in localities determine what gets done there and what does not. However, a place is not just the background, or the context, to any sociological research, but may be viewed actually as one of the actors that loses or gains in the negotiations between social actors. The land and physical environment itself is not a homogenous plain upon which people and organisations compete for dominance, but it is a varied entity which exerts an agency of its own over the uses to which it can be put. The existence of the appropriate type of landscape is a prerequisite for the success of any activity, be it building holiday homes or growing organic vegetables. And if Nature is mistreated or polluted, she will fight back, in one way or another.

The development of a place depends upon whose ideas about the present and future of that place become dominant at any particular time. These ideas may derive from a myriad of sources, from the utilitarian materialism of the property developer to the romanticism of the artist or the ecocentrism of the environmentalist. Human meaning animates places and gives them their resonance. Without human meaning, a place is just open space. Space becomes place by being named and 'by embodying the symbolic and imaginary investments of a population.'[56] Places are powerful markers of identity and sources of meaning. In his poem, 'Going Home to Mayo, Winter, 1949', Paul Durcan calls place names 'magic passwords into eternity'. An oak forest, for example, might be viewed on the one hand as an ecological and spiritual oasis by an environmentalist or, on the other hand, as a terrible waste of land by a farmer. One will want to conserve it, while the other might want to clear it. It is a question of whose views are allowed to become dominant within society. From the beginning to the end of this process, there will be local clashes of opinion and struggles over development issues. If our oak forest is named as part of a UNESCO World Heritage Site, for example, credence is given to the conservationist view over any other. It is likely that more people will become invested in the place. This will probably be heartily supported by local business owners who stand to gain from increased tourist numbers. A conundrum may then develop as the forest becomes more popular as a tourist destination, and the area gets more commercialised and ugly as a result. The original beauty of the area may become threatened and undermined by that same tourism. As the line from the old Eagles song went: 'Call someplace Paradise, kiss it goodbye.'

Places and Power

The ability to make places of spaces is therefore a question of power. Allied to this, the act of 'drawing boundaries in space is always a social act.'[57] Boundaries and borders did not exist before people intervened, imposing a privatised, socio-political order on space. The identity of a place emerges from the intersection of its location in the international 'scapes' already discussed and with the ways it is constructed as a community or locality by its inhabitants. The world is a series of culturally, socially and economically-interconnected and interdependent spaces. The consequences of globalisation for each place is determined by 'a territory's relation to other locations, by its prior locational histories, and by its social properties, as well as by the hopes, needs and actions of people, by its public policies and actual or potential political mobilizations.'[58] Places have been saturated with the meanings infused by the people who have lived in or passed through them throughout history. Some meanings have a bigger impact than others, like those of property developers or politicians trying to attract investment from TNCs. Especially at times of hardship, these meanings dominate all others. At times of war or ethnic conflicts, it is nationalist and ethnic leaders who attempt to 'fix' the meaning of places, in their bid to remain the 'face' of their nation or region.

There is no such thing as a simple story about a place, because, as I noted in an earlier work:

... any spatial area, being comprised of complex and varied physical realities and different sets of individuals, can produce varied results, or what we may term a *meaning-cluster*. Because of inequality between social actors, certain types of meanings become dominant and others subordinate at any particular time.[59]

It is artificial and politically biased to choose any one particular era or any one cultural symbolic package to represent the 'true' nature of a place. British geographer Doreen Massey reminds us that:

... we should question any characterization of place which is singular, essentialist, and which relies on a view of there having been one past of this place, one story to tell, most particularly where the story is an internalised one of the evolution of that place within its bounds.[60]

People engage in symbolic struggles in order to have their definition become the dominant one. In terms of the history of a place, Massey points out that:

> ... to fix on one moment, or one period, by which to characterise the ever-shifting medley of social relations which have taken place in that location ... is to make a claim about a particular moment in time-space as having a verity which others do not.[61]

Interpretations of a place's past, as well as its present, will always differ. We might think here of Nationalist versus Unionist versions of Northern Ireland, the Republican versus Democrat versions of the US, or the versions of China portrayed by the official state apparatus versus human rights activists. In the social construction of place, there is a constant struggle over meanings, because social actors are always biased in one way or another. A place is composed of its identity as a particular moment, a unique *meeting* place, in the network of global relations. Each place is 'constructed out of movement, communication, social relations which always stretched beyond it.'[62] Massey wants an 'extroverted' and 'progressive' notion of the identity of a place, where its inhabitants are aware of and open to its historical and contemporary connections to the outside world.[63] Each globalised place is viewed as an ongoing process and constantly under construction:

> The open-ended interweaving of a multiplicity of trajectories (themselves thereby in transformation), the concomitant fractures, ruptures and structural divides,

are what makes it in the end so unamenable to a single totalising project.[64]

We have already discussed that our experience of community is not now necessarily attached to particular places or localities. We can feel a stronger sense of connection sometimes with a disparate group of people from lots of other places, based, for example, upon a particular political philosophy or set of interests. It has never been easier to be part of a global social movement. Does this mean that we are therefore less connected to the places in which we live?

A debate that has surfaced since the 1980s surrounds the following problem: if associating community with fixed localities is now seen as retrogressive or passé, is it possible to recreate a progressive role for them in society as we now know it? In her highly influential work, *Spatial Divisions of Labour*, Massey imagines localities as 'a product of the combination of "layers", of the successive imposition over the years of new rounds of investment, new forms of activity … those layers represent in turn the succession of roles the local economy has played within wider national and international structures.'[65] She stresses that localities themselves should be viewed as ongoing processes, not as something stable and fixed, so we need to define them '*ab initio* [from the start] in terms of change.'[66] This applies to cultural and political aspects of society as well as economic ones, and it is emphasised that agents in local areas can also exert agency over international processes in some cases.

Using this schema, the sociologist can analyse the social dynamics of how and why certain individual agents and social groups become dominant in particular localities, which may be viewed as 'constructions out of the intersections and interactions of concrete social relations and social processes in a situation of *co-presence.*'[67] So the attempt by some people to assign essential, 'authentic' characteristics to a locality is artificial, as that locality, no matter where it is or what size it is, is itself the product of a variety of global relations, both past and present. These global relations articulate themselves in variable ways that are highly dependent upon the cultural context and the historical moment in which they operate.

Transnational Corporations (TNCs) in Irish Localities

The predominant Irish economic development strategy of relying upon export-led development has afforded us some interesting intersections of the global and the local and, hence, noteworthy globalised social dynamics in small places. It has meant that a small number of companies employ very large numbers of people in specific locations. Examples are Intel in Leixlip, County Kildare; Google in Blanchardstown, County Dublin; Pfizer in Ringaskiddy, County Cork; and Allergan in Westport, County Mayo. While the first two are in the information sector, the second two are in the pharmaceutical sector, which continues to be a major employer in Ireland. Pfizer makes Viagra, the fastest-selling drug in medical history. About thirty million men in one hundred and twenty countries take Viagra to treat impotence, making Pfizer the biggest drug company in the world.[68] The company employs five hundred people at their Ringaskiddy plant, transforming a small place into a very big earner – swelling its coffers, so to speak.

Westport, County Mayo

Allergan, with a base in Westport, County Mayo, is the US multinational company that makes another of the most popular and successful pharmaceutical products in the world: Botox. This drug, which was originally used to treat migraine, is now the cosmetic treatment of choice for those who wish to smooth away their facial wrinkles. The company opened in Westport in 1977, and it now employs eight hundred and fifty people. Its workforce is also due to expand to over one thousand in the next four years.[69] Amazingly, the entire world production of Botox is based in this small West of Ireland town, so it occupies a very important coordinate on the world map of the pharmaceutical sector. Local people are no doubt very happy to have this employer in their midst, especially during this recession. However, it is worth considering what might happen if any problems emerged with the use of Botox, or if another company were to develop a rival product to challenge its dominance in years to come. However, Allergan is keen to stress that they are constantly innovating and that an increased number of the products they are currently developing in the areas of eye care, neurosciences, urologics and medical dermatology have more therapeutic than aesthetic functions.[70] The current success of this company ensures that the fortunes of this small West of Ireland town will be heavily dependent upon decisions made in Allergan's Los Angeles headquarters for many years to come.

Westport is not the kind of place one would associate with cosmetically-modified Hollywood A-listers, unless they were on the run, hiding out from the paparazzi. It is on the itineraries of most tourists visiting the West of Ireland, however, because of the town's scenic good looks, as well as being a popular haunt for retirees. It was a planned town originally built around the 1730s by the owners of Westport House. A small town of around six thousand in population, its setting is extremely beautiful, on rocky terrain not far from Clew Bay on the Atlantic coast. The *Lonely Planet* travel guide calls it 'a genteel country town' that is 'Mayo's tourist honey pot'. It is well known for its frequent victories in the national Tidy Towns competition, so 'Westport is well and truly in the beauty business.'[71] Tourists are also attracted by its picture-perfect old pubs. Matt Molloy of the global superstar group The Chieftains owns one of these pubs, and it is well known now for its rollicking music sessions. Because of Molloy's global fame, tourists come here from all over the world for an 'authentic' Irish experience. Naturally enough, the more who come, the less authentic it will be, as the music sessions become literally staged to suit the tourist market. The introduction of the practice of applauding after each tune is an example of the changes brought about by tourism.

As well as the pubs and music, thousands of people converge on the area every year to climb nearby Croagh Patrick on the last Sunday in July, known as Reek Sunday. Some do it for the apparently stunning view of Clew Bay from its summit, while others do the climb barefoot, as a sacred pilgrimage. So some people come to Westport to get culture, some to get religion, some to get work and others still to extract profit from the area. They must be doing something right, however, having been voted in 2012 as the best place to live in Ireland, as discussed earlier.

The various products of this town could not be more different. The locality is highly globalised, so its residents 'can reside in one place and have their meaningful social relations almost entirely outside it and across the globe', and hence 'use the locality as site and resource for social activities in widely differing ways.'[72] The variety of the interpretations of its identity is what makes Westport what it is. The diverse constructions of this place appear to be in harmonious co-presence at present, and not interfering with each other's activities. Allergan is welcomed by the majority of the community, and local people are grateful for the company's presence. Imagine if the major local employer were a company that polluted the surrounding environment or endangered the local population – conflict would be inevitable, as the area is so dependent on tourism.

The region further north along the County Mayo coast has seen more than its fair share of conflict in recent years. There, Shell plan to build an over-land gas pipeline in the Rossport area. Many locals do not welcome these plans, and a social movement, Shell to Sea, has emerged to resist their actions. In this David and Goliath battle, five local men each spent 94 days in jail in 2005 for obstructing Shell from laying the pipeline on their land. When Willie Corduff, one of the so-called Rossport Five, was asked if he would be willing to serve time again for the cause, his response was, 'yes, definitely.'[73]

The Shell to Sea movement also has a global outlook, because it compares its concerns with other sites throughout the world that are facing similar plights. The group's basic concern is to defend a locality from a perceived aggressor.[74] Most people spend their lives living in localities without ever having to ponder such matters. However, if global economic forces, like Shell in this case, enter a locality, the people living there must decide whether or not such companies will be of benefit to the locality, and they must then act accordingly. The state in both Westport and Rossport more or less stands back and allows the TNCs free rein in Irish territory. When conflict occurs, as it has in Rossport, the Irish police force is at their beck and call when required, to defend their interests from protesters.

Decisions about TNC investment in such places as County Mayo are made by powerful actors on the global stage, and ordinary people have to live with the result of these decisions at the local level. If they are lucky, they will be beneficial, as in

Westport, or if not, as in Rossport, they might be potentially harmful. The national level scarcely matters anymore, as:

> ... the new pathways for the development of capital cut across national boundaries and intrude on national economic sovereignty, which renders irrelevant the notion of a national market or a national economic unit and undermines national sovereignty from within by fragmenting the national economy.[75]

Hence we can witness the increasing interpenetration from the global to local levels, with the state as a more or less irrelevance in between.

Localities in the Global Arena

Localities still matter because they provide the context in which people make sense of their world. They can be constructed in differing ways, as we saw in the Westport example above, but it is at the level of the locality that one has to start when looking at how people locate themselves geographically in global social relations. A nice story to illustrate this discussion is that of Amelia Earhart, who attempted to become the first woman to fly solo across the Atlantic in May 1932. Having taken off in Newfoundland, Canada, she subsequently landed in the middle of a field outside Derry. 'Where am I?' she asked the first shocked local upon the scene. 'You're in Gallagher's pasture,' he told her.[76] This was an instance of two world-views colliding. Clearly, such local detail was not much good to her, who saw the world in terms of countries and continents, latitude and longitude. The priorities of the local man, however, would have had to do with what the soil in that field was like and if it was possible to make a living from it.

As referred to earlier, large corporations now recognise the importance of engaging with local differences as a marketing strategy, in order to sell more of their products. They view the local level, both in the Western and non-Western world, as 'a site the inhabitants of which must be liberated from themselves (stripped of their identity) to be homogenized into the global culture of capital (their identities reconstructed accordingly).'[77] This approach was mirrored in the parallel development policy trend that suggested that capitalism's dominant modernisation ideology needed to be tempered with some local inputs. This realisation was exemplified by World Bank thinking and policy. This was the time when it became politically correct in aid agencies to actually consult with locals in developing countries as to what they wanted in order to develop their communities, rather than imposing what Western 'experts' thought was best for them. Before this, the non-Western locality and local people were seen in derogatory terms as idiosyncratic barriers to development, as zones of backwardness that were resistant to progress and inevitable modernised urbanisation. The change of heart was also connected with the increasing popularity of an ecological worldview, which recognised how important local environmental conditions were to the implementation of any development strategy.

It is now recognised as fruitful to view socio-economic development policy and practice as a '"battlefield of knowledge" within which different visions of needs and priorities are fought out.'[78] It can no longer be presumed that local people exercise no power over the economic and environmental policies that affect them. Their everyday, grounded understandings and experiences of global processes and policy innovations are now beginning to be integrated into sociological analysis. Even macro-level phenomena like globalisation are intelligible only in situated, concrete contexts. This means that any subject of social research needs to be analysed as a mediated and, potentially, transformed phenomenon, having been affected by various actors, either individually or in groups like social classes, and social structures. This approach sees knowledge not as a fixed given, but as a *process* which is ongoing, dynamic, open to change and, above all, socially based and constructed.

Knowledge is multi-layered, fragmentary and diffuse, rather than unitary and systematised.[79] It is produced, after all, 'not *in abstracto* but in the everyday contingencies and struggles that constitute social life.'[80] Therefore, development processes and policy initiatives cannot be viewed in a linear or deterministic fashion, because they can potentially be changed at any time by actors in different contexts. Actors can exercise choice in how they use information, pick and choose elements at will, continue to use their own ideas from their own knowledge repertoire, or choose to adapt new ideas to their own ends. It is the task of the social scientist to isolate the types of strategies used by different actors and determine the effects they produce in terms of structural outcomes.[81] All actors are thus viewed as being capable of strategic action of some kind, thereby potentially challenging more powerful official views.

Political Activism in Localities

The locality has also been the level at which many of the world's most interesting strategic actions have been taken by radical social movements over the past few decades. These movements have been termed 'nomads of the present' which create 'submerged networks and laboratories of experience' in the political arena.[82] They construct the local not as reactionary retreats to escape the global, but give us ways to place the local in the global, with no contradictions. As Irish writer John McGahern has said:

> Everything interesting begins with one person in one place, though the places can become many, and many persons in the form of influences will have gone into the making of that single woman or man. No one comes out of nowhere; one room or town or locality can be made into an everywhere. The universal is the local, but with the walls taken away.[83]

Localities have often been the locus of intense political struggles, where different groups battle over which version of that locality should dominate. Sometimes these battles can be based on the narrow principle of 'not in my back yard', or NIMBYism. This might be a group of local people opposing a perceived negative development in their area, like a dump or a mobile phone mast or wind turbines. However, these people are not necessarily self-centred and only interested in their own localities. It can often be the case that what starts out as a purely local campaign sends ripples out into the world, resonating with others and connecting with similar campaigns elsewhere. This has occurred in the women's movement, the environmental movement and the struggles of the world's indigenous peoples. In relatively stable democracies, such movements articulate sets of interests in the public sphere, giving their members a sense of belonging and reinforcing political identities. However, in times of crisis, they might form the constituency for the formation of new political parties, thereby exerting their influence on public life.

Major global movements are made up of people in localities doing things to improve their lives. When people feel disenfranchised by 'high' politics, they engage in actions at the micro-level in their own localities. By no means does that imply that these actions are small and irrelevant. As Doreen Massey says, 'localities are not internally introspective bounded unities. They have to be constructed through sets of social relations which bind them inextricably to wider arenas and other places.'[84] The global networks that result from these activities can be very powerful, especially because of the use of the Internet and social media like Facebook and Twitter.

US Civil Rights Movement

John McGahern, as quoted earlier, said that 'everything interesting begins with one person in one place.' An example of this is Rosa Parks in Montgomery, Alabama in 1955. At that time, the seats on public buses were segregated there, with whites at the front and blacks at the back. One black woman, Rosa Parks, refused to move from the front of the bus when told to do so. The police were called, she was arrested, the word spread among the black community, and the famous Montgomery bus boycott was born. This became a major turning point in the black civil rights movement, which spread throughout the United States and beyond. There were widespread demonstrations and boycotts, with the participants demanding an end to discrimination against black people in terms of employment, housing and education. These were sometimes attended by busloads of whites coming to the Southern states on so-called 'freedom rides'. In 1963, the legendary leader Martin Luther King wrote a letter from jail in Birmingham, Alabama, in which he said:

The nations of Asia and Africa are moving at jet-like speed towards gaining political independence, but we still creep at horse-and-buggy pace towards gaining a cup of coffee at a lunch counter.[85]

The famous rallying cry of that movement, 'We shall over-come', was adopted later by the civil rights movement in Northern Ireland, and continues to raise the hairs on the back of necks whenever it is heard. The civil rights movement later merged with other movements like the peace movement, the women's movement and the gay movement, to form what was called, in true sixties style, 'the counter culture'. Rosa Parks did not cause all this, but her actions were a major spark to action at the time. One person in one place. That infamous bus is now in a museum in Dearborn, Michigan. An extremely evocative picture was published in *The Guardian* newspaper in the UK in April 2012 of President Obama sitting on that same bus, staring out the window and no doubt thinking about the struggles African Americans have undergone thus far, as well as those yet to come.[86]

The Zapatistas in Chiapas, Mexico

One local movement that gained worldwide attention in the last twenty years was the *Ejército Zapatista de Liberación Nacional* (EZLN) (Zapatista National Liberation Army), more commonly called the Zapatistas of Chiapas, Southern Mexico.[87] This uprising of Mexican peasant farmers and indig-enous people began on 1 January 1994 to coincide with the implementation of the North American Free Trade Agree-ment (NAFTA). This agreement gave *carte blanche* to global business interests to buy what were previously communal lands in Mexico.[88] The EZLN movement has resisted the incursion of neoliberal economics into their area ever since: they resist the privatisation of their land and opening up the region to market forces. They demand self-determination and the inclusion of *campesinos* (small farmers) in national decision-making in order to sustain their local culture and ecology.[89] This movement has earned massive support internationally, helped by the inputs of their balaclava-clad leader Subcomandante Marcos, who is charismatic and enigmatic in equal measure. Marcos has a very strong Internet profile, via which he often engages with independent media. In a recent YouTube clip he spoke of what he terms the Fourth World War, against the powerless and disenfranchised peoples of the world. The Zapatistas' political goals are a constellation of struggles over indigenous peoples' rights, land reform and environmental conservation, all of which are threatened by neoliberalism.

The Chipko Movement, Himalayas, India

Many environmental campaigns start out at the level of the locality because of the diversity of environmental conditions. When the European green movement was founded in the 1970s, its slogan reflected this as well: 'act locally, think globally.' Environmental campaigns have taken a huge variety of forms, underpinned by a range of philosophies that vary in terms of their levels of radicalism. Many of the most inspiring examples of local environmental struggles have emanated from the developing world. One example is the Chipko Movement, which started in the Uttar Pradesh region of the Himalayas in the 1970s.

'Chipko' is the Hindi word for 'hug'. The movement's members literally hugged trees to prevent them from being felled by foresters. The clearing of the forests was part of the modernisation zeal of the Nehru government of the time. The movement sought access to small-scale tree felling for locals and more government aid for the region, as it was so poor. It was a heterogenous group: some of the members were regionalist, some were socialist and some were Gandhian, but all of them were against the commercial deforestation of the region.[90] It has garnered a huge amount of international support and, even now, the Internet contains thousands of pictures of earnest young people hugging trees to show their support for the movement. The actions of those involved in the Chipko movement led to a ban on tree felling in the region. So they were successful in their goals. However, forestry jobs were lost as a result.

An alternative separatist movement emerged in the 1980s, seeking a separate state called Uttaranchal. This regionalist movement sought to reverse the ban on tree felling in order to bring what they saw as development to the region. This type of expression of localism gains little sympathy internationally. Both movements wanted local development and control of resources, but they had different approaches and strategies. It is therefore clear that 'the local' means different things to different people and, hence, localities are 'frequently riven with internal tensions and conflicts.'[91]

These movements vividly illustrate the possibilities that exist for action when people feel threatened. They are role models for different types of social activism that people can use when the need arises. It is difficult to measure their actual effectiveness sometimes, but they are important because they show that 'issues of universal concern need to be instantiated in the everyday, local experience and "moral lifeworld" of the people.'[92] However, most people who live in localities do not experience this kind of drama. Local life is usually much more mundane than this, as most of us will never have to strap on a Kalashnikov or lie in the path of a tank to defend our locality from an aggressor. We are the lucky ones. Every decade we witness new groups of people who have to either fight for their locality or else run for their lives. Some situations, indeed, never seem to change, as in the case of the severely-oppressed Palestinians. The most recent images of people fighting against oppression on our TV screens are coming from Syria. Where will it be next year?

Social Class and Localities

Undoubtedly, we now live in an era of increased mobility. This does not affect everyone personally, though. Some cannot afford to move from their locality, even if they wish to do so. Due to a lack of money, education or useful contacts in powerful circles, they are localised without their consent. In the absence of the currency of cultural capital – the right school, college, accent or appearance – people develop coping strategies to maximise their situation. They may be forced to live with the identity ascribed to them in their social milieu, rather than having the freedom to develop their own. They therefore develop a new type of cultural capital based on knowing and being known in the locality. For people who have rarely left their own locality, connection to people or places in that locality is their main means of judging a person's value. If someone 'local' climbs Mount Everest or wins a Nobel Prize, they will focus on the fact that he/she is Mrs. O'Brien's young one rather than the details of their actual achievements. This is particularly prevalent in Cork, it has to be said!

In one sociological study of a working-class housing estate in Britain, it was found that 'those "known" on the estate are "in", be they black or white, manual or non-manual. Locality and local solidarity and loyalty become the central concepts of inclusion and exclusion.'[93] So territory and the rules and codes associated with it meant everything to this estate's inhabitants. Locals' power was based on who they knew on the estate, especially in the light of 'the decline in national identity, and the alleged breakdown of the concept of class.'[94] They have to build a strong local identity when they have nothing else, as it might be a source of employment, mutual aid and support among community members.[95] This is what the famous sociologist Robert Putnam calls 'bonding social capital', which is 'good for under girding specific reciprocity and mobilizing solidarity' or, in other words, 'getting by'. These people probably have low stocks of what Putnam calls 'bridging social capital', which is good for 'linkage to external assets and for information diffusion' or 'getting ahead'. The former is 'sociological superglue', while the latter is 'sociological WD-40'.[96]

The impact of globalisation is negligible in such settings, so the locality is still crucially important in people's lives. Even if we are not the ones doing the moving, other people around us are, perhaps changing the social composition of our own area. Most people are just at the receiving end of globalisation, finding their places transformed before their eyes by new shops, new images, new people – everywhere. This can sometimes generate racism and xenophobia in localities, causing major trouble for minorities, whether Pakistanis in Leeds or Koreans in Los Angeles.

Conclusion

Local life is what constitutes our everyday experience, most of the time. For most people, globalised modernity means 'staying in one place but experiencing the "dis-placement" that global modernity *brings to them* [and how] distant events and powers penetrate our local experience.'[97] While the Internet and global TV networks like CNN bring the outside world into our living rooms, we need to be careful not to overstate the extent to which this changes peoples' lives. People are immersed in their localities like fish in water. They are 'in the local setting bodily, with all their senses, ready not only to look and listen but to touch, smell and taste without having their fields of attention restricted, pre-structured for them.'[98] When we watch John Simpson reporting for the BBC from the latest war zone, the world is packaged in an easily-digestible 'McNugget' of information. We do not have to risk our lives or see dead bodies up close – if the images get too much for our delicate sensibilities, all we have to reach for is the remote control. The ways in which this instant access to the outside world changes peoples' lives in their localities are very subtle for most people, who still have to do the washing and get the kids out to school in the morning.

This chapter has attempted to shine a light on the impact of globalisation upon our localities and the places in which we live. The places people live in still matter. However, it is argued that we need to be realistic – that we cannot draw a boundary line around any village, region or country and that we all live in one huge, interconnected system. The more we know about that system, the more likely we are to be able to exert agency of our own to shape the futures of our own places.

4

Who Am I? Constructing Our Identities

Having addressed how we identify with our homes, families, communities and localities, it is now time to take a step back and address the ways in which we construct our personal and sexual identities. Because most of us, in the Western world at least, live in societies that are freer than they used to be, we are now more conscious and thoughtful about how we want to build our selves, from the ground up, so to speak. We make grown-up choices, having left the nest of our homes and communities, deciding for ourselves what the components of our personal comfort zone are to be. As I will show, the freedom to explore in this way is a product of social power that is not shared equally by everybody. This chapter begins by discussing sociological means of addressing questions of identities, before going on to focus upon sexual identities in particular, with a special emphasis on the role of the Catholic Church in Ireland in restraining those identities.

Defining Identities

When we are asked to prove our identity or age to gain admittance to a country or a nightclub, the main document that defines us, that determines whether we are welcomed in or refused entry, is our passport. The picture and text on this document gives information on aspects of our identity, including nationality, citizenship, skin colour, sex and age. My passport, for example, tells an airport official that I am a white-skinned, Irish, European woman. The possession of this passport confers rights upon me that others do not have, affording me freedom of movement virtually anywhere in the world. It is a valuable document which many world citizens would do anything to obtain. It is a symbol of relative privilege. However, as a representation of me as a human being it is extremely minimalist. It does not tell how I feel about the various aspects of my identity. For example, do I wear my Irishness or my Europcanness lightly or heavily? Is there anything about these identities that I would kill or die for? Which collective identity is the most important to me? Am I part of any movement that is founded on the fact of my Irishness or my femaleness?

My identity as per my passport is a fixed entity, a set of facts that does not change. In everyday life, however, aspects of my identity might change frequently, depending on my feelings surrounding my particular life circumstances and the actions I take as a result. These aspects of my identity are potentially multiple. I might, for example, marry a man from Algeria, learn Arabic and convert to Islam. Or I might decide that I need a sex change, that I would be happier living my life as a man. Or I might join an armed resistance group fighting for the rights of a religious minority in China. All of these are real possibilities, and this shows how narrow, bloodless and rationalised our passport selves are compared to the complexity of our real, everyday, irrational selves. This is about human agency or individual power, which has the potential either to support or to topple the structures that constrain and define us.

Forming Identities

Our identities are formed by the ways in which we attribute meaning to the world around us. Meaning may be defined here as 'the symbolic identification by a social actor of the purpose of his/her action.'[1] In other words, it has to do with the cultural reasons why we do the things we do. One of my identities, for example, is that I consider myself to be a dyed-in-the-wool feminist. I attach strong importance or symbolic weight to the fact of femaleness. It is a lens through which I see the world. I perceive that most problems associated with poverty and underdevelopment in poorer countries could be solved most efficiently and lastingly by the education and empowerment of women. The actions I have taken in my life and the ways that I interact with those around me are strongly influenced by my feminism. The slightest whiff of sexism gets my back up. Other people might attribute more importance to race, ethnicity or sexual orientation, and live their own lives accordingly.

What we think of as our inner selves are always formed by interaction with the social world around us. Of course, it is the connections between human beings that make life worth living. These connections can be, broadly speaking, to other people or to places, and they can be either chosen for us by others or chosen by ourselves. We have no choice as to where we are born and into what family. It is what we do with the social hand we are dealt – the people we associate with and the places we identify with in our adult lives – that is mainly of interest here. Identity 'bridges the gap between the "inside" and the "outside" – between the personal and the public worlds.'[2] We weave the fabric of our selves from both social and personal threads. The interaction between self and society is the bread and butter of social analysts. American social psychologist George Herbert Mead tells us that 'the self … is essentially a social structure and it arises in social experience.'³ What we think of as our 'selves' are created both by ourselves and by others, within the context of our social environment. In extreme cases, such as where children are reared in isolated circumstances, it is difficult for them to develop a 'self', as they cannot learn through communication with others. They may not know what a smile, a kiss or a wave even means, never mind be able to respond appropriately.

Identity formation is therefore a dynamic process during which we learn to know 'who's who' and, hence, 'what's what'. When you walk into a room full of people, whether at an art auction, a Jewish wedding or a dogfight, you just know whether you belong there or not. There are cultural markers that make you blend in or stand out. The way you look, dress, speak and behave will either get you ejected or handed a welcoming drink.

The process of identification involves classifications of various kinds and, hence, is usually emotion-led to some extent.⁴ We identify with our hearts. To decide that you are going to become a Rangers fan, a Hare Krishna, a Goth or a nun means that you will be wearing external symbols of the group with which you now identify. This means that you will be loved and included in some circles and utterly reviled in others. This is the process of *symbolising*, where wearing a particular shirt or piece of cloth on your head stands for something else that has deeper meaning for us. We symbolise the sort of person we want others to think we are through the clothes we wear and the ways we behave. We present various faces to the world at different times, and it is debatable as to what extent there is a 'real' or authentic self behind these various faces.⁵ To express oneself openly like this takes courage, as you might even risk your very life in some settings.

Wearing, or indeed not wearing, a particular piece of cloth can get you killed in certain contexts. Developing the courage of your convictions is what identity formation is all about. And it is never finished, complete, settled – change is always possible to a greater or lesser extent. The self you were at 18 years of age is very different from the self you are at 40 or 75. We all know the experience of meeting old school friends who knew only our childhood or teenage selves. They think they know you, but once the conversation moves on from reminiscing about the 'glory days' of the school years, there is often not a lot left to talk about, as they do not know, or perhaps want to know, your older self.

The Power to Choose

This ongoing process of identification might be conscious or not, actively chosen or passively inherited from older generations. The extent to which we can exercise choices around our identities is very much dependent upon how much power we have in the different aspects of our lives. Some young people have the personal freedom to acquire an education, study subjects of their own choosing and, consequently, develop a career and life-path that make them happy. They can express themselves culturally and sexually as they wish, living and loving as their whims take them. At the other extreme, some young people's life-paths are landscaped for them before they are even born; they have no choice about anything in their lives, slotting into the boxes that are predetermined for them. An extreme example of this is the continuing hold that the caste system has over Indian social life, despite countervailing social forces that are making that country wealthier.

For most of us, the truth lies somewhere in between, somewhere along that spectrum from complete freedom to complete oppression. For example, a person might possess more money than they could ever spend, while suffering severe restrictions upon their personal and sexual behaviour; we think here of those born into royalty, for example. On the other hand, a person might have complete personal freedom, but very little money, which would help them enormously in enjoying their liberty!

Another aspect of this question of the power to choose our identities is how much freedom you subjectively feel you have, compared to how others see your situation, or compared to any objective set of criteria. When I look back on my teenage years, I can now see that I had very little freedom to explore anything different from the cultural norms of rural Ireland in the eighties, but back then I felt that I was having a great time. Or when we look back at out grandmothers' lives, we may see nothing but drudgery, though it is probable that they did not view it that way at all, seeing it as simply 'normal'. Another contemporary example might be when some people wonder why young Muslim women protest for the right to cover their faces with a *niqab*: one person's oppression is another's freedom.

The question of just how much choice we have over our identities has divided different authors on the subject in recent years. It has become a popular perspective that in contemporary society one's identity is a very dynamic, fluid affair that can mutate, being invented and reinvented at will. It is said that endless options exist for how we want to live our lives, with our cultural identities becoming more 'open-ended, variable and problematic.'[6] One can decide I am no longer this, I am now that, choosing from the cornucopia of options that life offers. This applies to matters of ethnicity, sexuality, gender and politics, among many other things. There are, apparently, 'numerous possibilities for belonging.'[7] The mind-boggling pace of global connections across cyberspace facilitates this creativity *par excellence*, leading to the potential integration of all sorts of social networks in our lives. When 'released from the fetters of traditional social relations of work, family, consumption, the state and education, the individual is both more free and at the same time more reliant on alternative social bonds.'[8] This means that 'the self becomes a reflexive project'[9], and we have transcended all of our old identities like class and nationalism, leaving us room to develop our self-identities. This has been termed the process of 'individualisation', where there are no more social certainties and everybody has to compose a 'do-it-yourself biography.'[10] This is akin to an existentialist perspective, where one's social origins are seen as of little or no consequence in determining the development of the self.

However, not everyone agrees with this attractive idea. As sociologist Richard Jenkins says:

> ... where does it leave the many millions of people, in Europe and the United States, never mind anywhere else, who, for whatever reasons, do not spend much, or even any, time agonising over 'life narratives' and 'personal growth'? Who have other things ... to fret about?[11]

The implication here is that it is only privileged, Western, middle- and upper-class people who ponder on their self-identities and have the freedom to pursue their whims. Most of the world has to worry more about surviving in turbulent economic times rather than navel-gazing about their personal life projects. If they do play around with the 'who am I?' question, they are likely to turn to some form of religion as their saviour ... or football, or Facebook, or, in my case, shopping! Others concur with this, saying that the conception of identity as choice is elitist, that it excludes 'involuntarily localised or racialised individuals.'[12]

It seems to me that the level of personal freedom alluded to above does not reflect the experience of the majority. Vast tracts of the world still do not have electricity, never mind access to the Internet. In other cases, some societies attempt to restrict people's access to the Internet because it is seen as dangerous: politically subversive and morally corrupt. Also, millions of the world's sons and daughters are still not free from family obligations and social duties. Many still eventually end up doing more or less what their parents expect of them. It is still mostly difficult enough to 'come out' as a gay person, for example, or to marry someone from a different religious tradition. People's life experiences serve to fence off certain possibilities, and people usually behave as they are expected to by society. The habitus of a person, or group of persons, prescribes certain courses of thought and action, laying down the divide between what is appropriate and inappropriate behaviour in society. People usually end up 'condemning themselves to what is in any case their lot.'[13] People are usually more likely to accept the status quo than to attempt to change it, because it is difficult and challenging to raise one's head above the parapet, especially in small places. However, just because it is difficult does not mean that some do not try to be different, express their individuality or subvert power structures in various ways.

Sexual Identities

At this point, I wish to focus upon how this idea of individualisation transfers into personal and sexual relationships. British sociologist Anthony Giddens argues, 'sexuality becomes a property of the individual the more the life-span becomes internally referential and the more self-identity is grasped as a reflexively ordered endeavour ... [so] passion is secularised ... it is privatised and redefined.'[14] According to this perspective, open experimentation seems to be the order of the day. Sexuality is one of the most important and personal aspects of our identities. It is interesting sociologically because it 'functions as a malleable feature of self, a prime connecting point between body, self-identity and social norms.'[15] If our sexual selves are content, it is easier for other aspects of our lives to fall into place. However, if we are not *bien dans sa peau* (happy in our skin) sexually, it can have a ruinous effect on our lives. Like any other type of identity, our sexuality is heavily influenced by the prevailing sexual attitudes in society. These in turn shape sexual practices.

Sexual Behaviour

Sociological analysts are often interested in making a distinction between public discourses on certain subjects and people's ordinary behaviour behind the scenes in everyday life. I will discuss later in this chapter how sexual discourse was dominated by the Catholic Church up until the 1970s. However, it would be too simplistic to assume that people necessarily always followed the rules laid down by them. Of course they didn't. Once boys and girls (and boys and boys, and girls and girls) are driven by their hormones to get their hands on each other, they will do it – no matter what. Sex is a powerful force. As a young person, if you are told to do one thing, you generally want to do the opposite. As historian Diarmuid Ferriter says, 'during a century where there was an avowedly Catholic ethos, oppression and watchfulness, there was also no shortage of clandestine and illicit sexual behaviour.'[16] For example, historian Maria Luddy has found that many thousands of

Irish women worked as prostitutes between 1800 and 1940. The high incidence of venereal disease is also a pointer in the direction of clandestine sexual activity. Between 1926 and 1941, in two Dublin hospitals alone about two thousand five hundred people were treated for venereal disease every year.[17] No society has just one set of characteristics – like traditional, Catholic and repressive – at a time; there is always a challenge, defiance and resistance by some actors in society. And when it comes to sex, that defiance usually comes from young people.

Feminist Activism

The present generation of women (and, indeed, men) owes a huge debt of gratitude to the feminist campaigners of the 1970s. Access to contraception was illegal in the Republic of Ireland then, and feminists like Mary Kenny, Mary Maher and Nell McCafferty fought hard for the liberalisation of laws and attitudes. One famous example of their activism took place on 22 May 1971, when a group of Dublin-based feminists embarked on a train for Northern Ireland (where contraception was legally available) to buy up every form of contraception they could find and bring it all back to Dublin. The police and the media were waiting for them on their return, and their action had a strong popular impact. McCafferty recalls:

> It was the fervent hope of those who embarked on the Pill Train that the Irish government would arrest us on our return, making us instant martyrs and obliterating all our sins. If you want to progress socially in colonised Ireland … the first thing you have to do is go to jail …[18]

This kind of radicalism, humour, imagination, cohesiveness and courage now seems to be a product of a bygone era. In the censorious Ireland of the sixties and seventies it was more difficult than one can now imagine to obtain information on sexuality. At this time, people learned a lot from Angela MacNamara's 'agony aunt' column in *The Sunday Press*. Sociologist Paul Ryan, who analysed these letters from a sociological perspective, said that they 'are an incredible resource and paint an intimate picture of a people emerging from the cocoon of rigid religious fervour and examining their lives more closely.'[19]

Sexual Discourse

There is still relatively little mature discussion of sexual matters in Irish society, indicating an ongoing tension between traditional and liberal attitudes. Social psychologist Michael O'Connell reported in 2001 that he witnessed a conversation between a group of young Dutch and young Irish people about sex. While the Dutch were 'at ease, open and mature', the 'embarrassed and squeamish' Irish 'blushed, looked at the ceiling, joked or changed the subject.'[20] I can verify that I witnessed a similar attitude over ten years later in a third-year sociology seminar on sexuality in an Irish university. When it came to discussions of sexual experience and whether young men and women were equal in this regard, the students didn't quite blush, but they were shy and quiet, hoping somebody else would speak first. If this anecdotal evidence reveals anything it is that there is still a tension – a coyness – about sex among young Irish people.

These seminar students did reveal that there still seems to be a very patchy delivery of sex education in Irish schools, with most of them getting little or nothing from their supposed educators on the subject. With little sex education to guide them, it is probable that young Irish people still rely on the age-old 'hands-on' active-learning approach that we all used, fumbling our way towards the emergence of our adult sexual selves. They now have round-the-clock instant access to hard porn on the Internet as well, so this may set up unrealistic expectations of what sex is really like, for real people who do not look remotely like dolls.

I recently saw one enlightened group of students who set up a stall on an Irish college campus on the subject of sexual health. Their table was covered in educational literature, but the most eye-catching items on their table were two substantial pink vibrators. As older people have said since the dawn of time, 'that wouldn't happen in my day!' If only the media were as enlightened as these young students. If sex is discussed at all in the media, it is pathologised in terms of the 'problems' of promiscuity, sexually transmitted diseases, fertility problems or erectile dysfunction. It appears that some people are having too much of it, and others not enough.

Sexual Practices

So what do we know about people's actual sexual practices? Not much. It is not a subject with which many social researchers wish to get down and dirty. One source does give us some information, however. The Durex Global Sex Survey, conducted in 2005, produced some relatively reliable results. The company interviewed 317,000 people from 41 countries, including Ireland. While Durex is, of course, most interested in the use of its own products, some of the general information derived in the survey is relevant here. The following are some of the survey's findings:[21]

• The average age when Irish people first had sex was 17.3 years, which was concurrent with the global average. The youngest age was in Iceland (15.6 years) and the oldest was India (19.8 years).

- The average number of sexual partners in Ireland was 11.1, whereas the highest was in Turkey (14.5). The lowest number was in India (3), and the global average was 9.
- 58 per cent of Irish people have had unprotected sex, compared to the global average of 47 per cent.
- Irish people have sex on average 97 times a year, compared to the global average of 103 times. The Greeks do it the most, at 138 times, and the Japanese do it the least, at 45 times.
- 12 per cent of Irish people have had an extra marital affair; 62 per cent have had a one night stand; and 20 per cent have had a gay experience.

All of this sexual activity is hard work. While there has always been more pressure on women than on men to look sexually attractive, the pressure that is on young women these days is like nothing I experienced when I was younger. The 'freedom' to express one's sexuality openly comes at a price, both meta-phorically and literally. As Tom Inglis says, young women 'have moved from a Catholic culture based on the principle "Lord, I am not worthy" to a consumer culture based on the self-justification principle "I am worth it".'[22] The standard expectations for young women nowadays are heavily deter-mined by consumerism and dumbed-down celebrity culture. They have to be unnaturally thin (or at least feeling guilty if they are not), coated in fake tan, impeccably made up, waxed (ouch!) to within an inch of their lives and wearing extraor-dinarily high heels. Shoe designer and elite cobbler Christian Louboutin made the first 8-inch heel outside the fetish world in 2009. It appears that the shape of the heel arch in such high heels resembles the shape of a woman's foot during orgasm.[23]

Who knew! The kind of heels that girls now feel they have to wear to the local pub on a Saturday night were previously, shall we say, not made for walking, except up and down a man's spotty back in a cheap porn movie. When they do walk in these heels, they often look a bit like a newborn giraffe taking its first steps. Doctors continue to warn of the damage caused by the prolonged wearing of high heels too, but to no avail.

Looking like this, in the style of what I like to call 'pole-dancer chic', is not *instead* of being smart – women still have to be smarter than men to get promoted because of their possession of that pesky piece of kit called a womb. Can you imagine a man putting up with this torture? Not on your nelly! And I suspect that the sexual game is still not a level playing field for young women and men – girls are still called 'sluts' if they behave promiscuously, whereas boys are accorded much more freedom by society. Then, if young women do settle with a man, they must combine a variety of roles. They have to be Maggie Thatcher in the workplace (because people feel more cash-strapped than ever), nurturing and loving with the children (because Supernanny will come and find you if you are not) and Dita von Teese in the bedroom (because the porn industry sets the sexual bar higher all the time). What a relief that I am no longer 19!

Sexual Abuse

The dark side of sexuality relates to the sexual abuse of children and adults, which is common in Ireland. A child is usually more likely to be sexually abused inside the walls of his or her own home than outside of it. However, the closed nature of the discussion around this topic which has pervaded Irish society for some time has been due in no small part to the sense of shame indoctrinated in people by the Catholic Church. Support structures and networks for people who have been abused are still, unfortunately, few and far between. The most comprehensive report to date on this subject has been *The SAVI Report: Sexual Abuse and Violence in Ireland*, published in 2002. Based on interviews with a random sample of three thousand people in Ireland, some of the report's findings are as follows:[24]

• One in five women and one in six men reported sexual abuse during their childhood.
• One in five women and one in ten men experienced a sexual assault as adults.
• As many as 42 per cent of women and 28 per cent of men experienced some form of sexual assault or abuse during their lifetimes.
• A quarter of perpetrators of sexual abuse against girls were family members of the victims; half were non-family members but were known to the victims; and a quarter were strangers to the victims.
• One in seven perpetrators of sexual abuse against boys were family members of the victims; two-thirds were non-family members but were known to the victims; and one in five were strangers to the victims.
• In four out of five cases of child sexual abuse, the perpetrators were known to the abused person.

The recession is having a deleterious effect on support services for abused persons, like the Rape Crisis Centres. As of November 2011, the Dublin Rape Crisis Centre has had €320,000 cut from its annual budget, and the centre fears its budget is to be cut again. The centre took almost twelve thousand calls to its helpline number during 2011, including approximately three thousand three hundred people who were calling for the first time.[25] So, ironically, as soon as the culture on the issue of sexual abuse improves, the economy crashes. While people might now muster the courage to pick up the phone and seek help, there may be nobody available to answer their call.

Sex and the Catholic Church

Irish public discourse about sex throughout most of the twentieth century was dominated by the teaching of the Catholic Church, where sex was equated with sin, shame and guilt. The sexual act was for procreation only, to produce the next generation of believers. The idea that it could be a source of pleasure or fun was repressed and condemned. Any media images that gave a glimpse of a female thigh or bellybutton were swiftly censored. The work of sociologist Tom Inglis, with his ground-breaking *Moral Monopoly*, and historian Diarmaid Ferriter's magisterial *Occasions of Sin* provide the best available works on this subject. Inglis says:

> The Catholic Church became the means to the end of controlling sex and marriage. It provided the beliefs, moral values, prayers, rituals and sacraments which protected the 'sacred heart' of the family from contamination through sex and selfishness.[26]

Throughout the twentieth century, there is a plethora of evidence to show the cultural dominance of the Catholic Church in Ireland and its obsession with controlling sex. Sex was equated with sin and sin equated with sex. The Church did not show too much interest in any other kind of sin – morality was below the belt only. This obsession was especially obvious in the mind of Archbishop John Charles McQuaid, who was

Primate of Ireland and Archbishop of Dublin for over three decades, from 1940 to 1972. Among his many social interventions on matters to do with women's bodies and reproductive health, he even endeavoured to have tampons banned in 1944.[27] Despite the Church's avowed concern with the purity of its flock, we now know that hypocrisy was the order of the day. As the song goes, hindsight is 20/20 vision.

Historian Maria Luddy argues that after Independence, women's sexuality and even their bodies were seen as 'suspect and in need of restraint'.[28] This state-sponsored misogynistic ideology was needed in order to ensure that women stayed in the home and out of public life. For example, the Magdalene asylums (or Laundries) were where unmarried girls who got pregnant, or sometimes just poor or neglected children, were hidden away, treated as 'fallen women' who were not deemed fit to live in normal society. In 1956, for example, there were 945 women in these hate-filled institutions, indicating 'the collusion of state, society and religious orders in seeking to remove from public circulation perceived threats to a conservative moral order.'[29] As Diarmaid Ferriter also points out, the men who impregnated them were not considered to be 'fallen men', continuing to live their own lives as normal.

In February 2013, following the publication of a major report on these Magdalen Laundries, Taoiseach Enda Kenny made a full apology to the women who survived their time in these institutions. As part of this long, heartfelt speech, he said:

> I, as Taoiseach, on behalf of the State, the Government and our citizens deeply regret and apologise unreservedly to all those women for the hurt that was done to them, and for any stigma they suffered, as a result of the time they spent in the Magdalen Laundry.[30]

He also promised reasonable compensation and medical care for the women for the rest of their lives.

As well as the Laundries, the industrial schools were for so-called 'troublesome' children who went on to 'learn the meaning of the word "cruel".'[31] The reports that have recently emerged from these truly terrible institutions constitute a litany of shame from which this society may never recover. These places have been called 'brutal slave camps for children from underprivileged backgrounds … incarcerated for trivial offences or even for no offence at all.'[32] A whole genre of writing has now emerged, recounting people's experiences in all of these institutions. We cannot hear the place names Letterfrack, Artane or Goldenbridge now without a shiver running down our spines.

At a more 'ordinary' level, the schools that most children attended were often places where mental cruelty and physical punishment were considered normal. Ask anybody over the age of 50, especially men, about their experience of school, and the stories that pour out of them would make you cry. In many cases, that they learned anything at all is a minor miracle. Being slapped with leather straps on the hands or being made to drop your trousers in front of the class to be spanked on the bare bottom were not at all unusual. I heard of one priest who endearingly named his own leather strap 'Susie'. Another friend told me of a priest at his school who used to make a weapon from a bag of stones, the contents of which he had lovingly picked especially for the job of torturing children. At the same school, the boys were regularly hung upside down by the ankles from a second floor window. These are the types of memories that signify the fifties and sixties for many thousands of Irish people. And that is just the physical abuse – there are many more accounts of the horrendous sexual abuse suffered by thousands of Irish children in Church-run institutions. The overarching power of the Church ensured that such unacceptable behaviour was tolerated and therefore condoned.

So much has now been said on this subject in Irish public culture that it is impossible to find anything to add to the discourse, except to add one's voice to the chorus that condemns the abuse of children in any way. In this regard, Church and state operated like one big secret society. As Ferriter says, 'the challenge that various authorities set themselves was to keep the uncomfortable truths behind closed doors', concerning themselves only with 'keeping souls, not bodies, safe'.[33] It has to be said that there were exceptional individuals within the system, who managed to be encouraging and kind teachers, despite the culture of cruelty and banal depravity that surrounded them. These teachers were just doing their jobs, in classes that were much smaller than they are now, but they stood out as exceptional in that harsh environment.

Among Catholic priests, nuns and bishops it became normal to say one thing while doing another. The so-called moral guardians of the Irish people were often not so moral behind closed doors. Again, as Inglis reminds us, 'we used to think that all our priests and bishops were paragons of virtue, exemplars of the good spiritual and moral life, and yet some of them were having sex *and* children while others were having sex *with* children.'[34] Even those priests who were not doing it themselves almost certainly knew that others were and did nothing to expose it.

Since the 1990s, the Church's house of cards has come tumbling down. There has been revelation after revelation of physical and sexual abuse within the various institutions run by the Church and by individual priests and brothers. One would like to think that no child will ever again have to suffer because of the cloak of silence and complicity put in place by the Catholic Church in Ireland. Organisations like One in Four, advocates for victims of clerical sexual abuse, are now firmly established on the Irish political scene, providing a supportive structure for this new culture of openness. Change is, of course, slower within the Church itself than outside it, with only one figure, Archbishop Dr. Diarmuid Martin, seeming to show genuine compassion and leadership in this regard.

Secularisation?

So is the influence of religion now ebbing in Ireland? I think that we cannot assume that contemporary Irish society is completely liberal, secular and modern. Cultural influences ebb and flow, depending upon the influences of different social actors at certain junctures. To assume that secularisation is a straight path that is collinear with economic modernisation and social liberalism is a big mistake. I wish to justify this argument on both micro and macro scales.

On the *micro* scale, at the level of the individual, the role of religion in people's lives is very complex and difficult to measure. Such a qualitative phenomenon is difficult to analyse quantitatively: might I go so far as to suggest that the true extent and nature of spiritual sentiments at a national level are *unknowable*? While various statistical surveys exist of religious belief in Ireland and elsewhere, I choose not to quote from them here, as I do not trust their validity.[35] Just because a person chooses not to attend church, for example, does not mean that they do not have some form of spirituality in their lives, either derived from their church of origin or from an adopted one like Buddhism. Even if they do go to church, it might be more out of habit than based on any deep faith. Perhaps they just want to impose some structure on their week, rather than structure their morality. People may also use their church to perform baptisms, weddings and funerals, even though they may not step inside the church doors at any other time. It is probably the case that people pay less attention to the rigid rules of established churches and make up their own minds on moral matters. For example, it would be difficult to imagine people avoiding the use of contraception for religious reasons at this juncture. So it might be argued that organised religion has declined in importance in many people's lives, but 'individual belief and need for spiritual meaning seem as strong as ever.'[36]

Nowadays, bookshops are crammed with ever-growing sections on self-help and spirituality. This publishing growth sector services the needs of people who are looking for some sort of true path, or perhaps just for a means of de-stressing. The most recent trendy buzzword is 'mindfulness', originally derived from Buddhism. It would be an interesting piece of sociological research to figure out how an idea like this suddenly bursts on to the spiritual scene in the Western world. I think it is connected to the recession, when we are now trying to be happier with less and get pleasure from simpler things. The tumultuous welcome that Amma, the Hugging Saint from Kerala, South India, receives from many thousands of people on her visits to Ireland is a case in point.

The Benedictine monks of Glenstal Abbey, County Limerick are targeting this spirit-thirsty market as well, as they now rent out 'God Pods' on their grounds for up to €80 per night. These are small wooden dwellings with all the 'mod cons'. They, according to their website, 'offer a space to encounter self, a unique place for you to pray, slow down and refresh your spirit.'[37] This *spiel* sounds a little bit Lough Derg, a little bit Goa and a little bit health spa. The Church is now, it appears, getting in on the act of New Age mumbo-jumbo.

On the *macro* scale, it is impossible to say that religion is declining in importance. There is considerable evidence that religion is still a very powerful force and is strongly connected to nationalist and ethnic identities. Christianity, Islam, Judaism and Hinduism still provide many of the tenets that serve to underpin global wars – everybody thinks they are doing God's work. This is a huge subject in its own right, which is beyond the bounds of this work.

Western societies like the US, with its strong Christian right movement, and the UK, where bishops still sit in the House of Lords, are far from secular in every respect. France attempts to ban public displays of religiosity, based on its legal principle of *laïcité*, or laicism, which rigorously separates church and state. This is deemed offensive by some minorities, especially Muslim women who wear the *niqab* and *burka* as they go about their everyday lives. There are no questions on religion or ethnicity on the French census form, so there is no possibility of quantitative research on these matters.

Despite having expressed my suspicion over the concept of secularisation, there is still evidence that Irish society is much more sexually liberal now than forty years ago. People are almost certainly having more sex, sexual imagery is everywhere, and some would say we have reached a kind of sexual 'end of history'. While it is still not a free-for-all, more sexual kit is certainly for sale. As academic Sinéad Kennedy says, 'the country that banned *Ulysses* as a pornographic text for much of the twentieth century now has shelves full of pornography, Irish versions of "New Lad" magazines, a growing prostitution industry and a selection of lap-dancing clubs.'[38] These clubs allegedly have a connection with the dark, exploitative world of trafficking girls and women from Eastern Europe and elsewhere. Ruhama, the NGO that helps women who work in the sex industry, says that 'lap dancing clubs are part and parcel of the global sex industry and a gateway into prostitution and trafficking', and it says that it has worked with women who were trafficked into Ireland to work in these clubs and end up in prostitution.[39]

Two Big Issues

Abortion

The age-old difference between males and females is still that it is the woman who 'gets in trouble' after unprotected sex. Since abortion is still illegal and such a political hot potato in Ireland, many women who have unwanted pregnancies have to go to England if they want a termination. Between 1970 and 1996, 70,000 Irish women had abortions in England, with 5,325 in 1997 alone.[40] In 2000, the number of women who gave Irish addresses in English abortion clinics went up to 6,381 – 18 per day.[41] By 2011, this is reported to have dropped to 4,149.[42] Many more will have given fake addresses, and more again are forced to go through with unwanted pregnancies because they cannot afford the considerable cost of the journey, accommodation and the procedure itself. After all, an abortion in England currently costs between £530 and £1,926, depending upon the method used and how advanced the pregnancy is.[43]

Women who were interviewed for a major report on crisis pregnancy in the late 1990s said that they chose to have an abortion because of the abiding stigma of being a single mother in Irish society, the difficulty of their lives while trying to combine earning a living with having a child, and their perception that they could not properly provide for a child.[44] Choosing a termination was their way of taking control of the difficult situation in which they found themselves. Neither, no doubt, did they want to be 'put away' in Church-run homes to have their babies and have them adopted. Following the X case in 1992, the Supreme Court allowed for the girl in question to travel to England for an abortion because she was at a high risk of committing suicide.

A full twenty years later, still no legislation has been introduced on the basis of this case. Until 2012, very few politicians wanted to touch it. As a result, a number of UN human rights bodies have expressed strong criticism of Ireland, with the UN committee on torture 'asking questions' on Ireland's slowness in legislating on the X case.[45] In 2012, a lobby group comprised of 60 groups and individuals called the 'Action on X Alliance' attempted to push for the introduction of legislation allowing for limited access to abortion in Ireland. Emotions ran high on 18 April during the discussion in the Dáil of the Medical Treatment (Termination of Pregnancy in Case of Risk to Life of Pregnant Woman) Bill. Independent TD Mick Wallace cried as he read out letters he had received from women who had had abortions abroad. This was followed by a round of applause in the House.[46] However, all of this emotion was not enough to pass the Bill, as it was rejected by 109 votes to 20 in the Dáil vote. *Plus ça change.*

One event that occurred in October/November 2012 has led to pressure on the government to legislate for the X case. An Indian woman, Savita Halappanavar, died at University Hospital Galway at the end of October 2012. She reported to hospital in distress, apparently miscarrying her baby at seventeen weeks. She and her husband, Praveen, asked for a termination several times over a three-day period but were refused on the grounds that there was a detectable foetal heartbeat. They were told by doctors 'this is a Catholic country'. Savita died of septicaemia a week after going to hospital.[47] This tragic death led to popular protests in Ireland and negative media coverage globally, so the government was forced to act. One of the memorable placards at one protest read: 'Savita had a heartbeat too.' The year 2013 is likely to see intense wrangling on this issue before it is finally settled. However, the public hearings of the Oireachtas Joint Committee on Health and Children seemed to have been conducted in a fair, objective and democratic fashion that gave equal voice to all parties, including lawyers, doctors and representatives of all the main churches in the state. Veteran reporter Geraldine Kennedy says, 'we are in a different country and the debate has all changed now.'[48]

The Catholic Church still will not give an inch on this matter, however, and this body continues to have a disproportionate input into public debates of this nature. Women's bodies, with all of the potential health problems associated with pregnancy and childbirth, continue to mark the frontline of ideological struggles in Ireland, as elsewhere. The Catholic Church, led by a group of supposedly-celibate men, ironically has a whole lot to say on sex and relationships. It would be like me claiming unshakeable expertise and making confident public pronouncements on the latest debates on astrophysics or orthopaedic surgery, or even canon law! I am somewhat in awe, however, of the Church's unbounded, self-righteous arrogance, sheer brass-necked audacity and medieval misogynistic attitudes that attempt to maintain women's status as second-class citizens well into the twenty-first century. The arrogant and top-down approach of the upper echelons of the Catholic Church alienates and silences its most enlightened and liberated members – clergy and laity alike.

The law in Northern Ireland allows abortion when a woman's life is endangered. About forty abortions are carried out for this reason every year in that jurisdiction. This would be equivalent to about one hundred and twenty every year in the Republic of Ireland.[49] This is a very small number in proportion to the number of Irish women who travel outside the country for an abortion. Those who continue to lobby against even this possibility are 'fighting a phoney war of dead symbolism.'[50] They are trying to recreate a repressive Ireland that belongs firmly in the past. Even on the remote chance that abortion was introduced in these circumstances, it would not change the big picture. Most women's lives are not at risk in a narrow sense because of an unwanted pregnancy, but they may be at risk in a broader sense. They might be at risk of not living the life they choose, free from the kind of emotional and financial pressure that children can bring to those who are not ready for them – for whatever reason.

First-hand accounts of Irish women's experiences of abortion in England are few and far between.[51] The sustained silence around this issue prompted Kathy Sheridan of *The Irish Times* in early 2012 to seek the experiences of those who had been through it. Her goal was to 'open a forum for those hitherto silent voices who had had direct experience of an abortion.'[52] The experiences documented range from women who discovered that their babies were severely disabled while still *in utero*, to those who had suffered marital rape, to those who were just too young and unprepared for a baby. The responses were varied. One woman in her mid thirties said, 'I loathe the secrecy and stigma associated with this topic in Ireland.' Another explained her actions simply: 'wrong man, wrong time.' Another qualified, 'abortion is not a contraceptive method, it is a very big deal. It's not a nice thing to do, and of course it stays with you always.' One young woman took pills she had bought on the Internet to induce an abortion alone in her flat in Dublin. She had to sacrifice food to pay for those pills. The women encountered a range of attitudes from their confidantes, along the spectrum from fully supportive to deeply judgemental. One of the women who had had an abortion had to defend herself from a friend's comments by saying, 'until the day you walk in my shoes, don't you dare judge me.' Another felt angry at a state that 'forces women to travel abroad as if we are morally deficient people in a pure-white state.'

Caitlin Moran, in her best-selling book *How to be a Woman*, bravely recounts her own experience of an abortion. She recalls how one of the other women had come from Ireland to that London clinic on that same day. When it was over, and they were lying in the recovery room, she describes how:

> The girl from Ireland leaves after five minutes – she has to catch her bus, to catch her coach, to catch her ferry back home. She walks sore. It's blatantly obvious that she shouldn't have to come to another country to get her life back on track. I wonder if the judges in Ireland have ever seen a woman as pale as this, counting out fifties onto the reception desk in a country where she doesn't know a soul, and then bleeding all the way from Essex to Holyhead. I wonder if her father approves of the law because he doesn't think it applies to her – and whether he would hate that law if he knew it did, and has brought her here.[53]

As long as women still have to make this tortured journey to acquire a termination, instead of walking down the road to a completely secular, safe, clean clinic in our *own* country, we cannot say that the grip of the Church has loosened fully and Irish women are truly liberated. It seems that freely express-ing your apparently limitless sexuality is a risky business when you live in such a restrictive society. It is somewhat akin to getting married in a society that doesn't allow you to change your mind by permitting divorce, as in Ireland before 1997.

Even if you feel individualised, as German sociologist Ulrich Beck would have it, the laws of the state in which you live still ultimately hamper your activities. There is no clearer example of this than the case of adult Irish women being denied the right to choose to have an abortion if they see fit.

Homosexuality

There has, however, been positive legislative and attitudinal change in recent years to homosexuality in Ireland.[54] After a long fight for the decriminalisation of homosexuality by David Norris and Mary Robinson, among others, Norris won his case against the Irish state in the European Court of Human Rights in 1988, on the grounds of the protection of the right to privacy in personal affairs. As a result, the Irish state decriminalised homosexuality five years later, in 1993. Máire Geoghegan Quinn was the Minister for Justice at the time. She was apparently propelled into action by a meeting with the mother of a young gay man, who argued for the need for equality for her son.[55] Norris' legal actions were taken in the context of the broader-based political activism of the Irish Gay Rights Movement (IGRM), which was established in the mid-1970s, and later the Gay and Lesbian Equality Network (GLEN). The first civil partnership ceremony between a gay couple occurred in April 2011, and it was a cause for celebration among most of the Irish population. Aside from some red top scandalmongers and barstool bigots, most acknowledge that the time has come for gay people to enjoy the same marital rights as straight people. Gays argue, however, that the legislation does not go far enough, and their struggle is not yet over. For example, it is still illegal in Ireland for a gay couple to adopt a child. However, it is at least a step in the right direction. It is also illegal to discriminate against people on the grounds of sexual orientation.

However, attitudinal change often lags far behind legal change. For example, teenagers still use the word 'gay' as a term of abuse, whether or not they really know the true meaning of what they are saying. Sexual orientation is often the basis for bullying in schools as well. It is also not uncommon for teachers to express homophobic attitudes against pupils. The stigmatisation of young people for their sexuality is especially serious, as they are still in their delicate formative years, and they will not yet have developed the emotional strength needed to handle such ignorance and cruelty. A gay switchboard in Dublin in the late 1990s received six thousand calls in one year, with almost half those coming from people under the age of 25.[56] This illustrates the isolation felt by young gay people, even in the Dublin area. These problems are magnified in rural areas because of the lack of service provision. Sadly, but unsurprisingly, it has been found that 'teenage gays are disproportionately represented in Irish suicide figures.'[57] This issue applies to teachers too. One ex-teacher and gay activist recently said that he knows of gay teachers who have been passed over for promotion and who have been verbally abused and discriminated against in Irish schools, which still have a reasonably strong Catholic ethos.[58] Such religious employers are still allowed to take actions in order to ensure the maintenance of their particular ethos, regardless of state law.

Irish society is, as ever, a mass of contradictions. The problems of discrimination faced by gay and lesbian people co-exist with a liberal media, where being gay is completely accepted. There are many gay actors, TV presenters, artists, novelists and poets who contribute to public life in Ireland. I think it is safe to say that sexuality is no longer a problem, in this realm at least. Cork hurler, Donal Óg Cusack, has been brave enough to extend gay activism into the macho world of sport and the malodorous dressing rooms of the GAA. He revealed his gay identity in his autobiography in 2009. Since then, he has lent his name to a high-profile campaign against homophobic bullying.[59] Some prominent media figures have also taken advantage of the new civil partnership legislation. One of these is Michael Murphy, the dulcet-toned veteran of RTÉ, who has been the voice of the RTÉ news since I was knee-high to a grasshopper. He married his partner of 26 years in June 2011. On the day, he said that he felt 'tremendously affirmed', because it was 'a day of history, personal history'. He went on, 'we decided to do this to make it easier for others to take the plunge.'[60] It appears that across the Atlantic in New York, the gay community are even starting to whisper about 'gay wedding burnout', forcing friends into 'an awful lot of toasting and tuxedo wearing and travelling.'[61] Maybe you have to be careful what you wish for!

Nevertheless, it seems that all of this liberalisation of attitudes is starting to have an impact here in Ireland. An edition of *Gay Community News* was dedicated particularly to teenagers in July 2007. An 18-year-old was asked when he came out of the closet. His priceless response was, 'Darling, I was never in!'[62]

Conclusion

This chapter has sought to discuss the ways in which people can construct their personal and sexual identities and, hence, their personal comfort zones. It sought to clarify some sociological thoughts on identification. It went on to focus on the issue of sexuality in Irish society and, in particular, to trace the social impact of the Catholic Church over the years on sexual attitudes and behaviour. While most people in Irish society currently experience more personal freedom to express their individuality than they would have in the past, we still need to be cognisant of those social constraints that have not gone away – yet. However, Irish people cannot be analysed in isolation from the rest of the world, as we can be found in every corner of the Earth. This leads us to discuss in the next chapter how Irish society has been affected by emigration and immigration demographically, economically and culturally.

5

Migration and Hybridity

Another major factor that affects the components of our comfort zone is, of course, the phenomenon of migration. It may be either a forced or a voluntary decision to leave the nest of home, family and community. The world is full of people who have been forced from their homelands by economic necessity and political strife or persecution. For these exiles, to return home and to be able to live there in peace and prosperity is their single biggest wish. For others, voluntarily moving to other places is a source of pleasure, adventure and an opportunity to expand their personal freedom. The ways that different individuals relate to the economic realm of investment, work, money and employment creates a 'power geometry', where some groups, like poor migrant workers, have to just go where they can in order to keep body and soul together, while others, the corporate jet-setters, are actually in charge of the ways that the world is being globalised.[1] In either case, people need to adapt to their new location and change somewhat in order to fit in, in terms of language, accent, dress or demeanour.

Emigration and the Irish

The experience of emigration has become part and parcel of being Irish. We have always been a nation on the move, with emigration serving as a socio-economic safety valve. The most recent statistics available show that 40,200 Irish people emigrated between April 2010 and April 2011, with 57 per cent of these being male and 43 per cent being female. This compared to 13,100 in 2007.[2] This official estimate is very high, yet most analysts would argue that this is probably a gross understatement of the real figures, as many young emigrants are not included in any available official statistics on the subject, flying under the radar, so to speak. It has even been suggested that it could be fruitful to view Ireland as a place of 'pure mobility, dominated by movement and fluidity.'[3]

For those who are emigrating, however, the economic pressures to leave are in conflict with emotional and social pressures to stay. Huge loss is felt by out-migrants, as they have to sacrifice their sources of support and, perhaps, their sense of membership of a local community. Finance Minister Michael Noonan recently suggested that emigration was 'a free choice of lifestyle' for young people. Opposition politicians and the media lambasted him for his insensitivity to the feelings of the thousands who are forced to leave by the recession.[4] Ironically, there is anecdotal evidence that some young Irish men and women are even going to Eastern European countries like Poland for work, whence many of our immigrants themselves came in the last fifteen years. Now it is their turn to have a building boom – the steel-capped work boot is on the other foot.

The idealised 'cosy homesteads' view of family and community life expressed by De Valera in his famous 1943 St. Patrick's Day speech, that we saw in Chapter 1, is a far cry from the realities of most Irish people throughout the decades since. In political geographer Jim MacLaughlin's emigration survey in the 1990s, 13 per cent of the families analysed had three or more members living abroad. He asserts, the 'sanctity of the family as enshrined in the 1937 Constitution is in stark contrast with a reality which sees emigration, often of quite young teenagers, embedded in the economic landscape and political system of this country.'5 Being set up as pawns to be moved around a global economic chessboard is nothing new to us. This aspect of globalisation is also hard for the parents and loved ones left behind, who have to endure a terrible sense of loss. So 'even the man [sic] who never leaves home may feel that home is leaving him, as parents, children, lovers scatter around the map, taking pieces of him wherever they go.'6 One oft-quoted effect of emigration is that some small communities in Ireland find it difficult to compose a GAA team because of the absence of young players. This has even been experienced at county team level. The GAA has recently argued that employers should consider some positive discrimination in favour of their players in order to preserve its culture.

Feelings of Exile

When migrants return to their Irish homes after a long absence, they often experience feelings of confusion, disappointment or displacement. The place they encounter has changed perhaps quite drastically from the one they left years before. It is at once familiar and strange. In Colm Tóibín's novel *The South*, the following lines describe the feelings of his main character on her return to Ireland:

> It did not feel like a foreign country, but a world she had known at some time in the past, but could not now reconstruct fully or recollect completely: a world peopled by relatives, ancestors, friends, peopled by faces she was just one step from being able to name or associate with some event.7

Salman Rushdie is one of the most notable authors on the subject of migration and exile. He left India for the UK as a teenager and only remembers his Indian childhood in fragments. He argues that these fragments become all the more special because they are incomplete, comparing them to bits of ancient pottery found by archaeologists. These vessels were very ordinary at the time of their using, but acquire great significance many years later. He says that 'the shards of memory acquired greater status, greater resonance, because they were *remains*; fragmentation made trivial things seem like symbols, and the mundane acquired numinous qualities.' He goes on to say that it is our very humanity that shapes our memories, as 'we are not gods but wounded creatures, cracked lenses, capable only of fractured perceptions.' We build meaning from 'scraps, dogmas, childhood injuries, newspaper articles, chance remarks, old films, small victories, people hated, people loved' and 'perhaps it is because our sense of what is the case is constructed from such inadequate materials that we defend it so fiercely, even to the death.'[8] How ironic then that Rushdie himself was subject to a death threat after the publication of *The Satanic Verses* in 1989, and 'the great spokesman of the people who live everywhere becomes literally a man with no address, in a society of one.'[9]

The Irish Returning 'Home'

I have three siblings who have lived in the US for many years. They have now spent more of their lives there than in Ireland. Whenever they return to Ireland, it is a bittersweet experience for them. They cannot help comparing the reality they see around them now with the country they left back in the 1970s and 1980s. They feel that the Ireland they left was poorer and more conservative, on the one hand, but simpler, friendlier and safer on the other. They are now surprised at the high standard of the roads, the number of vast housing estates, the number of foreign languages audible on the streets and, above all, the perceived higher crime rate. They associate gangland murders and drug wars with the Bronx instead of Blanchardstown.

Peter Creedon, an emigrant interviewed by *The Irish Times* on these issues, raised some interesting points. He finds that when he comes back to Ireland his friends who have stayed here tend to keep him at an emotional distance: 'you become part of the community that has travelled away.' He said that he considers New York home now because he did a lot of his growing up there. He muses, 'I think I came of age there.'[10] Peter, as well as every other person who has followed the same path, suffers from what writer Pico Iyer terms 'the immigrant's bifurcation – torn between the home he carried in his blood and the one he had on paper.'[11] Returned emigrants may be involuntary cosmopolitans, despite themselves. Even if they want to be the same as everyone else, they are not. They do not take home for granted anymore, because they have seen and lived among difference in other places.

Remembered places have often served as symbolic anchors of community for dispersed peoples. Although 'the "homes" which ground and house identities can be denied people physically by enforced exile or lost through chosen migration, they still continue to resonate throughout the imaginations of displaced communities.'[12] This can lead to an absentee nationalism being expressed by emigrants, supporting causes back 'home' that those who actually live at home may abhor, especially those movements that have used violent political strategies. However, ultimately, emigrants can never properly return to the place where they grew up, as both they and the place itself have changed. It is probably not the place itself they miss most, however, but their own younger, more innocent selves. Maybe when they leave they ultimately buy an emotional one-way ticket, as they can never recreate the way things were, and other people move on with their lives, without them in it. They have also had experiences in their own lives that those at home could not even imagine. Rushdie says that 'the migrant suspects reality: having experienced several ways of being, he understands their illusory nature.' So, 'to see things plainly, you have to cross a frontier.'[13] Thus emigrants ultimately inhabit a shadow-land between insider and outsider. Being 'worldly' has its downsides as well – part of the messy ambiguity of modernity.

I lived in London during the World Cup of 1990, when Ireland got to the quarter-final stage for the first time. I visited home during that summer. I was grossly ignorant of how big Italia '90 was at home and, *quelle horreur*, did not know the words to our World Cup song, and, even worse, did know a few lines of the English one. I was taken under the wing of a complete stranger in a pub in Cork one night, and he would not let me go until I could sing, 'We're all part of Jackie's army' from beginning to end! My national identity was at stake, at a time when we were actually proud to be Irish for a change, albeit under the management of a gruff Geordie. In retrospect, the feel-good factor of Italia '90 was never again recreated. Perhaps we came closest to it when the English Queen and the US President visited Ireland in May 2011, but it was nowhere near the same.

Some emigrants did return to Ireland to be part of the Celtic Tiger boom. It has been estimated that returned emigrants constituted 20 per cent of the workforce aged in their thirties and forties during the noughties.[14] These are a major part of the group that economist David McWilliams terms the Hibernian Cosmopolitans, or HiCos. He claims that this group, which he numbers to be about two hundred thousand, are highly educated, career-driven and, with their plentiful contacts and networks, have even been important movers and shakers in securing foreign investment here. He also claims that this group are very aware of their Irish identity because of having lived in England or the US, and 'many came back to educate their children in the Ireland they invented in their heads.'[15] They name their sons and daughters Oisín and Maeve and send them to Gaelscoileanna, both to escape the reach of the Catholic Church and to learn some Irish to solidify their sense of national identity. McWilliams wants to see the Irish diaspora brought back home. He started the ball rolling on the idea of tapping into the intelligence and creativity of those who left Ireland to seek their fortunes. This idea was used most recently in the speech given by Taoiseach Enda Kenny on the occasion of the visit of US President, Barack Obama in May 2011.

In families like mine, where emigration has been a veritably defining element of our identity, their emotional cartography might stretch from Cork to New York and from Charlestown to Cape Town. When we think of members of such families they are associated in our minds with places across the globe. While cheaper flights and instantaneous telecommunications sweeten the bitter pill of separation and make travelling much easier, it still cannot be underestimated how challenging it can be for the emigrant to find their niche in a new place. After all, as we saw in Chapter 3, the idea that places are all becoming the same all over the world is grossly over-stated. In some cases, there can be divisions and resentments between those who leave Ireland and those who stay behind, between those who have an idealised view of Ireland from afar and see it as a land frozen in time and those who live in it every day. The situation emerges where siblings have to rely on snippets of information relayed in occasional emails, photos and phone calls in order to keep in contact. Those who leave might feel abandoned and that those at home have accrued all of the advantages of kith and kin, whereas those who stay might feel trapped and denied the chance to try their luck in the outside world. It seems we always want what the other person has got. Because of the nature of extended physical and emotional distance, communication can be minimal, and family members might get together only for weddings and funerals, if at all. While this might appear to be an overly dark portrayal of Irish family life, I am confident that elements thereof will resonate with most readers.

The night before one of my brothers joined the emigration trail to New York in the 1980s, we had a party that turned into something like what they used to call an 'American wake'. Everybody drank a bit, cried a bit and sang a few songs. One of the highlights of the night was when my mother sang an old song that we all had heard her sing ever since we were tiny. It was 'Far Away in Australia', popularised by the Wolfe Tones. This is a song in which the main character has to leave his girl behind as he goes to seek his fortune in Australia. Needless to say, there wasn't a dry eye in the house. Such songs speak to our souls, even if we feel a bit silly admitting it. There is the crop of older songs like this, but there was also a newer crop of them in the 1980s, like Christy Moore's 'City of Chicago' and 'Missing You', and the Wolfe Tones' song 'Streets of New York'. The Saw Doctors' 'N17', a hit in 1990, was interesting because it is about the main road that goes through County Galway instead of an actual place – Ireland's little version of Route 66, perhaps? These songs were massively popular because they tapped into the trauma of leaving and the sadness felt by so many Irish families when their young ones left home. We have yet to see if this core feeling resonates with the current generation of emigrants, as I have yet to hear any new songs that serve as a critique of this new wave of emigration or the structural reasons behind it. The old ones are just rehashed, perhaps just like the cycle of emigration itself.

The 'New Wave' of Irish Emigration

There is a weary familiarity about the new wave of Irish emigration: here we go again! Ireland has once again become the kind of place that people want to get away from, rather than the kind of place they want to go to. The aforementioned troubled diasporic identity is one that will have to be negotiated by many more young Irish people as they join the serried ranks of the latest wave of emigrants. Parents suffer and, above all, mothers suffer. I recently heard of an Irish Mammy who asked her son what kind of party he would like before leaving for New Zealand. He replied that he would love if she cooked a Christmas dinner with all the trimmings. This she did, as well as setting the scene with a Christmas tree and decorations. It was 12 August! Mothers like this may regret having borne children in a country that is underpopulated by European standards and, yet somehow, cannot provide a livelihood for its daughters and sons. This new wave will no doubt breed its own stable of storytellers in years to come. However, I find major differences between the cultural construction of my generation's emigration in the 1980s and that of the current bunch since the recession began. In the 1980s, it was serious. We had a fair idea that we were away, if not forever, at least for a very long time. We attempted to build careers and new lives in our new destinations. There was work to be had, and the Irish could be found in every single walk of life. Flights were relatively expensive, the Internet was unheard of, we wrote letters to keep in touch and a weekly telephone call back home was as close a contact as one could muster.

Nowadays, there is more or less a world recession, so work is limited, and only certain specialised workers are welcome in Australia, the US or Canada. While things are worse economically than the 1980s, ironically there is a paradoxical sense of denial among young people which obscures the very real pain of separation. They do not use the word 'emigration' to describe their actions, and often construct their time abroad as an extended holiday rather than a formative part of their futures. A recent online survey in *The Irish Times* revealed that when they go, they miss those elements of everyday life that we all take for granted while at home. These might be good sausages, the incomparable and peerless Tayto crisp, enjoying a few creamy pints and a chat in the local pub, but most of all the humour and 'making Father Ted jokes with strangers and them getting them.'[16]

However, these new emigrants have access to instantaneous communication, so they can text or Skype Mam and Dad back home to send out more cash when they run out, to buy more sunblock, beer, hash and Pot Noodles. Parents are now also expected to support their children to a much later age, serving as a buttress in their unstable lives. These people who rely on their parents for financial support well into adulthood are known as KIPPERS: Kids in Parents' Pockets Eroding Retirement Savings! When I was growing up, to rely on cash from home after leaving college was virtually unheard of, except perhaps for the children of the wealthy, but I didn't know any of those. Only time will tell what the result of all this will be.

Cultural Resonance

Our music, our literature and our poetry are suffused with stories about emigration and movement. Much of our national cultural catalogue is as much of other places as it is of Ireland.

The dominance of the Catholic Church stymied so much creativity here throughout the years. James Joyce, for example, would never have been published in the early twentieth century if he had not gone to live in other more cosmopolitan European cities like Paris and Zurich, and the aforementioned series *Father Ted*, produced by British broadcaster Channel 4, would never have seen the light of day if it were left up to our own national broadcaster to produce it. A musician, a writer or an actor can remain in obscurity forever if somebody does not give them their first break. Those who have had the faith and courage to back some of our best writers and performers have often come from elsewhere, evidenced of course by the huge success of so many Irish actors in Hollywood. Colin Farrell might still be an underpaid exotic dancer if he had never left Dublin. Colum McCann's novel *Let the Great World Spin* has been lauded as the quintessential work about the identity of New York City post 9/11. As well as this, the market for Irish cultural products is huge internationally, most especially in the United States. So 'the spectacle of Riverdance, the music of the Chieftains and the "new" Irish films cannot be understood as national cultural forms. They may be partly constituted locally but it is with reference to a global cultural market: they are local cultural keys turning global locks.'[17] Thus we see that it is not just the subject matter of these cultural products that is based on the major tropes of movement, adaptation, exile and loneliness, but the very conditions of their making, and indeed selling.

Immigration into Ireland

The immigration of different nationalities into Ireland in recent years has made the country much more ethnically diverse than previously. An immigrant who is asked the aforementioned ubiquitous question, 'where are you from?' may feel uncomfortable with it. They may feel that it is a mechanism to reinforce their difference from the apparently uncomplicated native Irish norm. They may have come from Poland, Lithuania or Latvia fifteen years ago, now have Irish-born children in school and be an expert on ancient Irish folklore, and still be asked that question. It is part of the complicated reality of an emerging cosmopolitan society that a person can have several forms of affinity to people and places throughout their life. As a nation, we have been on a steep learning curve recently regarding sensitivity to such issues. You have no choice over where you are born, or where your parents move during your childhood. The choices you make as an adult mean that you may move somewhere else to work, or escape war and persecution, or to follow a loved one or family member to start a new life.

Official estimates of immigrant numbers are usually much lower than estimates by those who work with immigrants. This is due to a proportion of them who are in the country illegally and, therefore, who may not fill in the census. They may also come from places that have given them very good reasons not to trust any state authorities. However, these statistics are the only relatively reliable statistical source we can access. At the time of the 2011 Census of Population, 544,357 non-Irish nationals were said to be living in Ireland. The top ten nationalities and numbers of immigrants included 122,585 Poles; 112,259 UK citizens; 36,683 Lithuanians; 20,593 Latvians; 17,642 Nigerians; 17,304 Romanians; 16,986 Indians; 14,699 Irish Americans; 12,791 Filipinos; and 11,305 Germans. Other very significant groups were US citizens, Chinese, Slovaks, French, Spanish, Italians, South Africans, Czechs, Hungarians, Pakistanis and Brazilians.[18] It is impossible to generalise about these immigrants, as they are an extremely heterogeneous group in social terms. They work in all economic sectors, from manual to professional. They made a huge contribution to every sector during the boom years of the Celtic Tiger. They had to learn a lot quickly, including the Irish sense of humour. I once overheard a conversation where an immigrant was complaining that an Irish co-worker had called him a 'Lithuanian bollocks'. His Irish friend replied, 'Ah, sure, that's a compliment – that means he likes you!'

On a much more serious note, these immigrants did not always receive the welcome they deserved: there has been far too much exploitation of vulnerable immigrant workers. In 2004, the Migrant Rights Centre of Ireland published a report documenting widespread exploitation and maltreatment of foreign domestic workers in Irish middle-class homes. One of their female interviewees said, 'the problem with parents who don't respect foreign workers is that they pass these attitudes on to their children – treating us without any respect becomes normal.'[19] Neither were male immigrants off the hook. The case of the scandalous exploitation of the GAMA road construction workers, which came to light in 2005, was a case in point. This group of Turkish men were often paid as little as €2.20 per hour and accorded little or no basic worker's rights.[20] As well as this, many immigrants are often placed in segregated temporary accommodation, which serves to cut them off from the rest of the population. This serves to perpetuate social inequality, especially in the context of the continued 'suburbanisation of Ireland [which] has also meant that many individuals have withdrawn into exclusive enclaves, devaluing public spaces and reproducing class and racial segregation.'[21] There have also been too many racially-motivated attacks evident on our streets in recent years. While there have been many beatings and stabbings, these have sometimes culminated in death. For example, two young Polish men,

Pawel Kalite and Marius Szwajkos, were viciously stabbed to death with screwdrivers on a Dublin street in February 2008.[22] Another young Polish man, Lukasz Rzeszutko, was savagely beaten to death in Dublin in October 2010.[23] The perpetrators of these extremely brutal murders are now serving life sentences.

Many of Ireland's immigrants have been returning to their home countries since the onset of the recession. For example, in 2009, 30,100 people from the Eastern European accession states left Ireland, over two thirds of whom were male.[24] Among the immigrant groups to have come to Ireland, this group was the one that was most heavily affected by the downturn in the construction sector. They will only stay in Ireland if they have work and/or if they start a family here. Of the 118,000 foreign nationals aged 15 or over who were assigned Personal Public Service Numbers (PPSNs) in 2004, only 33 per cent of them worked at all in 2009, so Ireland is no longer as attractive a destination for immigrants seeking work.[25]

'Blow-Ins' in Rural Ireland

Some migrant groups have been in Ireland for longer than those who just arrived during the Celtic Tiger years. Certain rural Irish communities, particularly the prettier areas near the coast like parts of West Cork, Kerry and Galway, have become very attractive to counter-urban migrants, or 'blow-ins', as locals often call them. This group usually come from the UK and mainland Europe, but it can also include migrants from Irish cities. Using the easy distinction between 'local' and 'blow-in' is but a means of simplifying the social picture of local communities. One author, anthropologist Chris Eipper, has suggested that locals have pejoratively termed incomers as blow-ins 'as a device for class levelling'.[26] People are of course much more complex than such simple labels or stereotypes. Like all stereotypes the pure forms thereof certainly exist, but there is a huge grey area between the two ends of this social spectrum and, indeed, this is just one spectrum among many others that have a bearing upon people's lives. However, I stick with the use of the term blow-in here as it is still the most common term used for this type of urban-to-rural incomers, though I disapprove of its pejorative connotations.

These refugees from urban settings have been coming to rural Ireland for decades now, leaving behind their busy lives in Europe's cities and seeking a less stressful environment in which to either rear children or to live out their latter years. One blow-in I know has his West Cork home phone number listed on his mobile phone as 'Paradise'. Newcomers to these areas start off with a slate so clean they could eat their dinner off it. They can ignore all of the social alliances, divisions and cliques, as well as family ties, duties, obligations and arguments, of which every community is composed. They are free to be whatever they want and talk to whomever they want. They can totally reinvent themselves, put aside their old identity and create a new one if they so desire. Nobody really cares one way or the other what they do, as long as they do not frighten the horses! They can choose whether they want to become enmeshed in social networks or not, like becoming involved in local sporting organisations, or religious or cultural activities. They have a choice, perhaps unlike a local person who sings in the church choir or plays football because he or she is made to feel that everybody in the community expects it of them.

While it is difficult to generalise, most of these migrants who seek a new life in rural Ireland tend to come from middle-class backgrounds, and have something like an ecological world-view. An anthropological study of a remote rural community in the north of Scotland also found that the in-migrants there were mostly of a middle-class or upper-middle-class background. This group does '... not come to the countryside to practice their previous professions but to make a radical change in their own style of life.'[27] One study of West Cork newcomers found a similar situation amongst over half of the sample, as well as a generally counter-cultural approach to life.[28] In my own research in West Cork, I found a similar class profile among the blow-ins whom I met.[29]

Class is a blunt tool with which to analyse this group, however, as these people have relinquished most of the trappings of their former wealth and changed their lives completely. This counter-urban phase of their lives has lowered their position on the social class 'totem-pole'. They now wear Wellington boots to work instead of hand-stitched Italian leather shoes. However, their educated backgrounds have given them great confidence in maximising the benefits of moving to the Irish countryside. They are generally a very hard-working group, having made brave life-altering decisions to commit to independent counter-cultural lifestyles. They sometimes bring new entrepreneurial ideas with them. For example, they have been to the forefront of the food revolution that has turned the region of West Cork into a Silicon Valley of new food enterprises. While little thorough research has been conducted on these people, many of them have a public profile, based on their activities around environmental issues, organic food production and farmers' markets.

Local people have mixed feelings about the impact of blow-ins on the social geography of the countryside, with their attitudes ranging along a spectrum from total acceptance to total rejection. The former is much more common than the latter, as there is usually a genuine openness to and interest in other cultures; a newcomer would have to somehow offend a local for the latter to occur. There is a very high level of tolerance for different people in the West Cork I know, as long as they are judged to be generally decent folk who wish to do no harm. 'Live and let live' is by far the most common attitude, with very few exceptions.

However, where disputes between locals and newcomers do occur, the most serious of these are usually about land or property. This particular group of incomers usually buy up old properties in which locals show little or no interest; perhaps outsiders, who have an objective point of view, can see the development potential of those properties that locals associate with poverty and the past. One local man in West Cork said to me, 'people used to look down on the people who lived in cottages, but the *best* of people are moving into them.' There is, in actuality, little competition between locals and blow-ins for particular properties. However, raising the cultural bar can in time lend a certain prestige, or exclusivity, to particular areas, which no doubt could raise the asking prices locally. This is of course exacerbated when the individual blow-ins are celebrities. However, the machinations of the property market are ultimately more important than this in determining prices. One can now buy properties at a fraction of their Celtic Tiger prices. Outsiders buying into the countryside results in the rural equivalent of urban gentrification, where professional, middle-class people move into former working-class areas and restore them according to their own middle-class aesthetic. One researcher, anthropologist J.H. Gilligan, found that this was a big issue in Padstow in Cornwall:

Local service shops have been bought up and replaced by 'tripper-trapper' shops, and such dispossession is compounded in residential terms with the displacement of Padstonians from 'downtown' to the outlying council housing estates, as outsiders have gentrified the older unmodernised slate and stone cottages.[30]

This social change can be interpreted, on the one hand, as either restoring new life to an abandoned area or, on the other hand, as an invasion of outsiders who, with more money than sense, artificially inflate the price of property, thereby pricing local people out of the market. There can be a grudging appreciation among locals for the work done to old houses by newcomers, improving the overall look of the area. Those who have sold old properties to such blow-ins are undoubtedly delighted with their luck, as locals usually steer clear of older properties, preferring to build large new houses for themselves. For them, newness is a guarantee of no history, no baggage, no associations: a *tabula rasa*, a clean slate. Their size, and frequently their lavishness, is a means of acquiring status in the community for those who may be the first generation of their family to escape real poverty. If they cannot, or do not want to, move away geographically from their place of origin, they can at least move away in terms of social status, enjoying their underfloor heating, stainless steel kitchens and 50-inch plasma TVs.

Conversely, the blow-ins live in a parallel universe, as they generally care little about status, but just want to create their own little bit of Heaven behind their own gates and doors. In some cases, they create very exclusive properties that are tucked away in the West Cork hills. Sea-front properties are in most demand and fetch the highest prices. One quarter-acre site sold outside Kinsale, County Cork in 2005, during the Celtic Tiger years, for €650,000. I am rarely surprised anymore to hear of which wealthy celebrities have bought one of these: Jeremy Irons, Neil Jordan, Graham Norton, Christy Moore, Maureen O'Hara and David Putnam are all well established in West Cork by now. Some of the blow-ins who own these properties are more or less reclusive, while some others are consciously enthusiastic about getting involved in local community affairs, always on call to cut the ribbon to launch the local festival or regatta.

Social researchers have found in several places that the women among incomer groups are more active than the men in establishing and maintaining social networks. This can be either through their children attending local schools or various women's activities.[31] For male blow-ins social acceptance is enhanced when they show that they can work well, perhaps providing a service in the local area that might not exist otherwise. For example, finding a handyman during the Celtic Tiger years was a near impossibility, so if an English or German newcomer, Jeffrey or Joachim, was available for small jobs, that would have been very welcome. Nowadays, it is possible that skilled tradesmen would have emigrated for work, so Jeffrey or Joachim might have found his local role once again. This is a good way to break down barriers and get to know people, thereby becoming more integrated in the area. Being adaptable to what the local job market demands is essential for any newcomer. They may also speed up the integration process if they already know people in the area, or are there because of chain migration. This occurs when one person encourages friends or family to move to a particular spot, producing a cluster pattern of certain nationalities or types of people. Also, it has been found that when the local population has been reduced due to out-migration, incomers are more likely to be accepted.[32] They liven up the area in various ways, bringing money, children and ideas, so 'through the immigrants' fresh perceptions of the environment, new ways of making a living, new values and creativity are constantly being introduced.'[33]

The longer these incomers stay around, and are not deterred by feeling isolated or, indeed, the seemingly relentless wet weather, the more they are appreciated. But how long it would take to be actually called a local, escaping the tag of 'blow-in', is up for debate. As one author reminds us, 'the politics of claiming to be an insider are also often the politics of claiming power.'[34] I know one local West Cork octogenarian who originated in Connemara, but who, having married a local girl in the 1950s, went on to rear a family of nine children locally, and he still jokes about being a blow-in. However, he prefers to refer to himself as 'imported talent'. There is an unspoken rule that blow-ins are expected to strive to become more like the locals, and their efforts in this regard are rewarded with social acceptance. This was also found by anthropologist Adrian Peace in 'Clontarf'. He found that:

Some of these [blow-ins], even after a decade or more are considered, and consider themselves to be, marginal to the mainstream of community life: others within a shorter period have become actively involved in that mainstream.[35]

This has been found in virtually every piece of research on counter-urban incomers in rural areas. In a village in the north of England, locals said, 'they've got to summer you and winter you and summer you and winter you afore you mak' friends in Gosforth.' It was thought that this process could take twenty to forty years there.[36] In Dutch writer Geert Mak's ethnographic study of a village in the Friesland region of Holland, he found the question of belonging to be a complex one: not just black and white, but with many – if not quite fifty – shades of grey:

There were 'natives' and there were 'import', and then there was the difference between Frisian import and non-Frisian import, and besides that there was also a difference between active and non-active import. In short, all was not lost in advance for those townspeople who wanted to come and live here.[37]

The longer blow-ins live in an area, the more committed they are to it, and the more they may resent newer incomers. In a study of a village in the Yorkshire Dales, the 'old incomers', who lived in the area for between fifteen and twenty years or more, resented the 'new incomers' who built second homes, and who were not committed to contributing to the long-term future of the area.[38]

It is inevitable that the onus is on the newcomers themselves to learn the local way of doing things. Social interaction can be very subtle in rural Ireland, with much being said in a restrained manner, via virtually undetectable body language. It is possible that this is like learning a whole new lingo for some incomers. Being very direct is not a good idea. Blow-ins have to 'learn to communicate with more thought and care', like 'keeping their mouths shut in order to avoid offending anyone.'[39] They have to learn very quickly who's who and what's what. The intricate webs of family relationships in rural communities and the ways in which people are related to each other can be amazingly complex, for example. The newcomer therefore has to learn very quickly not to criticise anyone in public, because the person to whom they are speaking may be at least a far-out cousin of the person being criticised. Keeping the peace between neighbours is of paramount importance.

The norm of delayed reciprocity is another important one for blow-ins to learn. If Seamus does a small favour for the aforementioned Jeffrey or Joachim – maybe he might give him a lift to town or give him a loan of his trailer – Seamus will be grossly insulted if the incomer attempts to pay him in cash. Jeffrey or Joachim must instead buy Seamus a couple of pints the next time they meet in the pub. That, indeed, means that the newcomer has to first actually go to the local pub. Jeffrey or Joachim must learn the intricate subtleties of gift exchange, which will help him to bond with his new neighbours. The same applies with conflict resolution. Perhaps it is a historical hangover that it is only as a very last option that country people will resort to the law. They prefer it if things are worked out slowly, gently and indirectly.

Blow-ins therefore have to assimilate if they care about social acceptance locally. Some like to view regions like West Cork as romantic, multicultural 'melting-pots', where many languages are audible and various cultural influences visible. If West Cork were a true melting pot, locals would make an effort to communicate with their new neighbours on their terms and in their language, literally and metaphorically. There would be a two-way process of learning, leading to the emergence of a new type of cultural system. However, I would contend that this is actually uncommon, as blow-ins either keep to themselves or become so absorbed into the dominant culture that they mask their differences, eventually becoming more Irish than the Irish themselves. Those outsiders who go to the trouble of adapting like this are always far more popular with the locals than those who do not. If a newly-arrived family contributed a skilful young player to the local GAA team, for example, they would rise several notches on the status totem pole.

There may also be a sense of pride in being part of the blow-in minority in regions like West Cork. Newcomers to such regions usually have no family history in the area upon which to rely for identity, so they know they are outsiders as well as internationalists or citizens of the world.[40] They are members of globalised networks that stretch well beyond the local area. These are 'affectual tribes' which endeavour to form communities based on emotional connections, seeking warmth and companionship to shelter them from an often cold and rationalised world.[41] Blow-ins, therefore, walk the tightrope between the local and the global, leaning first one way and then the other.

Hybrid Identities

The ways in which various types of immigrants adapt to the expectations of their host communities and develop their own cultural confidence leads to the emergence of some fascinating forms of hybrid identities. We can never assume that space, place and culture are isomorphic, because of the permeable borders that surround each of these: there is a constant movement of people and ideas throughout the world. As sociologist John Tomlinson argues:

> Culture cannot be thought of as having these inevitable *conceptual* ties to location, for meanings are equally generated by people 'on the move' and in the flows and connections between 'cultures'.[42]

This is especially true of young people and the next generation, who change significantly as a result of assimilation. One school in Balbriggan, County Dublin has a majority of African pupils who are delighted to learn the curriculum ordained for them by Irish teachers. The principal says that 'we have great ambitions for these children – they have great potential and they are as bright as buttons ... some speak several languages and are learning Arabic at weekends. Irish is no problem to them.'[43] Who knows what contribution these children will make to Irish society in the future?

I recently witnessed the young, teenage daughter of German immigrants translating some Irish for her parents at a West Cork St. Patrick's Day parade. She, and many thousands like her, is well able to negotiate both worlds, that of her parents and of her school and wider society. I wonder whether she feels that her two cultures are conflicting or harmonious. A disadvantage of this hybridity could be that she feels different to everyone else, and therefore not fully at home in either cultural setting. A major advantage is that she speaks at least two languages fluently and has a close affinity with another country, and this will open up more options to her in later life. I would imagine that she is well aware of both the advantages and the disadvantages of her situation, but children and teenagers are remarkably resilient and adaptable. Interestingly, Kerry man Michael Fassbender, who is the most recent global movie star to hail from these shores, is a product of mixed Irish and German parentage. The delicious randomness of human life threw this young man from making toast in the Killarney restaurant in which he was reared to himself being the toast of Hollywood awards ceremonies!

Narrow national identities are challenged by such cultural difference, where minorities are not just melted into the host culture but are a source of innovation too, in one way or another. As Salman Rushdie says:

> … to migrate is certainly to lose language and home, to be defined by others, to become invisible or, even worse, a target; it is to experience deep changes and wrenches in the soul … but the migrant is not simply transformed by his act; he [sic] also transforms his new world. Migrants

may well become mutants, but it is out of such hybridisation that newness can emerge.[44]

Diaspora communities, whether of the Irish abroad, or, for example, of Polish, German or English people in Ireland, develop new cultural forms which are a mix of the old and new world, the old and new ways. This idea is threatening to some and exciting to others, but, regardless, we must live with the social effects of cultural difference, transition and displacement. Cultural theorists David Morley and Kevin Robins forcefully argue that:

> In a world that is increasingly characterised by exile, migration and Diaspora, with all the consequences of unsettling and hybridisation, there can be no place for such absolutism of the pure and authentic.[45]

Cultural purity is a myth, as mixing has always occurred. In trying to understand the complexities of cultural hybridity, it is instructive to learn from the experiences of other ethnic groups, like those of the Asian and Afro-Caribbean communities in Britain.

Probably the most sophisticated and influential attempt to make sense of cultural hybridity to date has been cultural theorist Paul Gilroy's *Black Atlantic*. In trying to understand the 'doubleness and cultural intermixture'[46] of the experiences of British blacks, he deems it necessary to rise out of the strictures of national boundaries and write their movements across the 'Black Atlantic' into the heart of his analysis. This serves to highlight the connections between British blacks and those in the Americas and the Caribbean, foregrounding their agency as political activists and cultural producers and not just as

passive victims of slavery. Gilroy suggests that cultural histo-
rians should 'take the Atlantic as one single complex unit of
analysis … and use it to produce an explicitly transnational
and intercultural perspective.'[47] He finds the image of the
slave ship useful in thinking about this. These ships, as well
as being symbols of racial terrorism, were ultimately a means
of connecting black people globally and a conduit for political
dissent and the creation of new hybrid cultures. He unearths
little-known black figures who excelled in politics and the
arts, and who used their experiences of exile and displacement as sources of inspiration 'in the difficult journey from
slave ships to citizenship.'[48] Gilroy argues convincingly that
such inputs are best analysed as transcultural products, born
out of movement and travel between fixed nation states.

Music

Music has always been a cultural medium that lends itself
very readily to expressing hybridity. It is impossible to build
walls around genres, styles and types of music. For example,
Bhangra music originated from the folk music of the Indian
Punjab region, but having been mixed with Western music
styles like house, garage, hip hop and reggae, it has been transformed into the voice of British Asian youth since the 1980s.
Its catchy tunes and irresistible rhythms have ensured that it is
growing from strength to strength.[49] It is a product of the Asian
diaspora and a confident expression of the ability of its culture
to hybridise and attract wide audiences, even if they do not
understand the lyrics. It is difficult to hate an ethnic minority
who produce great music (or art or food) because 'hybridity
unsettles the introverted concept of culture which underlies
romantic nationalism, racism, ethnicism, religious revivalism,
civilizational chauvinism, and cultural essentialism.'[50] This is

an example of a global counter-current, where a non-Western cultural form exerts a significant impact upon its host culture in the West.[51] While this might appear trivial in the bigger scheme of things, cultural products like music, food and language can help enormously in integrating minorities into the broader community and in breaking down racist ideologies.

In Ireland, the winds of change are also blowing the cobwebs off fusty old ideas about purity, tradition, and 'the way things have always been done' in music and culture. Christy Moore's song 'Continental Céilí' ably and humorously captures how people are coming to Ireland from all over the world to learn Irish music. Of course, this has reached epidemic proportions since *Riverdance* achieved global domination in the 1990s. This applies to the Irish language as well. In fact, Oideas Gael, the organisation dedicated to teaching Irish to adults, teaches about one thousand five hundred adults annually, with half of the students coming from other parts of the world like mainland Europe, Australia, the US and Japan.[52] The Irish language organisation Gaelchultúr estimates that about four thousand people are studying the Irish language in the US and Canada alone.[53] As well as this, even people who have never set foot in Ireland are learning how to sing, play and dance to Irish music, probably from DVDs of *Riverdance* and *Lord of the Dance*. For example, there are twenty Irish dancing schools in Russia, Ukraine and Belarus, as well as regular feiseanna, or dancing competitions.[54]

At the annual festival of Irish culture, Oireachtas na Samhna, in November 2011, one of the highlights was a performance of sean-nós dancing by a black Zimbabwean man, Cuthbert (Tura) Arutura. Tura has been living in Belfast since he was a teenager in 1993 and has been learning the Irish language for the past five years. His beautiful, fluid movements blend elements of his own traditional dance style from his homeland, tap and contemporary dance with the ancient anarchic style of sean nós. Even a short moonwalk was detectable! While no doubt challenging to purists, his brave performance was a breath of fresh air that was a powerful antidote to racial stereotyping.

Another interesting artist from this point of view is Róisín Elsafty, the child of a sean-nós singing mother from Connemara and an Egyptian doctor. She sings beautiful old Irish songs, but a very subtle Middle-Eastern influence underlies her singing style. In her hands, the two cultures are very much in tune and seem very much at home together.[55] She uses her music, for example her song 'An Phalistín', to raise funds for children in Gaza refugee camps. Another song, 'Alí: Dílleachtín Gan Bhrí' is a humanitarian statement against the war in Iraq. She and her parents are heavily involved in the Galway branch of the Palestine Support Group. It would be difficult to find a finer example of a young person who is more connected with both sides of her family heritage. She is a cultural conduit who conveys an ancient style of music to the wider world and concurrently transfuses important political issues from the outside world into the beating heart of Irish music.

The enormous and timeless contribution of Irish musical giants like U2 and Van Morrison to global rock and popular music is beyond the bounds of this discussion.[56] Artists like The Clancy Brothers and Tommy Makem, The Dubliners, and The Chieftains, however, have popularised Irish traditional songs and tunes globally. The latter are well known for their collaborations with popular musicians from across the globe. For example, in The Chieftains' Grammy award-winning album, *The Long Black Veil*, we hear Sting sing a local Irish song from Coolea, County Cork, 'Mo Ghile Mear'. He sings it phonetically and makes a very good stab at it! We also hear 'The Rocky Road to Dublin' performed by the Rolling Stones. In their 2012 album, *Voice of Ages*, old songs are given a new lease of life, with Imelda May singing 'Carolina Rua' and Lisa Hannigan singing 'My Lagan Love'. Other British and American artists add to the anarchic mix.

The world-famous *Riverdance* show was hybridised too, as the form of Irish dance it stems from was very 'tarted up' and modernised, and it also incorporated other types of dance, like tap from New York and flamenco from Spain. The creators of *Riverdance* released a new show in 2013 called *Heartbeat of Home*, along the same multicultural lines. As well as this, Irish fiddler Martin Hayes, who lives in Seattle, fuses tunes from east County Clare with American jazz to produce some wonderfully unique sounds that appeal to wide audiences on both sides of the Atlantic.

Irish Music in Britain

Some of the most major artists and bands on the British music scene since the 1960s have been of Irish extraction. Take a look at the following list: Lonnie Donegan; Paul McCartney and John Lennon of the Beatles; Donovan; Kate Bush; Morrissey and the Smiths; the Gallagher brothers of Oasis; John Lydon (a.k.a. Johnny Rotten) of the Sex Pistols; Kevin Rowland and Dexy's Midnight Runners; Boy George (O'Dowd); and Elvis Costello.[57] This is an impressive line-up. In the case of most of these artists, the fact of their Irishness, either first or second-generation, is not often acknowledged. It is brushed under the Axminster carpet of the dominant culture of Englishness, in a society where being Irish was, until very recently, about being the butt of abusive 'Irish jokes' and/or associated with trouble of one kind or another.

Historically, in Victorian Britain, 'the Irish were viewed as a stubbornly "unmeltable" minority and seen as a threat to hegemonic notions of respectability and industry.'[58] More recently, the Irish minority in Britain have usually been framed in terms of being problematic in some way, with poor health, poor education or a poor level of assimilation in an inherently superior host culture.[59] Little or no attention has been paid specifically to the second-generation Irish experience or, more importantly, to the ways in which these people have contributed positively to English culture. Anti-Irish prejudice in England (and especially in London) has now been well documented, with the characteristics of 'stupidity, easy recourse to violence, innate predisposition to alcohol abuse and blind adherence to religious dogma' composing the 'Paddy' caricature.[60] This prejudice was complicated further with respect to second-generation Irish people, who were often called 'Plastic Paddies', 'a derisive allusion to the perceived *inauthenticity* of the second generation's identification with Irishness.'[61]

Second-generation Irish artists represent a hybrid 'migration mélange', where their culture is a mix of 'home culture and language' (Irish) and 'an outdoor culture' (English).[62] Rather than trying to force square pegs into round holes, it is much more accurate to view these artists as deriving from 'a hyphenated Irish-Englishness that is not reducible to either dimension, and which facilitates a flexible, fluctuating and (sometimes) fractious identification with both.'[63] They are half-and-half, occupying a borderland between two cultures that have a historically troubled relationship. They are not *either* Irish *or* English, but *both* Irish *and* English. As a case study of this hybridity, where better to look than at the music of the Pogues, who are second-generation London Irish and directly challenged narrow essentialist notions of both Irishness and Englishness.

Seán Campbell provides the most comprehensive and perceptive account of the Pogues' lives and work.[64] In his wonderful book *Irish Blood, English Heart* he tells us that the

Pogues iconic front-man, Shane MacGowan, while born in Kent, spent a large part of his childhood in his parents' place of origin in rural County Tipperary. He avidly absorbed the Irish music and dance to which he was exposed there. They moved back to England when he was a young child, which he found very traumatic. He was a clever but troubled youth plagued by drug and alcohol abuse; he was expelled from school and spent a spell in a psychiatric hospital. The emergence of the punk cultural movement promised a psychic home for such disaffected youth in 1970s Britain. Shane, however, wanted to express his specifically Irish identity within this genre, calling himself Shane O'Hooligan. The Pogues' music, then, emerged as a fusion of Irish folk and English punk. Their first name was 'Pogue Mahone' ('kiss my ass' in defiant Irish) when they formed in 1982. They were the trailblazers in expressing the very particular experience of being London-Irish. Cáit O' Riordan, their bass guitarist, said that it was very difficult 'growing up London-Irish in the 1970s, having this funny name and parents who had this funny accent, with bombs going off.' She went on to say that it 'was a kind of soul-bending experience that could break you if you couldn't let it out.' Her interpretation of their gigs is that they were a cathartic experience for their audiences, a cultural pressure valve for a lost generation.[65]

Prior to The Pogues' emergence, the only Irish experience to be had in London was to listen to old-fashioned show-bands crooning away on the stages of the huge stereotypical dancehalls or little Irish clubs of Camden Town, Kilburn or Cricklewood. That might suit the parents, but not the kids. They needed something that spoke directly to them, and that provided a bit more dirty fun than waltzing chastely with your auntie to 'Spancil Hill' or 'Boolavogue'.

The band's music attracted the opprobrium of both British music critics and also some in Irish traditional music circles.

Music newspaper *Melody Maker* said they were 'spoilt, lying Londoners' performing a 'pale, anaemic imitation' of a music 'they really have nothing in common with.'[66] In Ireland, the critics were not too understanding of them either. Musician Noel Hill famously called The Pogues' style 'a terrible abortion' of Irish music.[67] Their cultural hybridity, their 'inbetweenness', was therefore seen as a threat. They were not trying to be more Irish than the Irish themselves, but were precisely London-Irish. It was challenging music that did not sit well with an ethnic minority who were trying to prove that they were just as good as the English in the 1980s. They sang of unsavoury people that did not meet with middle-class approval, to put it mildly. Sociologist Kieran Keohane reminds us that they sang of:

> James Joyce and Jessie James, Brendan Behan and the Banshee, labourers and intellectuals, God, the devil, some angels and a scattering of saints; Paddy the builder, Paddy the boozer, the soldier, the dreamer, the brawler; Paddy the racist, sexist, bigoted bastard; Paddy the socialist idealist; the rebellious, the broken-spirited, the dead and the resurrected.[68]

The Irish immigrants of whom they sang were the poor, the raucous, the homeless and the excluded, and their songs give the listener 'a maggot's view from inside the Big Apple, a sewer rat's view of London.'[69] And the London part of their identity should not be forgotten: after all, their beautiful love song is called 'Rainy Night in Soho', not 'Rainy Night in Ringsend' or 'Rainy Night in Salthill'.

The most famous song of all to emerge from MacGowan's gap-toothed maw is of course 'Fairytale of New York'. That such a deeply uncomfortable, subversive genius of a song could be commonly deemed the best Christmas song of all time is nothing short of a miracle. A duet between a couple of drug addicts in a New York homeless shelter (the female half sung by the late and much lamented Kirsty McColl), this 'secular carol' brilliantly captures a very dark version of its setting: 'it is an aria that invokes the city it hymns not as a place where emigrant dreams come true, but as a dream-busted landscape of the down-and-out – the lonely, the drug-addicted, the drunken, the homeless, the old, the incarcerated.'[70]

The song invokes the contradictions that every migrant knows: longing for the sense of connection to their homeland and yet, at the same time, glad they got the hell out of it. They listen to the NYPD choir singing 'Galway Bay' and express a bittersweet yearning for Ireland, or an aspic-coated, 'John Hinde postcard' version of Ireland. At the same time, the 'cars big as bars' and the 'rivers of gold' represent the materialistic dreams that brought them to New York in the first place. They are 'torn between the binding power of particular tradition and the cosmopolitan forces which promise the dissolution of the strictures of tradition and that promise us fresh air to breathe.'[71] It summons the unique vibe of the Irish bars in the Bronx, a potent mix of horrible sadness and, yet, a sense of freedom and possibility, that maybe tomorrow will be the day when you get your big break. The barman knows a guy who knows a guy, and if you keep giving him good tips, he might just let you in on the action. As Kris Kristofferson wrote in 'Me and Bobby McGee', 'freedom's just another word for nothing left to lose.' This is the peculiar mix of social solidarity and naked capitalism that makes New York what it is. The Irish community who left Ireland in the 1980s did not want to be 'one of the hod-carrier peoples of the world'[72] forever, but would do whatever it took to get on and get out.

Places and Hybridity

This unpredictable mixing and cultural hybridisation is often reflected in the composition of real places, where the arrival of particular ethnic groups or nationalities changes places that might have been quite homogenous in the past. This mixing has a long history, and one that is often far from benign. The imperial past of Western countries like Britain or France impacted upon both the places of the coloniser and the colonised. As cultural theorist Edward Said asks:

> Who in India or Algeria today can confidently separate out the British or French component of the past from present actualities, and who in Britain or France can draw a clear circle around British London or French Paris that would exclude the impact of India or Algeria upon those two imperial cities?[73]

Visit the sari shops of Southall in London or the halal butchers of Belleville in Paris and you will see how the inhabitants of the former colonies have now come home to roost. Author Andrew Hussey, in his book *Paris, the Secret History*, recommends one of his favourite walks through Paris:

> It begins at the corner of rue d'Oran and rue Léon in the 18th arrondissement. From here you can take any number of directions towards the city centre – towards the market at Doudeauville, or the rue Myrha or rue Polonceau. At any point, depending on your angle of vision, you could be in Casablanca, Algiers, Dakar, Tirana, Beirut, or the backstreets of Bucharest. But you always know that you are in Paris …[74]

This cultural mixing creates vibrant local communities for the inhabitants and often intoxicating urban experiences for the visitor. These hybrid sites are fascinatingly contested zones that simultaneously serve the needs of several different communities.

The experiences of the different members of these mixed communities vary according to the amount and types of power they can exercise in their lives. Gender is massively important, as girls and young women among immigrant – especially Asian – communities may have to struggle to compromise between the often patriarchal expectations of their elders and the opportunities offered to them in secular European societies. These themes are usefully explored in such thought-provoking movies as *Bend it like Beckham* and *East is East.*

So it is not only ethnic identities that are in question here, but also identities based on gender and sexual orientation. To walk through Madrid's gay area, Chueca, you could easily forget yourself and think the whole world was gay. Behaviour that would be frowned upon or legally punishable in other places is de rigueur here – what gets you laid in one place can get you killed in another. There is a safe and friendly atmosphere, where gay people can celebrate their sexuality and lifestyle with abandon in the heart of a country with some very conservative tendencies. In the US, The Castro in San Francisco is now world famous as a gay destination, a safe zone where people can express their sexualities without fear. The movie *Milk* is a solemn reminder that San Francisco was not always as open and tolerant as it is now. Harvey Milk, the 1970s gay activist who led the gay community to create The Castro area, was assassinated for his actions. The existence of separate zones like this is a constant reminder that it is prejudice in the broader society that creates the need for them in the first place. It can lead to a sort of ghetto identity, where inhabitants rarely leave the area, as 'attachments to gay neighbourhoods are the result of complex relations between social marginality and geographical (im)mobility.'[75] The ambiguity of meanings is a constant theme of social life, especially in mixed urban settings where very different social groups live cheek by jowl.

London

In a global city like London, its demographic history can be read in the contemporary composition of its communities. The mixing of different nationalities has a long history there. From the late eighteenth century, London's population, and in particular its working classes, may be likened to a popular drink of the time called 'All Nations': this intoxicating mixture sold in 'dram shops' was made up of the dregs of different spirits.[76] This multicultural history undermines any coherent, essentialist notions of Englishness. There is a constant ebbing and flowing of ethnic and class identities in certain regions, cities and districts. This exciting hybridity can be a money-spinner for those who are clever enough to cash in on it. Culture is a very marketable commodity for entrepreneurs who know that visitors like to engage in a little bit of virtual travel, without having to bother getting in an aeroplane: 'ethnic' districts have become key selling points for cities now, as they compete for the global tourist. It is important, however, to differentiate between the intentions behind creating such districts and their consequences, both intended and unintended.

One interesting example of this is Brick Lane, one street in East London that is a microcosm of multicultural Britain, with all of its achievements and setbacks. Brick Lane was historically virtually entirely Jewish owned, but only one famous bagel shop, Beigel Bake, remains now. In latter years it has been reinvented as 'Banglatown', after the influx of Bangla-deshis in the 1960s and 1970s. It is now renowned for the unbeatable curries to be had in its Indian restaurants, as well as its Asian supermarkets and street festivals. The street names in this district are now bilingual, in both English and Bengali. In Monica Ali's novel *Brick Lane*, it is even said that Bangladeshi-Muslim-owned businesses put statues of Hindu gods and goddesses in the windows just because they look colourful and interesting. The accuracy of this fictional anec-dote would have to be checked.

The history of this one street has been an ideological ethnic battle for dominance. Most of the time, people muddle along in one big hybrid mix, but there can sometimes be trouble between groups. There have been racist attacks by skinheads in the past, and the appearance of drug dealing and alcohol-related anti-social behaviour has made the area a bit more dangerous for young and old alike. It has also been reinvented as 'shabby chic', making it popular with artists like Tracey Emin, fashion designers and trendy media types. The tradi-tional Sunday street market, although much changed and diminished from olden times, attracts thousands of tourists who want to add a bit of edgy street life to their itinerar-ies. Impossibly cool young fashion students are thick on the ground, selling 'last season's unwanted fashion, not the broken belongings of poverty-stricken lives.'[77]

Some aspects of Brick Lane social life are gone; others, reinvented; and others, totally new. The effects of this all depend on your perspective as to whether this is positive or negative overall. On the one hand, the area is much cleaner and safer now than it was in the 1970s, when many lived in utter squalor and racist thugs used to harass Asian families. On the other hand, the area has become gentrified and the old working-class culture has been marginalised and pushed to the very edge, both socially and geographically. Gains for some groups cause losses for others, leading to power struggles in such urban environments. Such are the ebbs and flows of social life, whether on a small or large scale. Urban hybrid sites like Brick Lane reflect par excellence the changes brought about in communities by events occurring far away, perhaps on the other side of the globe. No locality exists in a bubble, even if it is not as ethnically diverse as this one. There are always varied meanings and conflicting constructions that may or may not happily co-exist.

Dublin

In Dublin, the Moore Street and Parnell Street area has become an urban hybrid site in recent years. For as long as anyone can remember, the traditional street market traders on Moore Street have shouted out the prices of their bargain fruit, vegetables and flowers to passers-by: 'Pineapples: two for a pound', or 'apples: ten for a euro' are familiar calls. The stallholders are often well-known characters and have been the cultural guardians of this market's distinctiveness for decades. Behind these stalls, there are now a variety of nationalities doing business, providing the tastes of home for Dublin's immigrant communities. There are East European, Nigerian, Vietnamese and Chinese food stores, restaurants, Internet cafés and hairdressers operating side by side.

In the last few years, the Moore Street Mall opened, offering a multicultural shopping experience to consumers, with various types of African, Asian and Eastern European produce on offer. Here, you can have your hair done in an elaborate African style, buy some Hungarian wine or Polish pierogi and eat some authentic Chinese hoisin duck for lunch, all in the one afternoon. Immigrants have been attracted to this area by low rents, and many of the shopfronts are far from aesthetically appealing. The Dublin Civic Trust, while it welcomes the renewed vibrancy of the area, feels that proper planning needs to be put in place to raise the area's profile and to restore the traditional facades on the buildings. The Trust recommends the creation of an 'oriental enclave' in the area that would showcase Asian architecture without impacting on the streetscape nearby.[78] This shows that different versions of a sense of place are not always harmonious. However, in nearby Smithfield, Chinese New Year is celebrated every year with a dragon-bedecked colourful festival. This has become one of the major events in Dublin's cultural calendar.

Gort, County Galway

Immigrants are sometimes clustered in particular places, as in the following example of Brazilians in Gort, County Galway. According to the 2006 Census, one-third of all 4,388 Brazilians then living in Ireland lived in County Galway.[79] Read another way, the Census shows that 40 per cent of the town's residents were non-Irish, with 83 per cent of these being Brazilian.[80] During the Celtic Tiger years, Gort became a hub for Brazilian immigrants. A small group of skilled workers were brought here initially in 1999 to work in Kepak, a local meat plant, which has now unfortunately closed down. Following on from then, the town became a magnet for Brazilian workers and their families. They were employed in various sectors in the region and set up lots of small businesses like food shops, hairdressers and Internet cafés. Even a cursory visit to the town revealed how the culture of the town was visibly affected by their presence. The town was transformed by their positive spirit, as were the coffers of local businesses and landlords. They formed the *Associação Brasileira de Gort,* which provided assistance and advice to the community.[81] Every year they organised a 'Carnaval' festival that celebrated their exciting and vibrant music and culture. The colourful and exotic feathered costumes they wore became an annual sight to behold in the rain-sodden Connacht town. Events like this help immigrants to bring a little of their own culture with them, as well as helping the host populations to learn more about their places of origin. Remembered places, like Brazil in this case, often resonate in the imaginations of dispersed or displaced peoples and serve as symbolic anchors of community to sustain them in hard times.

This immigration story was largely a positive one for several years, with Gort being 'a flagship for other communities on how integration should work.'[82] That is not to deny that exploitation probably took place too, as some of the immigrants worked only on the most casual basis and for the most menial wages. It was usually possible to see the Brazilian men standing on a particular corner of the town square, hiring themselves out for casual work on local farms and businesses. This sad scene was reminiscent of the Irish men who used to stand on Cricklewood Broadway in 1980s London, whose immediate concerns did not extend beyond making enough money to pay their rent and drink a few pints at the weekend.

Since the recession began in 2008, many of the Brazilian immigrants that had moved to Gort have since gone back home, as their lives became unbearable due to unemployment and poverty in Ireland. In 2008 an Irish journalist, Ruadhán MacCormaic, visited the southern Brazilian city of Anápolis, from where many of the Gort immigrants originated. He found evidence of new wealth, with extravagant houses amidst poorer, older ones. One house was even painted in the green, white and gold of the Irish flag. He met children there who spoke with Galway accents, played hurling and pined for Ireland. The connection is so strong between Vila Fabril (the suburb of Anápolis where many of the immigrants came from) and Gort that it is 'talked about as if it were a neighbouring townland.'[83] So it appears that the hybridisation that they had brought to Gort has now been reversed, with Irish influences being visible in a random city on the other side of the world. Such is the surprising richness that migration and hybridisation can bring to social life.

West Cork

In rural Ireland, the West Cork region may be viewed as a hybrid site that incorporates many nationalities. As referred to earlier, the widespread perception of the region as a beautiful place has meant that people have come from all over the world to live here. This clean, unspoilt image of its environment is now being capitalised upon by Fuchsia Brands Ltd, a recent rural development initiative that markets West Cork tourist enterprises and food products under its own indigenous brand and logo.[84] Newcomers to the region, as discussed earlier in this chapter, have been very much to the forefront of this developmental strand. The CEO of Fuchsia Brands Ltd feels that the multiculturalism of this sector is an asset to be celebrated and encouraged, and part of the distinctiveness of West Cork. These entrepreneurial incomers are viewed as contributing to the local economy by providing employment.[85] Even for those who never move from their homes, little bits of the wider world have come to them: the mountain has come to Mohammed. It is a Mecca for artists, writers and food producers from all over the world. The routes that these people have taken in their lives affect the social makeup of places like Clonakilty or Skibbereen, where local people have their roots. When a local farmer goes into town to sell his cattle or sheep on a Saturday morning, he might encounter a farmers' market on the street where French people sell their crêpes, Germans sell bratwurst sausages, Austrians sell waffles, and there might even be a Japanese woman selling homemade sushi. These transnational forums encourage local people to step outside their comfort zone a little, experience a smidgeon of cultural difference and add a little spice to their lives, both literally and metaphorically.

It is common to find these street markets, which are more associated with mainland Europe, throughout West Cork, as well as car boot sales, which one might associate with England. These latter emerge from an eminently sensible culture of thrift, which Irish people would have been too shy to get involved in up to recently. The town of Kinsale is home to 324 UK citizens, while 132 UK citizens live in Skibbereen, the highest numbers of UK citizens for any towns in the country.[86] Also, English and mainland European New Age travellers have been coming to live in West Cork for many years now. Despite frequent criticism from locals over the years, these newcomers are often much more interested than locals in preserving, and indeed revitalising, such traditional craft skills as thatching and basket making.[87] Ecological concerns are indeed now part of the mainstream cultural norms of the region. Another example of this ethos is that Clonakilty became Ireland's first Fairtrade town in 2003, an initiative that sees local businesses endeavouring to stock Fairtrade goods whenever possible. This open, cosmopolitan outlook is typical of the region.

Conclusion

No matter where we live or where in the world we move to, we are never fully removed from the operation of global socio-economic forces. Geographers Alison Blunt and Robyn Dowling provide us with the following productive and useful guideline to help us accommodate to globalised spaces and hybridised cultures:

> Rather than view home as rooted, located and bounded, and often closely tied to a remembered or imagined homeland, an emphasis on 'routes' invokes more mobile, and often de-territorialized, geographies of home that reflect transnational connections and networks.[88]

Each field, town, city, region and country has a place in the global order and is a product of socio-historical change. The best we can do is try to adapt to our environment and play the hand we are dealt. Geographer Doreen Massey argues that 'a large component of the identity of that place called home derived precisely from the fact that it had always in one way or another been open; constructed out of movement, communication, social relations which always stretched beyond it.'[89] This is not just a recent phenomenon, but stretches back hundreds of years. We all have to try to find our comfort zone, carving out our own paths in a world that can seem like an imposing and scary jungle at times. The cultural differences between people are a product of a shared historical process that differentiates and connects the world at the same time, producing endless social and cultural variations and possibilities for interaction. The combination of our personal stories and the precise components of the times we live in is what makes us who we are and provides us with our sense of identity.

This chapter has attempted to address the complexities of Irish identity, taking into account our long history of emigration and our more recent identity as a destination for immigrants. Our communities are more ethnically differentiated at the same time as being challenged by recession and high rates of emigration. The hybrid identities that result from all of this human mobility are endlessly fascinating, stirring things up and keeping us on our toes. I argue that this aspect of migration is exciting and dynamic, creating new cultural forms and more interesting places in which to live. In the next chapter I look at the question of the impact of different types of people moving around the world. Does it always necessarily have a positive impact on social life? I unpack the concept of cosmopolitanism, and introduce four people who I think embody this idea and provide an example for how to live open, cosmopolitan lives.

6

Cosmopolitanism Is Not Elitist

It is clear by now that assumptions can no longer be made about people's identities, connections with their communities or their sense of place in the world. The core question is how can we live in such a complex, mixed-up world and create for ourselves a sense of self and of connection with the places we inhabit, as well as be informed by a global sense of social justice? I want to argue here that *cosmopolitanism* is a key philosophical idea that can help us to live lives that are other-centred rather than self-centred. It is a complex notion that needs to be unpicked in order to be useful in thinking about these issues. Some forms of it take us outside our comfort zone, while others challenge us hardly at all.

Origins of Cosmopolitanism

So, to set the scene, where did this term come from? The origin of the word 'cosmopolitan' is from the Greek '*kosmos*', meaning 'world' and '*polis*', meaning 'city'. The Stoics of ancient Greece argued, 'each person lives in both a local community and a wider community of human ideals, aspirations and argument [based on] the equal worth of reason and humanity in every person.'[1] So to say that someone is cosmopolitan is to say that he/she is first and foremost a citizen of the world, over and above being a citizen of any state. The term was also used in the Enlightenment in the eighteenth century, most especially in the work of Kant, who coined the German term '*weltbürger*', meaning 'world citizen'. He was concerned with just conduct and cooperative relations between equal human beings.[2] In contemporary political philosophy, the principle of cosmopolitanism is based on the idea that every person in the world deserves equal respect and consideration, that everybody is treated impartially based on universally applied rules, and that these are acknowledged by everyone.[3] Because of human difference as well as human bias, this is not necessarily an easy principle to live by, as we will see throughout the following discussion.

A person is not born, but rather becomes cosmopolitan.[4] Cosmopolitanism is not the product of social class or status, but is something to be *worked at*. We can invent and reinvent it on a daily basis. It is not a cultural resource that is passed on by one's forebears, and it does not exist in a pure form. *Webster's Dictionary* defines it as 'not bound by local or national habits or prejudices; at home in all countries or places.' Cosmopolitanism 'is first of all an orientation, a willingness to engage with the Other. It is an intellectual and aesthetic stance of openness toward divergent cultural experiences, a search for contrasts rather than uniformity.'[5] The cosmopolitan can be in his/her comfort zone in many parts of the world and among many types of people, recognising 'the real, networked spatial hybrids and institutionalised syncretisms of which the real world exists.'[6] He/she can find some essential feeling of connection with people from cultures that are very different to his/her own culture of origin. Being cosmopolitan also means 'having a cultural disposition which is not limited to the concerns of the immediate locality, but which recognises global belonging, involvement and responsibility and can integrate these broader

concerns into everyday life practices.'7 Society is always changing and to feel comfortable with that is often a challenge. For
example, the cosmopolitan welcomes immigrants into his/
her community, viewing them as an enhancement of the local
cultural mosaic. This is the complete opposite of the xeno-
phobic perspective, which ultimately fears 'different' outsiders
and views them as a threat to the local culture. Of course,
these two perspectives lie at opposite ends of the spectrum,
and there are many permutations in between. People can have
different types of experience out in the big, bad world, leading
to varying attitudinal responses.

People on the Move

There is no doubt that we are witnessing much more geographical mobility now, with more people going places and doing
things that they might never have imagined before, either as
migrants or tourists. This increase in tourism transforms our
social identities, which, it has been argued, are formed around
three elements: space, time and memory.[8] Firstly, the spaces
that are created for tourists can alienate the locals who actually
live in them. They might feel that their place is not for them
anymore, when mown down by hordes of tourists. Those who
are not making any money from these same hordes probably
feel especially disgruntled. I think particularly here of coastal
cities that serve as stopovers for cruise liners. Slews of tourists
d'un certain âge wander around the main streets for a couple
of hours, getting in the way of locals who are trying to get the
kids to school or deliver kegs of beer.

Secondly, tourism involves a skewed perception of time.
For example, visitors might like to sense that a rural idyllic
village is taking them back in time to a simpler life. I once
stumbled upon a medieval festival in a remote Spanish town.

It was very strange to see everybody dressed up in medieval costumes – men in tights and women in wimples – while drinking cheap wine from plastic glasses and speaking on their mobile phones.

Thirdly, the memory of a place is always packaged very conveniently for tourists by the heritage industry. There can be disputes over whose version of history should be represented in that package, especially in societies that have experienced ethnic conflicts and wars.

However, just because you move to another country, or visit a country as a tourist, does not make you particularly interested in becoming a cosmopolitan. Just because you physically go to another place doesn't mean that you necessarily learn much at all about that place. And just because aeroplanes can take us to very different places in under a few hours does not mean that we have become an intimate 'global village'. We may be able to overcome physical distance by applying technological fixes, but overcoming cultural distance still takes some work.[9]

Most international travel starts with a journey on an aeroplane. In a plane, you are completely removed from the real world beneath you. You are in a metal box that is going very, very fast above the clouds, giving you no idea about the type of terrain over which you are travelling. You might get an occasional glimpse of a stretch of coastline or a mountain range that gives you a clue as to where you are – 'that must be the Pyrenees/Himalayas/Rockies' – but the job of the aircrew is to make the journey as removed from reality as possible. They distract you with dodgy meals, soppy Hollywood movies and flight statistics on how many hours it is to your destination. Imagine if you took that journey – from Madrid to Buenos Aires, for example – over land and sea instead. You would have to use trains, buses, cars, boats, or even bicycles and mules. Some of it you might have to go on foot. This kind of adventurous travel is not for the faint-hearted. Imagine how different those experiences would be. Imagine all the places you would see and the people you would meet. Imagine how smart you would have to be to come out of such an experience unscathed. Imagine the skills you would need to negotiate your way across the world. Plane travel dispenses with the need for all these kinds of intelligence. You just need a valid passport and ticket and to be able to read the signs saying 'entrance' and 'exit', 'departures' and 'arrivals'.

Types of Cosmopolitanism

To help us think through this question of what travel does for us, I wish to develop the idea of cosmopolitanism by dividing it into two categories, which are further subdivided into two subcategories, as displayed in the following figure:

Types of Cosmopolitanism

	Involuntary	Voluntary
Passive	Business travellers	Package tourists
Active	Immigrants	Independent travellers

The first division is between what I term *passive* and *active* cosmopolitanism. Within each of these types, there are people who adopt them voluntarily and involuntarily. There is a sociological 'ideal type' of traveller that fits into each of the four boxes. I will discuss later how some people rise out of this fixed typology throughout their lives, but, for the moment, it might be interesting to stick with them. I want you to imagine our four types of travellers emerging out of an aeroplane in Charles de Gaulle airport in Paris, for example. They vary according to their motivation for coming to Paris, how their travel expenses were paid for, the experiences they have in the city and the effects their type of travel has upon their destinations. Each of these will be discussed in turn in the case studies below. It should be stressed here that these ideal types are entirely fictional, based on general observation.

Passive Cosmopolitanism

Passive cosmopolitanism comes to us before we leave home at all. This is in the form of watching the Travel Channel on TV, eating Thai green curry on a Friday night or observing Chinese New Year celebrations on our own main street. This type of cosmopolitanism is easy and is firmly at the core of our comfort zone. Nobody has to learn a new language, speak to anybody new, get hot and sweaty or perhaps even leave his or her couch. This is a 'seepage' of a banal type of cosmopolitanism that permeates everyday life.[10] It just sort of sneaks up on us, whether we like it or not. The media has a role to play, of course, in exposing viewers to other places and cultures they might not otherwise get to see. However, there is only a remote chance that people will take any form of cosmopolitan political action of any kind following that exposure. To do anything meaningful with the fleeting images we see on our TV screens has to come from a deeper place within ourselves, 'ultimately from within the situated lifeworld of the self … no amount of technological sophistication can make us cosmopolitans online.'[11] When people travel passively, they have such sheltered, packaged experiences that they may as well not have been there at all. They have little or no interest in the surrounding society and are only there to achieve very limited goals. This is a shallow form of cosmopolitanism that looks at 'other cultures' exclusively as a resource to be used or consumed to 'cosmopolitanise' the urban, Western and the 'core'; they propagate the ideological illusion that in 'consuming' ethnicity we are contributing to global multiculturality.[12]

The Business Traveller

The first type of traveller represented in the figure above is the business traveller, who embodies a passive form of cosmopolitanism, as detailed in the following case study:

Case Study 1: David

David works for a software firm and has to travel a lot for his work, liaising between Head Office in New York and sub-offices all over the world. By now, he hates travelling and would much prefer to be at home. He is therefore in the 'involuntary' box, because he is only there to keep the company running smoothly. Paris is the last place he wants to be. He has been there lots of times before and finds it cold and alienating. Nobody likes to speak English to him, and he finds the food very oily and unhealthy. He is trying to get healthier because his blood pressure is high. The company pays for his travel, of course, even though they complain about having to stump up for business class since the recession. He is transported into his hotel in the city by taxi, or perhaps the company will send a driver to fetch him. He only stays in five-star hotels, as he needs to have excellent business facilities available to him at all times. The environment in his preferred hotel chain is nice and neutral and, more importantly, the same all over the world. He doesn't like surprises. He does bring a picture of his wife and son with him, however, to make him feel at home. He never has time to sightsee, as all of his time is taken up with meetings. To relax at night, he watches the news on CNN and maybe a little porn. The only tourist sights he knows are the ones he can see from his hotel room window on the fifteenth floor. He has never been to the Louvre. He is not interested: he would much prefer to be playing baseball with his son than traipsing around strange cities. He rarely ventures outside of the air-conditioned confines of his hotel. He knows that a drink costs ten times more in the hotel bar than in the local bars, but he doesn't care because he puts them on his expenses account anyway. He sometimes chats to lonely businesswomen in the same situation as himself, and, like Bill Murray's character in the film *Lost in Translation*, he has sometimes been tempted to take it further. The only local people he meets are the ones who work in the hotel, and they are all well trained to deal with English speakers, especially in order to get as many tips from them as they can.

In the everyday use of the term 'cosmopolitanism', most people might think of global jet-setters like David as being typical of those who fit this category. It is associated with wealthy people who can afford to travel the world, accumulating worldly experiences. These are 'a cultural elite with the means to rise above the petty concerns of the everyday.'[13] Inherent in this elitist approach to the world is a denigration of everything local as backward and parochial, and looking down upon people who may never have travelled outside their own country. These are jet-setters who get on planes like most of us get on buses, who can boast of staying in fancy hotels from Dubai to Darwin. They know things like the contents of various cocktails (including the one *called* the cosmopolitan) and how to handle chopsticks, and they will regale dinner party guests with their dastardly tales of gambling in Las Vegas or of exceedingly thorough security checks at LAX airport.

They appear to have seen and done everything, and this is reflected in their faintly jaded attitude to the world around them. Different world cultures serve as noisy, colourful backdrops, viewed from the twenty-first floor of a Beijing or Tokyo office building, or from the holiday village that is hosting their company's annual conference. These business travellers have contacts (rather than friends) in various locations who interpret the local idiosyncrasies for them, giving directions to taxi drivers, ordering food at local restaurants and maybe hooking them up later on in the evening, to indulge their particular peccadilloes. I believe, however, that this kind of passive, involuntary cosmopolitanism does little to expose people to different cultures or make them feel like global citizens.

The Package Tourist

The second type of traveller from the figure above is the package tourist, as outlined in the following case study:

Case Study 2: Rosemary

Rosemary really wants to be in Paris, so she is placed in the 'voluntary' box. Rosemary is travelling with a group where everything is pre-organised for them. She is a little over 50 and has spent her entire life in southern England. She is now looking for some adventure in her life. However, she wouldn't be brave enough to do it alone because having to speak French would be scary, and she wouldn't be able to manage getting around such a big city by herself. Anyway, she likes being in a group because she wants to meet some new people. Her everyday life at home is quite mundane and isolated, so she feels it is time to try something new. She has always heard that Paris is beautiful, and she wants to see it before she dies. That old Marianne Faithful song about driving through Paris 'with the warm wind in her hair' was one of the main reasons she came. She has been to Spain before on a package holiday, but this is her first time in a big European city. She had to dip into her limited savings to do this trip, but it was all paid for up-front, so she knew from the start what it was going to cost.

The group is picked up from the airport in a hotel coach. Their three-star hotel is on Boulevard de Sebastopol in the 2nd arrondisement. The tour guide tells the group that it is good to learn about these different sections of the city in order to help them get around. The hotel is near lots of shops and nightlife, on the Right Bank of the river Seine. They have five days in Paris, so the schedule is packed. They have to see all the sights: the Eiffel Tower, Sacré Coeur, Notre Dame, the Louvre, the Champs Élysées, the Arc de Triomphe and a boat trip on the Seine. Rosemary gets to see everything, so she can tick all the boxes on her tourist itinerary. She is glad of the bus that takes them around because the Metro looks very complicated. They are brought to restaurants that serve familiar food, and where they have menus in English with handy little pictures of each plate. Some of the others want to try eating snails, but she doesn't fancy it. She can now tell her neighbours all about her trip when she gets home, and she feels quite proud of herself.

Several years ago, I asked the woman in a local video shop where she got her great tan. She replied, 'Spain.' I then asked, 'Oh, what part?' Her answer was, 'I don't know, but it was near the airport!' She didn't know where she was, and she didn't care. Much package tourism is of the 'home plus' variety: 'Spain is home plus sunshine, India is home plus servants, Africa is home plus elephants and lions.'[14] In our case study above, Paris is home plus culture. This type of experience asks little or nothing of the tourist, because everything is already organised for them, and they are brought to a resort that is isolated from the surrounding society and pointed towards convenient bars and restaurants that serve the same kind of food they eat at home. Think of the English people in the movie *Shirley Valentine* eating nothing but egg and chips – in Greece!

People choose these kinds of holidays specifically because everything is paid for up-front and because they are convenient, presenting no challenge to them. This is possibly the biggest investment of the family finances for the whole year, so it is important that they are guaranteed a good time. This concern is intensified by the fact that there is much less money to go around these days because of the recession. It may be the case that they work in tiring jobs with low pay, long hours and short holidays. People in this situation may not want to risk usurping their precious, brief holiday time with more challenging travel that may end up costing more money in the long run. Doing this kind of travelling with young children in tow is not for the faint-hearted either. Especially when one comes from a place where the climate is cold and rainy, perhaps to sit in the sun by the pool drinking mojitos is just what the doctor ordered. It may also be that they have small children and need a break in a resort where there is organised childcare. To hand over the kids to childminders, especially where the sun is shining, can be a holiday in itself for people at this stage of life. In the case of older people, they might not be able for challenging situations and need some care and protection. Or, finally, it might be that some people are actually afraid to engage with different cultures because they are unable to speak the language and lack the confidence or self-esteem to give it a try. They might fear that something will happen to them and they won't be able to cope in a strange place. This might be partly related to one's social-class background and level of education, but not necessarily. I studied French for my Leaving Cert and knew (way back then) every grammar rule that existed, yet was still very shy ordering a cup of coffee the first time I went to Paris, several years later. Some people have the chutzpah and interest to give it a go and others do not. It takes courage to risk looking silly speaking a language badly, or to risk paying too much for a train ticket, or to try to speak to someone on a dark street in a strange city, or to eat something new that looks weird to us.

Active Cosmopolitanism

Active cosmopolitanism is harder work. It is much more of a challenge – physically, emotionally and culturally. It has little to do with formal education and has more to do with a particular orientation to the outside world, 'a mode of managing meaning.'[15] The active cosmopolitan challenges him/herself to develop a *cultural competence* in order to actively engage with people who are very different to them. This is a two-way street between what we are exposed to in the first place, and our personal ability to deal with it, to interpret it, make sense of it and even love it. The active cosmopolitan is therefore able to adapt in different places and in different situations, developing a mastery over culture. Sometimes people do not necessarily want to do all of these things, but are forced to by their life circumstances.

The Immigrant

The third type of traveller is the immigrant, as described in the following case study:

Case Study 3: Ashraf

Ashraf is an immigrant from Algeria, a former French colony. He has come to Paris looking for work, as he has been unemployed for too long now back home. He was very sad to have to leave his family behind, but he knows some people in Paris who can find some work for him. He does not want to be there, so we can place him in the 'involuntary' box. He had to borrow money from his cousin to make the trip to Paris, and he hopes that he will find work soon so that he can start paying him back. He has been promised that he can stay on another cousin's couch until he finds his feet. Without the kindness of these family members he could not do this.

He gets the RER train into the city from the airport. He has never been on such a train before, and he finds the station very intimidating. However, he cannot afford anything else, so he has to do it this way. He goes straight to his cousin's apartment in Belleville in the 11th arrondisement. This is an immigrant neighbourhood, where almost everyone is from a North African background. Both Arabic and French can be heard on the streets, and the vibrant, colourful street markets remind the inhabitants of a taste of home. One can buy the big bunches of mint needed to make mint tea and halal lamb to make a tagine. The men sit in street cafés smoking their shisha pipes, exchanging news of the day. The people here watch out for each other, as they say that they are experiencing much more police harassment since 9/11 and the other attacks attributed to al-Qaeda.

Ashraf feels exiled from his own country, and he has very little interest in French culture. He is just interested in keeping his head down, remaining in the circle of his own people. Any skills he picks up are just used to function in this big new place without attracting any trouble.[16] He learns what he needs to learn in order to work and send money home – no more and no less. Therefore, a migrant like Ashraf probably has very limited experience in France, his host nation. He is not interested in the tourist sites but is very adept at managing himself in this city. He is 'street smart', the kind of cultural competence that counts when moving to a new country, especially as part of the Muslim minority in France.

Ashraf is not alone in this. It is common for expatriate groups to prefer to stay among their own ethnic group, with very little mixing with the native population of their host country. They may not even try to learn the host country's language. Some Irish emigrants also 'have effectively remained in an Irish bubble, living away from home.'[17] Meeting only other Irish people, both at work and at play, does not widen their horizons much, whether living in Boston or Melbourne. It leads them down a kitsch cul-de-sac, pointing towards the same old clichéd 'shamrocks and shillelaghs' version of Irishness. However, they have to be able to earn a living, so they must engage with local people to some extent. This is a kind of functional, begrudging cosmopolitanism. There is an active engagement with the rhythms of their host localities, but the primary motivation is earning money. They have no choice in the matter.

The Independent Traveller

The fourth type of traveller is the independent traveller, as in the case of Jill in the following case study:

Case Study 4: Jill

Jill is bursting with curiosity and definitely fits into the 'voluntary' category. Jill has travelled a lot, but somehow has never been to Paris before. She cannot wait to work on her French so that she can travel in other French-speaking countries afterwards. Her next idea is to volunteer in an ecotourism project in the Caribbean island of Guadeloupe, so she will need good French for that. Like Ashraf, she gets the RER train into the city, but she could do this with her eyes closed, as she has been to lots of other cities. She will be couch surfing with a girl she met online who lives on Rue Oberkampf. This, she hears, is a very cool, 'shabby chic' street at the edge of Belleville. It has lots of ethnic restaurants, and she would love to try them all. She is determined to get to know Paris well, walking everywhere and chatting to everyone along the way. She has an open, positive attitude and loves to stretch the limits of her comfort zone. She has a real, heartfelt interest in other people's lives. She has had to save up for this European trip, as it is more expensive than most places she goes, like India and Southeast Asia. She worked in a bar in London for a while to this end. She will have to watch her budget, so she will mostly shop in local markets for her food. She never stays anywhere for too long and is happiest on the road. She writes a blog and does the odd bit of freelance journalism. Facebook makes it possible to hook up with people all over the place, so there is a couch for her to sleep on in many parts of the world.

While in Paris, she will take a quick look at the major tourist sights, but she is far more interested in improving her French and learning about people's lives in this city. She would much prefer to chat to a little old lady and sip Pastis than spend her time staring at the Mona Lisa in the Louvre.

In fact, she will boast to her friends that she *didn't* visit the Louvre, so there is a form of elitism in Jill's type of travel as well. She is a kind of reverse snob, looking down on people who 'collect' world tourist sites. She went to Cairo and didn't bother going to see the pyramids, for example. She is the kind of cosmopolitan who wants to be free to immerse herself in other cultures. She wants to 'be able to sneak backstage rather than being confined to the frontstage areas.'[18] She was always very much an individual, never one to run with the pack. When travelling, she loves to blend in, not stand out from the crowd. She knows she is breaking her parents' hearts, as they wanted her to settle down and choose a profession many years hence. Maybe it is too late now, so she just has to keep moving.

This kind of travel takes travellers completely to the outer edges of their comfort zones, but that is exactly what they are seeking. See my section on the adventures of the legendary Dervla Murphy later in the chapter.

Sometimes one of the best parts of this kind of travel is the advance preparations we make for it. This often involves poring over detailed maps, which I have always loved. Irish travel writer Mary Russell evokes the richness of maps when she writes:

The large atlas lies on the kitchen table, in a pool of warm light, opened at the page where Asia blends into Europe. As I stare at it, the boundaries of the table, of the kitchen, of Dublin itself, melt away into the darkness and I am in Georgia, land of Colchis, of Jason and the Golden Fleece.[19]

I love it when the map comes to life. I love nothing more than standing on a street corner in a new city, navigating my way around from the piece of paper in my hand and the co-ordinates in my head.

Of course, younger people tend to eschew paper maps for everything that the Internet can offer. Before a recent trip to London I went to my local photocopy shop to copy the few pages from my 'London A-Z' that I needed, rather than carrying the whole book. The young man working there was amused. He asked me why I couldn't just use Google Earth on my mobile phone instead. Naturally, I only thought of some decent responses to this after I got home. I can think of nothing more off-putting and stupid than staring into a mobile phone screen to navigate new streets. Over-reliance on such technology removes control from our lives, in my opinion, rather than adding to it. The phone may not work in a different place, it may be lost or stolen, or the map it gives me might not match my exact needs. During the moments in which I am staring at a screen, I am not as observant as normally and vulnerable to being mugged or followed. I am much happier with a piece of paper that I can peruse discreetly and at my leisure, giving me a great sense of control over my surroundings and orientation in a new environment. Neither is there any risk that someone is going to snatch it out of my hand. And there is always the rich resource of the local knowledge of the inhabitants to fall back upon in times of need, and the entertaining encounters we can have with the locals as a result.

Merging Types of Travellers

At this point, let us look at how the four types of cosmopolitan identity, as evidenced in our four travellers above, can merge and blend into each other – or even change completely – because of the various trajectories of a person's life course. Take David the businessman, for example. He did a lot of travelling after college, so he used to be an independent traveller before he had to don the universal uniform of the business suit. He actually donates US$50,000 a year to an orphanage in Vietnam that he used to volunteer in, but the only one who knows about that is his accountant. So he used to be like Jill.

Rosemary later decides to move to a cottage in the west of Ireland, and she becomes an immigrant who finds it difficult to blend into the local community. Money is short so she grows vegetables to sell at farmers' markets during the summers. She finds that she is most comfortable in the company of other English people. In a lot of ways, she becomes like Ashraf.

Ashraf decides to fulfil his dream of going back to university in order to complete his PhD in electronic engineering. He then gets a job as an academic and starts to travel all over the world to conferences in his field. He always stays in very nice hotels and has little interest in where he is. So Ashraf becomes a lot like David.

As Jill gets older, she finds that she prefers to travel in groups, as being alone can get so lonely, and she has developed health problems. She still goes to exotic regions like Goa or Cancún, but her experiences are really more like those of Rosemary now, as she goes on organised trips to touristy resorts rather than hitchhiking on back roads through countries like Zimbabwe.

These are only a few examples of the unpredictable swings and roundabouts of life – there is a plethora of others that I will leave to your own imagination, involving jobs, relationships, changes in health or accidents.

Putting Active Cosmopolitanism to Work

Active cosmopolitans apply their cultural competence at home as well as abroad. Because of their experience and knowledge of different cultural worlds, they will experience a certain feeling of detachment, not taking their home milieu for granted as the only 'normal' way to live. They will have a questioning attitude about their *own* cultural assumptions, leading to 'an *ongoing dialogue* both within [them]selves and with distanciated cultural others.'[20] Allied to this may be a sense of 'irritation with those committed to the local common sense and unaware of its arbitrariness.'[21] When they go for a drink at the local pub, they may be quite bored with the gory minutiae of the local gossip. When people stay where they are reared, either voluntarily or involuntarily, it means that they must invent an identity around their place. 'Tradition' is a powerful trope through which people do this, adopting some old elements of it as well as inventing some new ones. Active cosmopolitans may feel excluded by this local sense of tradition, having missed out on its evolution over the years. They may feel like what writer Pico Iyer terms 'offshore beings' rather than having an unquestioned sense of belonging.[22]

This type of cosmopolitan is also open to immigrants and learning about the newer cultures that are in our midst in the Western world. Some people can be oriented towards cosmopolitanism without even travelling outside of their locality at all.[23] They may never have had the opportunity to travel, but they, nevertheless, retain a strong interest in other peoples' localities. Perhaps it is the case that it is difficult for active cosmopolitans to settle down fully once they have been away, always fighting off boredom, hankering a little for the piquancy of cultural difference. Local people may view these people as 'someone a little unusual, one of us and yet not quite one of us.'[24] There may also be a sense of resentment against them, perhaps grounded in feelings of jealousy. This depends sometimes too on how these cosmopolitans behave upon returning home. For example, there is a plethora of jokes about the 'returned Yank' in Irish popular culture. We have all encountered Irish migrants who, having lived in the US or UK for some years, display a quasi-racist attitude towards everything to do with Ireland. They complain about the roads, the service in restaurants and how we all are out of shape and drink too much!

Active cosmopolitans have a positive attitude towards their own homes and the localities where they were brought up. This is very different to just viewing moving around the world as a shallow means of accumulating distinction, putting them apparently above their neighbours in terms of status. On checking into a County Wicklow B&B once, I replied, 'Cork' when the owner asked me where I was from. She thought for a second and responded, much to my amusement, 'Ah, yes, but *well-travelled* Cork.' Active cosmopolitans are not afraid to have roots of their own (in Cork or otherwise), even if much of their lives are spent charting routes through new territories. Several of the authors in this field term this 'rooted cosmopolitanism', which has both 'roots' and 'wings'.[25] Ghanaian cultural theorist Kwame Appiah describes the position of such a person as 'attached to a home of his or her own, with its own cultural particularities, but taking pleasure from the presence of other, different places that are home to other, different people.'[26] Without the connections these cosmopolitans feel to their own home and locality, 'there can be no genuine sense of obligation to the universal and, moreover, one's local loyalties and experiences provide an experiential basis for the constitution of a postnational or cosmopolitan morality.'[27] So one does not have to choose between being a local or a cosmopolitan, as one can happily encounter at least these two levels of life experience at once, with perhaps several others in between. What I term the active cosmopolitan 'is precisely someone who is able to live – ethically, culturally – *in both the global and the local at the same time.*'[28]

The Dunnes Stores Strikers, 1984

I wish to stress one more time that this type of active cosmopolitanism is not necessarily a product of middle-class identity. One does not have to have had a university education or even to have travelled much in order to show global solidarity, for example. This was shown to great effect by the actions of eleven young Dublin women who worked in the Henry Street branch of Dunnes Stores, the Irish supermarket chain, in 1984. Mary Manning started it all: she refused to handle South African Outspan oranges at the checkout at which she worked. The oranges were a symbol of the economic output of South Africa. She and her fellow strikers thereby lodged a public protest against the oppressive apartheid regime that was in place in South Africa at the time, and sowed their solidarity with the local black population whose lives it affected. This was done despite their having only a rudimentary knowledge of the political situation in South Africa, well before the advent of the Internet and global social networking. Their cosmopolitan form of activism was driven by a very straightforward sense of right and wrong and of moral outrage.

The eleven workers were backed by their union, surviving for the almost three-year duration of their strike on just IR£21 strike pay per week. This brave action was taken during the bleak years of the 1980s recession. Eventually, three years later, and due to popular pressure, the Irish government agreed to ban South African fruit and vegetables. These women were not part of the Irish Anti-apartheid Movement at the start of the strike, but their actions served as a great boon to its profile. It was like throwing a stone into the pool of public discourse, producing ripples that resonated with a wider public more effectively than a university-based movement ever could.

Archbishop Tutu later praised the strikers, and Nelson Mandela later said that the stand they took helped him to keep going during his long years of imprisonment. There is now a plaque outside the Henry Street store dedicated to the strikers. Mary Manning was also honoured by having a street named after her in Johannesburg.[29] These young working-class women were certainly living in the local and the global at the same time. They were risking their livelihoods and living in poverty, all because of a profound sense of justice. The Outspan oranges at the heart of the dispute were like the baton in a relay race, passed between the hands of working-class people in very different parts of the globe.

The Fairtrade Movement

While this serves as an example of *worker's* solidarity with people living in an undemocratic country in the developing world, it is more common now to find solidarity being expressed by Western *consumers* of goods. The Fairtrade movement is an evocative expression of active cosmopolitanism, because its supporters show a very strong sense of empathy with producers of food and craft items from developing countries. This is what I call 'caring without borders', or what sociologist Ulrich Beck terms, 'the globalisation of emotions'.[30] We should all be familiar by now with the Fairtrade logo that can be seen on products on our supermarket shelves, in some clothes stores and in Oxfam shops. The following is a statement from the website of Fairtrade Ireland:

Fairtrade is about better prices, decent working conditions, local sustainability, and fair terms of trade for farmers and workers in the developing world. By requiring companies to pay sustainable prices (which must never fall lower than the market price), Fairtrade addresses the injustices of conventional trade, which traditionally discriminates against the poorest, weakest producers. It enables them to improve their position and have more control over their lives.[31]

The typical products supported by Fairtrade are tea, coffee, chocolate, bananas, orange juice, honey and cotton, even though the range of products has expanded hugely in recent years. There are Fairtrade fashion items available now as well, both in retail outlets and online.[32] Fairtrade helps producers and craftspeople to circumvent open competition on the global market for these goods. Direct links are made to producers and their co-ops. This turns globalisation into something positive, building international linkages that strive to act on global inequality and injustice in the world trade system.

This idea emerged in the early 1990s, led by a group of UK aid agencies. This kind of activism 'questions the assumption of uniformity in the global development project and asserts the need to respect alternative cultural traditions as a matter of respect and global survival.'[33] Other examples are indigenous movements throughout the world, local cooperatives in developing countries, as well as the Zapatistas, who were already discussed in Chapter 3. This approach to activism has been termed 'cosmopolitan localism' because it 'seeks to amplify the richness of a place while keeping in mind the rights of a multi-faceted world. It cherishes a particular place, yet at the same time knows about the relativity of all places.'[34] It is about improving the lives of ordinary people in localities, whether these are in India, Kenya or Nicaragua. It has a powerful appeal because it connects us with the place where our consumer goods are produced.

In recent years, however, I have noticed some companies selling coffee, for example, using packaging that makes it *look* like it is Fairtrade when it is not. Such a cynical marketing strategy makes it all the more important for us consumers to develop the savvy to tell the difference between fakes and the real thing. It is an attempt at a co-optation of the alternative marketing idea led by Fairtrade. Notwithstanding this challenge, Fairtrade has grown from being a drop in the ocean when it started to being a ubiquitous label that greets us wherever we go now.

A Nicaraguan coffee farmer visited Ireland with Oxfam in the mid-noughties, at the height of the Celtic Tiger. While in Dublin, he tasted a cappuccino that cost €3.50. This cup contained 10 grammes of coffee. With this same money, you could buy 2 kilos of coffee directly from him. This inequality is truly staggering. Because he deals with Fairtrade, he at least gets more than double the money for his coffee than he would otherwise on the open market. This helps him out of a cycle of poverty that leads to dependence on the use of child labour on coffee farms in the region. Instead, Fairtrade helps with improving educational facilities for children in the region and also with encouraging economic diversification.

Black Gold, a film made in 2006, sought to raise awareness of these issues. This dealt with the poor prices paid to Ethiopian coffee farmers for their produce. Even when dealing with Fairtrade exporters, the profit accrued to the farmers was US$1.10 per pound of coffee. This is enough to make 52 espressos, earning about US$160 for the retailer. The film shows malnourished workers depending on handouts from aid agencies in order to stave off starvation.[35]

Fairtrade has not been without its critics, for a variety of reasons. Some say that farmers in the developing world need to improve their production methods and enter the world market in order to improve their lot, rather than to be protected in a closed-off section of that market. This right-oriented perspective sees integration into the machinations of world markets as the best development approach. However, it seems to me that we have seen more than enough of the inequalities of that market to know that this is certainly no panacea for these farmers.

Others say that Fairtrade traps farmers into producing the same basic unprocessed goods, rather than diversifying into higher-value goods. It is of course true – in theory – that diversification is a desirable goal. However, the reality on the ground in developing countries is that most farmers find it financially difficult to take a risk on new, unknown commodities and to switch from one product to another. They can only afford to stay on the path of least resistance, because their very survival is at stake. When only scarce resources exist, this has to be a very finely-tuned calculation. It is worth quoting anthropologist Sutti Ortiz at length to explain the nature of risk involved:

> When any individual, whether peasant, Western businessman or farmer becomes aware that a particular action entails a risk, he evaluates it and decides how to act. The number of elements are numerous and relate to his income, cost of the enterprise, the pay-offs, the type of assets he holds, whether his livelihood may be threatened, the alternative opportunities he foregoes, means of insuring the well-being of his family, his social status, etc. If on occasion a peasant hesitates to take a risk this does not imply that he always shies away from a gamble.[36]

Smaller farmers will invest in a new initiative, naturally enough, only when there is a high level of confidence that it will not threaten their subsistence. It appears to me that they may as well receive some extra support for what they are probably going to continue to do anyway, in a very hostile global financial environment.[37] These farmers often have to work in harsh physical environments that might be unsuited to diversification anyway.

Fairtrade recognises the massive inequalities that exist in world trade. It wants to improve livelihoods *now* rather than wait for some future nirvana when things will be better for the farmers of the developing world. It undoubtedly helps enormously in improving the lives of the farmers it supports, but there is a question as to whether it can go further, to 'mobilize public education and consumer purchasing power to democratise the global market.'[38] It is ultimately no substitute for deeper reforms of the world trade system, stacked as it is against poorer countries, upon whom we ultimately rely for much of the food we eat and even our morning cup of java.

Voluntary Work

Another means of expressing active cosmopolitanism at an individual level is volunteering with a non-governmental organisation (NGO) in a developing country. This has become very common in Ireland now, especially since the onset of the recession. This is part of 'the drive to self-realization in lifestyles which are themselves open to an expanded mutuality.'[39] While it is very difficult to know the exact numbers doing this, anecdotal evidence tells us that they are quite high. Almost everybody knows somebody involved in some overseas charity work. My own particular volunteering experience was with the Hope Foundation (a.k.a. HOPE), which works with the poor of Kolkata (formerly Calcutta) in India. I spent six weeks in Kolkata in late 2009, researching a book that was a fundraiser for the charity.[40] This was a short period compared to the other Irish volunteers, who were spending at least three months – and usually six or nine months – volunteering. One exceptional woman, Annemarie Murray from County Clare, has been there for ten years working on public health projects in the slums.

The team of young Irish volunteers whom I befriended were highly dedicated. They worked as teachers in the children's homes, schools and crèches run by HOPE, as well as counsellors, social workers and sports coaches, among other things. They were resilient and professional, working tirelessly in this tough old city to help impoverished children and youths. Kolkata is one of the world's poorest cities, with new migrants pouring in every day to live on its streets and in its slums. Despite India's emerging wealth *on paper*, this has little impact on the poor who can barely survive in its chock-a-block cities. The experiences these volunteers have are unforgettable; they stay in their minds for life. They all say that they get back far more than they put in. It definitely enriches your life to witness with your own eyes just how hard life is for the majority of the world's population, and the survival strategies they are forced to adopt. It ensures that you never again take for granted even the small things that make life worthwhile: a warm bed to sleep in, a decent school to study in or a fair election to vote in. Appreciation of cultural difference is important, of course, but awareness of the gross injustices suffered by the majority of the global population takes you to a deeper level again. It gives you an active cosmopolitan outlook, which Ulrich Beck defines as 'an everyday, historically alert, reflexive awareness of ambivalences in a milieu of blurring differentiations and cultural contradictions.'[41]

This everyday reflexive awareness serves you well when tramping the highways and byways of other countries. The active cosmopolitan retains the curiosity of the toddler who keeps asking 'why?' The greatest legacy bequeathed to him or her is a profound sense of perspective. Home is never again taken for granted. Having returned from a poorer part of the world, your character has grown, you have become more patient, learning not to complain about small things. When you see *with your own eyes* what life is really like for the world's peasant farmers, child labourers, beggars, sex workers, rag pickers, rickshaw pullers and destitute mothers of hordes of children, who are powerless to control their fertility, our own lives look very lucky and wealthy in comparison. What seem like big problems turn out to be but minor inconveniences compared to the hardships endured by others. Also, when you endure some physical hardships when on the road – extreme hunger, thirst, heat, cold, exhaustion – your needs become very basic, and you are reminded of the simple humanity that transcends all ethnicities and classes: when on a long-distance bus in the middle of nowhere, everybody equally needs to eat and drink and pee and poo!

Cosmopolitan Politics

This humanistic perspective is a form of relating to others that is, in my opinion, more powerful and steadying than any form of spirituality. To have the clarity to really focus on the links with people in other localities in other parts of the world is worth striving for, worth *working at*. You can learn a lot just by hanging around and working on the language by chatting to local people. Once you find a local café or bar where you get known a little bit, you can take part in the daily rhythms of local life and observe how things work. This provides food for the brain and the soul, as well as food for the body. This is what geographer Doreen Massey terms 'a progressive sense of place.'[42] So this kind of active cosmopolitan world-view gives one a 'distanciated identity', or a wider perspective on local life, embracing 'a sense of what unites us as human beings, of common risks and possibilities, of mutual responsibilities.'[43] It is also an excellent foundation for the development of a meaningful political consciousness that transcends parochial concerns and petty power plays.

At the higher level of institutionalised politics, the principle of cosmopolitanism can be of great help in trying to improve the quality of democracy, because it means 'taking cultural diversity seriously'.[44] This requires a politics of inclusion where no minority feels excluded from decision-making. It means completely separating church and state and being guided by 'secular-humanist values'.[45] This spirit of inclusiveness has become more mainstream in Irish society in recent times, as, for example, it is no longer socially acceptable to use racist or sexist language in public now. It caused a huge public outcry when in May 2005, the Fianna Fáil Minister for State at the Department of Foreign Affairs, Conor Lenihan, called Turkish construction workers 'kebabs' in the Dáil. This was appallingly insensitive, considering that the people to whom he was referring were seriously-exploited workers, employed by GAMA to build roads here. He was forced to make a public apology. Positive attitudes toward intercultural relations and ethnic minorities have permeated the cultural and political spheres due to an increase in cosmopolitan values.[46]

The ruthless egalitarianism of environmental threats, in particular, makes it all the more crucial that what Beck terms 'a realist cosmopolitanism' guides our political actions.[47] Nuclear radiation and air or water pollution do not stop at international political boundaries, so ways have to be found to work together on such common threats. One finds that 'risks explode self-referential systems and national and international political agendas, overturning their priorities and producing practical interconnections among mutually indifferent or hostile parties or camps.'[48] So cosmopolitanism is not some vague notion that has no effect on real people's lives; in fact, it can have very real socio-political implications when taken seriously by 'the entrenchment of accessible and open public fora.'[49]

Four Active Cosmopolitans

At this point, I want to introduce four individuals whom I feel have dedicated their lives to being active cosmopolitans. This is a very personal selection, reflecting my own particular set of interests. They all have engaged actively with the wider world in different ways. Each of them has been unhampered by national boundaries and has shown a deep interest in and love for people in other places.

Maureen Forrest (b.1946) – Founder and Director of the Hope Foundation

The Hope Foundation, the Irish charity that works with the poor of Kolkata (formerly Calcutta), is the brainchild of Maureen Forrest. Even when she was a younger woman rearing her family of three children, she has always had an interest in global development issues. During the Ethiopian famine in the early 1980s, she started fundraising for GOAL. She says, 'famine was brought into our sitting rooms for the first time on television.'[50] She later went to work in the refugee camps in Somalia. She says, 'it was a horrendous place to be. You were dealing with gunfire every minute of the day.' She recalls one incident where her camp was shot at, and she remembers lying on the ground thinking, 'I don't want to die on my own in a foreign country.' It was hard on her family at home because they literally didn't know if she was dead or alive.

Over the years, Kolkata was always on her mind, which she attributes to the world-famous work of Mother Teresa among its poor. Kolkata, whose name has been synonymous in the Western mind with terrible Third World poverty, is a mass of contradictions. It was a vitally important port city that remained capital of the British Raj until 1911. During that period, it was second only to London throughout the British Empire. This city also views itself as the cultural capital of India and has been the home of three Nobel Prize winners. At the same time, many millions live cheek by jowl, enduring some of the harshest conditions on the face of this earth. It really has to be seen to be believed. The poorest among the locals, like the rag pickers and the beggars, endure lifetimes of humiliating and backbreaking work to earn less than €1 per day. It is like somebody has waged war on the poor: they are forced to the edge of the cliff of survival. The environmental conditions are also among the worst in the world. It is like the whole city has had a heart attack, with its veins clogged by pollution and garbage. This mixed bag is what makes it so horrendously fascinating: reeking of poverty and pollution, but also reeking of character.

It was into this setting that Maureen accompanied then Irish President Mary Robinson when she visited aid organisation GOAL's Kolkata projects in 1993. She was horrified – 'it's the scale of it.' She refers especially to the rickshaw pullers, who are 'treated as animals'. She compares it to the apartheid era in South Africa and asks, 'Can people not see the injustice all around them?' After her experiences in Africa, she viewed the slums of Kolkata as refugee camps, because many of the slum-dwellers in this city are the descendents of those who were displaced by Partition and the creation of Bangladesh. She asks, 'How can India be called a democracy? It suits the West to call it that because they want to trade with it. They choose to overlook big issues like the trafficking of children, child labour, children who go missing, dowry issues and child marriage.'

After her initial visit to Kolkata, she then decided to volunteer with GOAL, who funds local partner organisations there. She went initially for six weeks, where she met her colleague Geeta, whom she subsequently invited to work with her in HOPE. Together they set up schools in the slums, which taught Maureen that the key to the success of slum children's education was to involve the mothers in the education process as well.

After this, she then went to work in the emergency relief camps in Goma following the genocide in Rwanda in late 1994. It was absolutely horrific, with 350,000 people living in the camps, and many of them suffering from cholera. She also visited refugee camps in Swaziland on the border with Mozambique. All of this experience had a huge impact on her. Her experience of emergency relief taught her that she preferred the sense of continuity in development work, 'where you can see a child progress.'

Kolkata was still on her mind, so she returned in 1998 and started to set up an organisation along with Geeta. They tackled enormous legalities, with the initial goal of running a home for 25 children and raising IR£25,000 a year to run it. It snowballed into the size it is now, taking in over €2 million a year and employing a staff of almost 800 in its homes, schools, crèches, clinics and hospital. It therefore grew much bigger than anticipated. Maureen and Geeta learned that the way forward was to work closely with established partner organisations that have expertise in different areas.

Now in her sixties Maureen says that she might retire at 70, but, she insists, 'I don't worry about that; sure I'm still a young one!' She sees herself as part of an extended family, and she is helped hugely by her sister Jenny Browne, the Overseas Director who spends most of each year in Kolkata. They have affected the lives of about twenty-five thousand children in Kolkata, but the number could stretch to millions if you take into account Maureen's work on relief in Africa and in Gujarat and Tamil Nadu after the huge tsunami in 2004. HOPE is very committed to keeping its running costs down. Maureen takes no salary at all herself, and only occupies a room in the girls' home when in Kolkata. The conditions are basic, and she and her sister Jenny live right next to the rescued girls in adjacent rooms. I asked her if she would not think of getting an apartment in the city that would be more comfortable. Her answer was, 'No, I'd hate to move out; it would make me lose touch with the dynamic of the thing. My only concern is that we're using a room that children could be in.'

She sums up their modus operandi like this: 'It's all about trying to get as many children into education as possible, and as many women into work as possible.' There is a clear focus on addressing gender discrimination. She has found so often that in any one family the girl child is starved while the boy is fat and healthy. There is also a focus on educating mothers on their reproductive cycles, thereby contributing to women's empowerment. Education is the only way to achieve long-term success – coercion is not an option. So many of the women are illiterate that educating them can be difficult, so the organisation focuses on the use of condoms for contraception and HIV prevention, and tubal ligation for long-term contraception.

Keeping the funding coming in is the organisation's major priority, and the HOPE team are very imaginative in coming up with new ideas. Maureen has a doggedly-determined spirit: 'There's no such thing as a real *no*; there's always a way. There's always another source.' The organisation gets no direct grant aid from the Indian government, but their partners do, to various extents. She is thankful that they have not had to cut any projects like some other NGOs due to the recession, as she asks, 'Where would you start?' The organisation is targeting private Indian donors now as well, since there is now more wealth in the country than before.

India's economic growth is very impressive at the moment, but this growth is pointless and unjust unless attempts are made to ensure that everybody benefits from it. As the Nobel-Prize-winning son of Kolkata Amartya Sen reminds us, 'The basic point is that the impact of economic growth depends much on how the *fruits* of economic growth are used.'[51]

With improved access to health and education services, healthy, educated and confident citizens can therefore become agents of their own destinies, rather than waiting patiently for the next crumbs to fall from the rich men's tables.

Despite all its problems, Maureen says, 'I love Kolkata. I love the people: they're very cultured. And I love the children, of course.' She lets nothing get in her way to achieve her goals. While she could have stayed in her comfort zone, living the life of an ordinary Irish, middle-class homemaker, she chose instead to establish and run a charity in one of the poorest cities in the world. No border or bureaucratic red tape got in her way. As the quintessential active cosmopolitan, she pushed herself to do what she could for the children of Kolkata. This is now her new, expanded comfort zone, and she would not be happy without it, without a life that involves extraordinary stress as well as extraordinary satisfaction. Lots of Westerners go to places like Rishikesh in India, which is now called 'the yoga capital of the world.' They go there for the 'bells and smells' of self-indulgent alternative therapies in order to find inner peace. Instead, Maureen Forrest went to the heart of the teeming city of Kolkata, in order to make things better for some of the world's poorest citizens.

Martha Gellhorn (November 1908–February 1998) – War Correspondent

Martha Gellhorn was one of the foremost war correspondents of the twentieth century.[52] She left a privileged background and dedicated her life to bearing witness to global suffering and exposing the true horror of war. She lived, travelled and wrote throughout virtually the entire twentieth century, working right up until very shortly before her death in her eighty-ninth year.

Martha was born in St. Louis, Missouri of a well-to-do, liberal Jewish family. Her father was a gynaecologist and obstetrician, and her mother was an early suffragist and social reformer. She went to the elite Bryn Mawr College in Pennsylvania but left after two years. She started to get into journalism, writing in local papers, but found that she couldn't settle down. She felt bored and restless, so she left for New York in the winter of 1929. Shortly after, in spring 1930, she got on a ship for Paris. In those years, many British and American writers lived in Paris, including Ezra Pound, Gertrude Stein, F. Scott Fitzgerald and, of course, Ernest Hemingway, whose novel *The Sun Also Rises* had been published in 1926.

Martha dedicated the next couple of years to partying and travelling, before finally returning to the US in 1932. She went travelling across the US and did some reporting for a local paper. In this way, she honed her writing and reporting skills. She also got as far as Mexico, where she spoke to Diego Rivera as he painted his famous murals at the National Palace. She was always very adept at using any social connections she had to make her way around and gather stories. She then went back to Paris, where she worked at *Vogue* and, hence, had a very glamorous whirl of a social life. She also used her time there to write a novel. At this time, she also protested against the rise of Fascism and of Hitler's popularity in Europe.

In the autumn of 1934, Martha went to work for Eleanor Roosevelt, wife of President Franklin Roosevelt. In fact, the First Lady became a life-long close friend. This was the time of the Depression in the US, when its population suffered enormous poverty. As part of his 'New Deal' strategy, the President wanted to sct up a welfare scheme called the Federal Emergency Relief Administration to tackle this deprivation. Martha was hired as one of a team of researchers who were sent out into the rural areas on fact-finding missions to determine the real extent of this poverty and the needs of the people. She found widespread starvation and related diseases among the population. Around this time, her novel *The Trouble I've Seen* was published and met with very good reviews. She actually stayed at the White House at this time.

Martha had a lot of affairs with men throughout her life, but it was around this time that she met the man with whom she is most often publicly associated: Ernest Hemingway.[53] He was still married to his second wife, Pauline, at this time. The two had a lot in common, including a passionate hatred of Fascism, especially as it was manifesting itself in Spain. So she decided to go there to see for herself what was happening. In a letter to a friend, she said, 'Me, I am going to Spain with the boys. I don't know who the boys are, but I am going with them.' The Spanish Civil War attracted 40,000 people from all over the world to join the International Brigades in order to stop the onward march of Fascism.[54] It also attracted lots of writers, artists and poets, because Spain represented something positive to fight for that was lacking in their own worlds. Martha arrived at the northern border on foot with US$50 in her pocket and a knapsack full of tinned food. She got the train to Barcelona, from where she cadged lifts and made contacts. She got as far as Madrid and stayed at the same hotel as the other reporters. She met Robert Capa, the famous war photographer, who became like a brother to her until he was killed, years later, by a landmine in Vietnam.

Ernest Hemingway also stayed at this same hotel. He was widely regarded as the best writer on war at the time. He was a blustery, charismatic figure who always seemed to have supplies of luxury goods at his disposal. It was at this time that Martha became his lover. While Hemingway's journalism was composed of macho reports from the battlefields, Martha's forte was reporting on the everyday life and suffering of local people. She was 28, reporting on her first war for *Collier's* magazine. She found it impossible to be neutral in this and other wars and freely admitted that she didn't believe in 'all that objectivity shit'. She was in fact very much on the side of the republicans. She wrote: 'How can I explain that you feel safe at this war, knowing that the people around you are good people?' She and Hemingway returned to the US to raise money for the cause. She did a lecture tour of the US, raising awareness and support for the republic, before returning to Spain.

Years later, she wrote in *The Face of War*, 'All of us who believed in the Causa of the Republic will mourn the Republic's defeat and the death of its defenders, forever, and will continue to love the land of Spain and the beautiful people, who are among the noblest and unluckiest on earth.'

Following a period in which she did a lot of travelling and reporting throughout Europe, she followed Hemingway to Cuba at the end of 1938. They rented a house while he wrote *For Whom the Bell Tolls*. During this time, Martha went to

Finland to report for *Collier's* magazine on the Russian invasion of Helsinki. In November 1940 she married Hemingway,
which was promptly followed by a three-month 'honeymoon'
in China. She could have lived an elitist life of glamorous
parties, but she chose instead to continue her war reporting.
Her restlessness was evident in the fact that she went travelling in the Caribbean islands, where she got seriously ill with
dengue fever. She continued to live in Cuba with Hemingway
and a menagerie of animals. However, she was always writing,
working on novels and magazine pieces, as she was continu-
ally interested in the minutiae of people's lives. She then went
to London in 1943, which had been devastated after the Blitz.
She wrote about the British army, going to Algiers and Italy
with the soldiers. From this trip she wrote a letter to Hemingway saying, 'I'll never see enough as long as I live.' After this
she returned to Cuba. She found that she was very unhappy
on her return, so the relationship with Hemingway ended.

She then found herself in London again. On 6 June 1944,
subsequently known as D-Day, she discovered that she was
being sidelined in favour of male reporters to cover the invasion of France by the Allied troops. Her way of handling
this was to bluff her way onto a hospital ship that landed at
Omaha Beach. She helped with casualties on landing there and
wrote a very affecting piece on her experience. She always
turned being a woman to her advantage, using the assets of
her good looks, as well as her courage and her blatant disre-
gard for authority. She spent time with Allied soldiers in Italy
and flew with the US air force on a mission over Germany.
She was always interviewing people in order to get human-
interest stories. It was during this time that her divorce from
Hemingway was finalised.

A major turning point in her life came when she went to
Dachau concentration camp a few days after it was liberated

by Allied troops. She was driven to actively bear witness to the darkest corners of her world. She wrote: 'I look at anything, you see, because I do not admit that one can turn away: one has no right to ignorance, one has no right to spare oneself.' Dachau tested her principles: thirty-three thousand people had been there for up to twelve years. She interviewed the Nazi camp doctors who had carried out the unspeakable 'experiments' on the inmates. Her journalism remains a crucially important record of that terrible time and place. She felt very guilty that the Allied forces were so slow to act, as well as a sense of personal guilt that she herself had done nothing to expose it. She was actually in Dachau when she heard that the German Army had surrendered to the Allies. She wrote: 'Dachau seemed to me the most suitable place in Europe to hear the news of victory. For surely this war was made to abolish Dachau, and all the other places like Dachau, and everything that Dachau stood for, and to abolish it forever.' She went to Belsen camp as well. In subsequent years, she never showed any sympathy for any German citizen, despite the fact that their cities were flattened by the Allies. She later attended the Nuremburg Trial and described each of the infamous Nazi officers. She said of Goering that his 'terrible mouth wore a smile that was not a smile, but only a habit his lips had taken.' Keitel was 'nothing, a granite bust badly made of inferior stone.'

Deeply disturbed by what she witnessed in wartime Europe, Martha moved to Mexico, where she rented a house. She enjoyed her time there, but there remained an emotional gap in her life. In 1949 she went to Naples to adopt a child from an orphanage she had visited there during the war. She brought home a beautiful baby boy, whom she named Sandy. When Martha decided she wanted something, she let nothing stand in her way and was completely undaunted by obstacles of any kind.

Later that year she visited Israel, where she enjoyed the spirit of the fledgling state. She said, 'Israel is a model of sanity among the nations, and no more aggressive than Denmark.' She was very pro-Israeli throughout her life, and was totally indifferent to the plight of the Palestinians who had been displaced in their own country. Perhaps everybody has at least one blind spot, and this was a very serious one in her case. She in fact took a very anti-Arab stance, comparing them to Germans, which was not a compliment from her perspective.

In the early 1950s she moved to London. She married her second husband, Tom Mathews, in 1954. Throughout the 1950s she lived a sedate life in London, where she wrote novels and short stories. However, all throughout her life she dreaded boredom more than anything. She discovered Africa in 1961. This was a new chapter in her life, and she returned there often. She declared Africa 'the capital of my soul'. Kenya was her favourite country. She travelled a lot in Africa, becoming interested in wildlife and environmental issues. No matter how rough the travel was, she didn't mind very much, because at least she wasn't bored. She said that the open road was her 'first, oldest and strongest love'. In 1963, she discovered that her husband was having an affair, so she promptly divorced him and bought a house in Kenya.

Over the years, Martha was becoming more and more critical of US politics. In the 1950s, McCarthyism and the resulting communist witch-hunts had horrified her. Of course, the CIA kept a file on her as a communist. She was deeply upset by John F. Kennedy's assassination. This was the second big turning point in her life after Dachau. She found herself increasingly pessimistic about political change. The Vietnam War incensed her, so in the summer of 1966 she went there to cover it, at the age of 58. She strongly disapproved of US intervention in the region and said that they displayed 'natural Fascism'. She felt it her duty to bear witness to the suffering of civilians, so she visited refugee camps, hospitals and orphanages. She was concerned especially with the effects of the war on the local children. She was horrified by the use of napalm. It worked, she noted, because it was jellied gasoline, and the jelly stuck to the flesh while the gasoline burned. She also described that white phosphorus gnawed at the flesh like rat's teeth. She wrote a major series of articles for *The Manchester Guardian*, as none of the US papers would take her work due to its critical stance. Following the publication of these articles the South Vietnamese Government refused her a visa to make return visits. She continued to rail against the war in whatever ways she could. She said that 'it left a stone on her heart'.

In her older years, she lived in a flat in London and a country cottage in Wales. She continued to travel and do some reporting. In the 1980s she wrote about US intervention in Central America: El Salvador, Nicaragua and, later, Panama. She hated Reagan's personal vendetta against the poor of Central America. She wrote: 'Combined with economic blockade, the undeclared war by proxy is punishing the poor people of Nicaragua whose only crime is their will to be free in their own land, and free of gringos.'

At the age of 80, she befriended younger writers and journalists like John Pilger, Rosie Boycott, Nicholas Shakespeare, John Simpson and Jon Snow. She would have social evenings at her flat where they would discuss politics and argue into the wee hours. At the age of 85 she took a trip to the city of Salvador in Brazil to write about street children being killed by murder squads. The result was published in the *London Review of Books*. This was her last big piece of investigative reporting.

In her elderly years her biggest problem was the rapid decline of her eyesight. This meant that she couldn't read and write, her two great passions. In February 1998 she decided to die. She somehow got hold of a 'bye bye pill' and thereby took control of her own death. She asked for her ashes to be scattered on the out-going tide of the Thames, 'for my last travels'.

Martha Gellhorn was the consummate active cosmopolitan. She was a true citizen of the world, challenging herself physically and emotionally to report from places where most people did not want to go. She felt a strong empathy with people who were from completely different backgrounds to herself and exhibited a deep humanitarian ethos. She let nothing stop her in her endeavour to educate people as to what life was really like for the inhabitants of the world's trouble spots. She developed a wide-ranging cultural competence as she travelled and also lived in many different countries. She once wrote, 'who said, "I think, therefore I am"? Descartes? I think it wrong. I act, therefore I am. We must be the product and sum total of our actions.'

Alan Lomax (January 1915–July 2002) – Song Collector and Folklorist

Texas-born Alan Lomax was a colossus of the music world.[55] He was best known as a song collector, but he was also a world famous folklorist, musicologist, archivist, singer, DJ, filmmaker, photographer, writer, radio and TV producer, and concert promoter. Without him, we might never have heard of Lead Belly, Woody Guthrie, Muddy Waters or Jelly Roll Morton. He dedicated his life to bringing the music of African American people to a wider audience and promoting the appreciation of cultural diversity. It is difficult to know where to start on relating where his influence ends, but we do know where it started – with his father.

Alan's father, John Lomax, was a song collector himself. He lectured in English in Texas, but went on to study further at Harvard, where he initiated a study of cowboy ballads. He combined lecturing and song collecting on his tours across the country. He became known as quite a character on the academic circuit, as he would happily break into song to illustrate his talks on folk music and culture.

Alan, born in 1915, was pushed very hard by his father to achieve well in school. He was an excellent student, but he was put under enormous pressure, which often manifested itself in physical illness. He went to university in Austin, which was near his home. There, he was drawn to black people's music, hanging out at their clubs to hear live musicians. He went to Harvard the following year, but a combination of forces brought him back home after a short time. His father lost his job, so money was tight. Alan's health was not strong, and, as well as this, he discovered Communist politics and got himself arrested at a protest in Boston. The combination of these factors meant that his early college career was doomed. Back in Texas, he convinced his father, John, that he should revert to touring again, with Alan as his driver and assistant. John secured a contract for a book on folk song, and in 1931, on the back of the publisher's advance, embarked upon a tour across the US with his two sons, Alan and John Junior. Conditions were basic, and accommodation was usually in the form of a tent.

In the summer of 1932, with sponsorship from the Library of Congress, John and Alan toured right across the Southern states, recording singers with a huge, cumbersome voice recorder. One of the first people they recorded was an old black washerwoman, who gave Alan his first epiphany. He wrote: 'The voice of the skinny little black woman was as full of the shakes and quavers as a Southern river is full of bends and bayous.'

Alan and his father visited plantations to record black workers. On one occasion, a worker made up a song about their tough working conditions, so Alan soon realised how political song collecting could be. They discovered the importance of work songs when they recorded sawmill workers and also attended black Sunday services to hear the spiritual music. They also went to prisons, which they thought to be important cultural enclaves of pure black music, uncorrupted by outside influences. They wanted to reveal the creativity that languished behind those prison bars. The prison wardens were often suspicious of them, and they frequently had to cajole and name-drop their way inside.

At one prison in Louisiana, called Angola, they met a prisoner called Huddie Ledbetter, or Lead Belly, who played the 12-string guitar. He had written a song called 'Goodnight Irene' that was later to become a global classic. At a prison farm called Parchman Farm, one of the prisoners who was picking cotton there treated them to their first airing of 'The Midnight Special'. Alan said, 'the people who sang for us were in stripes and there were guards there with shotguns. They were singing there under the red-hot sun of Texas, people obviously in enormous trouble. But when they opened their mouths, out came this flame of beauty. This sound matched anything I'd ever heard from Beethoven, Brahms or Dvořak.' These were the songs and stories of ordinary working people and the poor and the down-and-out. However, John was reflexive about their own role when he said, 'Worse than thieves are ballad collectors, for when they capture and imprison in cold type a folk song, at the same time they kill it.'

John started to consult with social scientists and convinced the Library of Congress to let him work for free, gathering and collating folk songs. He published his book, *American Ballads and Folk Songs*, and went on a book tour to promote it. In this way he met with academics like Charles Seeger, father of well-known folk singer Pete Seeger. He also met Mary Barnicle, a professor of English at NYU and a leftist feminist scholar who was to become a research collaborator later on. John and Alan also met Zora Neale Hurston, who was the only black person they knew who was a trained folklorist.

John hired Lead Belly as his driver on his release from jail. On his tours, John would perform on stage along with Lead Belly, who had no compunction about passing around a hat to collect some money, even at the most elite black-tie university dinners. Alan was to write the first ever singer biography on Lead Belly, followed by a radio programme on him. Once, while in Washington DC, the men couldn't find a hotel that would take them both together, because of racial segregation. Lead Belly's response was to write the famous song 'Bourgeois Blues'.

At the ripe old age of 20, Alan went on a collecting tour of the Southern states with Barnicle and Hurston. They got themselves arrested, as they made a suspicious looking trio in the 1930s South. On this trip they recorded the famous folk song 'John Henry' for the first time. This trip also took them to the Bahamas to record music there. Alan then got a job as a clerk at the Archive of American Folk Song in the Library of Congress. While the salary was very low, it bought him some status in academic and political circles.

At this time, under Roosevelt's New Deal strategy, the time was right for celebrating the creativity of ordinary people. Both the President and his wife, Eleanor, were personally very interested in folk music. Alan attempted to record music all over the country. It was very tough going, travelling in very isolated areas to find America's 'homemade music'. He had to take time to befriend people before they would trust him enough to sing for him. He wanted 'the songs of the forgotten people of modernity, the music of those at the bottom of the greased pole of life.' Later, he got to perform at the White House. However, because he was suspected to be a communist by the FBI, the security staff frisked him and kept a close eye on him for the evening. In fact, the FBI investigated him and kept his file open for 30 years.

He started graduate classes in anthropology at Columbia University in New York at the age of 23. During this time, he was constantly performing and scouting for music as well as studying. He joined a group whose goal it was to raise funds for the Spanish Republic in 1937, so perhaps he crossed paths with Gellhorn and Hemingway too! He negotiated with two record companies, Columbia and RCA, to make folk recordings. He hired his sister Bess and Pete Seeger to help him in his task.[56] They had to sift through existing recordings, listen to them all, catalogue them and decide which ones were the best. His influence was growing, and he was asked to do a major series on radio to educate children on folk music.

He met Jelly Roll Morton in Washington DC, a singer and pianist who was the originator of jazz, stomps and swing. Alan recorded his music, as well as his autobiography. Morton was eloquent on the importance of jazz music and its origins in the multicultural mix of New Orleans. Jazz was 'a cosmopolitan musical argot'.

Another major musical figure discovered by Alan was Woody Guthrie. His performances were like a 'country opera', inventing a whole 'new idiom'. Alan saw him as a self-made intellectual with enormous promise. Alan recorded his oral history, as well as hundreds of songs. They planned a book called *Hard Hitting Songs for Hard-Hit People*, but no publisher would take it until 1967. However, Alan got a recording contract for Woody at RCA to make an album called *Dust Bowl Ballads*. At this time, he also produced an album of Lead Belly singing prison songs.

Alan was asked to participate in a major research project on black music in the South. It was to be on the musicology and sociology of black music in the Mississippi Delta region. This showed how seriously Alan's work was taken in academic circles. He also devised a radio programme on the Tennessee Valley Authority (TVA), an ambitious New Deal develop-ment project. His remit was to record how local people felt about the effects of the dams built for hydroelectricity and the new agricultural methods introduced. As he travelled for this project, he met with a guitar-playing, barefoot cotton plantation worker in raggedy overalls who went by the name of Muddy Waters. His music, the blues, was an artful response to pain, suffering and oppression whose roots were in Africa. Unsurprisingly, the local police often harassed Alan as he made his way through the South. Undaunted, he recorded the music of many types of people, from children and old ladies to cowboys and prisoners.

He had to enlist in the army in 1944, but even during that time he never stopped recording. The army was still segre-gated at that time, and he recorded the chants of black troops while they were doing drills. This was such a success that the songs were taught to white troops to make them run faster and train harder. Alan was not reticent about publicising his views on prison reform and civil rights for blacks. Some artists were afraid of the political repercussions of this, but Alan never was. It was impossible to separate the music from the context when the songs were about 'the tribulations, humilia-tions, and absurdities of black life in the South, of chain gangs, lynchings, being tracked by dogs, but also of the pleasures and violence of jukes and barrelhouses, and of the blues as a medium of stories, a record of a way of life, a source of joy and an escape from pain.'

In 1950, Alan drew up an audacious plan with Columbia records to produce 30 LPs (long-playing records), which was to be entitled *The World Library of Folk and Primitive Music*. This was an enormous project. The company provided just the recording equipment, while Alan had to foot the rest of the expenses himself, because of his lack of institutional support. So he became a 'one-man foundation'. This was to lead to his spending eight years in Europe, collecting music, making radio programmes and producing albums. His initial base in Paris didn't yield much for him, but he had better luck in London, where some people at the BBC were very interested in his work. His first collecting trip was to Ireland. He whizzed around the country in six weeks, collecting enough for an album. Seamus Ennis was his guide in this risky endeavour, recording the likes of Elizabeth Cronin in Ballymakeera, County Cork and Mickey Doherty, the Donegal fiddler. In England, he recorded Ewan MacColl, among others, and in Scotland, he was fascinated especially with the rhythmic songs of the tweed workers on the Isle of Lewis. He saw strong parallels here with African American music. In Spain, he spent seven months recording, producing 45 hours of music, which was whittled down to enough for eleven brilliant albums. He absolutely loved Spain, but the Guardia Civil constantly followed him while there, 'like black buzzards, carrying with them the stink of fear.' He then spent ten months in Italy, where he was robbed several times and threatened by local mafiosi. All this time, he worked very hard, living in cheap fleapits and scrounging for money all the time.

Back in England in 1954 he found that skiffle music had burst onto the scene, an English musical movement parallel to rockabilly in the US. Lonnie Donegan was a pivotal figure of the movement, going on to influence Van Morrison, John Lennon and Mick Jagger's early musical efforts. When Alan returned to the US in 1958, he found that rock and roll had revolutionised the music scene. While he loved that this was happening, he worried that music was straying too far from its roots in the blues, and that, broadly speaking, white people were stealing black people's music. He then embarked upon a new collecting trip in the South, where he found folk music 'with the bark still on it'. This led to a series of seven albums, issued in 1961. One of the most important artists he found on this trip was the now legendary Mississippi Fred McDowell. At this point, he wanted to return to some academic research, to develop an idea he was working on. This was called 'cantometrics', the study of comparative musical styles. He was made a Research Associate at Columbia University, an honorary position he would hold for 27 years.

When the civil rights revolution took off in sixties America, Alan decided that he wanted to contribute to the black people's struggle by making documentaries and radio programmes on black music and culture. His radio series *The Black Encyclopaedia of the Air* was an African American cultural history, made with the intention of portraying black culture in a positive light. He also co-edited an anthology of African American poetry to this end. He felt that 'the country's internal crisis lay in some form of multicultural awareness, a process of making all peoples aware of their histories, and creating pride in what America had achieved with its cultural mix.' These kind of utopian goals kept him going.

Over the years, there were always new book, radio and recording projects simmering away either in his mind or in reality. His life was a constant flow of ideas and quests for the money to make them happen. In 1978, he took another trip to the South to record a documentary series for the

Public Broadcasting Service (PBS) called *The Land Where the Blues Began*. This was very successful and won him accolades and awards. Later on, in 1993, an accompanying book was published of the same title. It exposed the uncomfortable truth about the extent of the racism that existed in the South in the 1930s and 1940s. It won the National Book Critics Circle Award in 1993. In 1986, President Reagan presented Alan with the prestigious award of the National Medal of the Arts. In the same year, ironically, his income was only US$11,500. After all his work and achievements, he was actually ranked among America's poor.

In the late 1980s he came up with a huge idea: to transfer all of his enormous collection of folk recordings onto digital media. He could see, well before the development of the Internet, how important this was to become. This goal, which he called the 'Global Jukebox', was a utopian one, but, at the age of 76, he managed to secure a huge grant of US$1 million to achieve it. However, he was now becoming elderly and unwell. He had surgery on his carotid artery in 1995, after which he had a stroke. He was poor and unable to cope, so his daughter moved him to Florida to live with her. The 'poet laureate of the folk' died in July 2002 at the age of 87.

Alan Lomax lived life on the edge. He was always short of money, as he was never part of any institution. The singers he recorded often asked him for money, and he always found a way to pay them. He spent a huge amount of time chasing research grants. He was constantly coming up with new schemes to spread the interest in folk music. He was at the coalface of cultural creativity, constantly dreaming up new ideas like books, radio programmes, popular theatre, music festivals, concerts and academic symposia. He was always interested in the links between music, culture and social structures, yet he was always on the periphery of the academy. He never showed deference to those in universities, behaving the same no matter who his audience was. Nevertheless, he was very much respected among music scholars, despite his lack of formal training in any field.

Alan lived the life of the true active cosmopolitan. While much of his work was conducted within the one country, the US, his goal was largely to introduce blacks to whites, the South to the North. In such a socially-segregated country, these cultures were very separate, and mainstream white culture had marginalised black culture to a huge extent. He was driven by his love for music and a desire to bring the sad beauty of the blues and the exuberance of jazz to a wider audience, into the heart of mainstream American culture. He didn't separate culture from politics and economics, however, and never minded nailing his political colours to the mast. He brought this enthusiasm to the highways and byways of Europe as well, recording the music of Irish Travellers, Spanish Gypsies and Scottish women workers, among others. He truly belonged to a global family of musicians, making links between disparate types of people in different places. His cultural competence and his boundless energy drove him to unmask the origins of musical styles across the world.

He began his work in Texas, where he was from, but, in true active cosmopolitan style, he crossed racial barriers to reach out to the most oppressed people in his own midst, in the fields and prisons that most white people preferred not to think about. Even today, almost 100 years later, this would still be an enormously radical idea.

Dervla Murphy (b.1931) – Travel Writer

Certain words are over-used these days. Words like 'heroic' and 'legend' are often used to describe people who have done 'awesome' things of 'epic' proportions. While these words are often used to describe people who were good at kicking a football around a field or playing the violin well, it is justifiable to use all of these epithets to describe Dervla Murphy. This woman takes her place in the pantheon of brave women travellers like Freya Stark and Isabella Bird. She has served as a heroic role model to generations of people interested in world travel. This is especially the case for those of us who are Irish and female. She was one of our own, and if she could do it, maybe we could try it too.

Like many other readers, I have been reading Dervla's books since I was a teenager, taking me out of the small world in my head and introducing me to the possibility of a bigger one. Paul Theroux recently called her 'a national treasure' on Irish TV. This is no exaggeration. She never sets out with a particular agenda, preferring to believe what her own eyes tell her. One journalist said that she is:

> ... not exactly politicised – Dervla has never given allegiance to any particular party, or for that matter, country, seeing herself as a *citizen of the world* – but she came to feel that it was the duty of writers to enter into the lives of those they portray – 'to sleep on their floors', as she puts it.[57]

Perhaps this observation is now obselete, as Dervla has become a strong supporter of the Palestinian cause, more of which later.

When most of us consult a world map, we might be able to point to certain places to which we have flown. Dervla Murphy, however, would not point to particular spots, but to the land route she took to get there. She will have made friends along the way, and she would know the details of the terrain, the cultural mores and how much a beer costs in each place on the route. While she has known many such routes throughout the world, her *roots* are in Lismore, County Waterford. Literature featured strongly in her household, and her parents always encouraged her love of reading and writing. She recalls, 'at Christmas or their birthdays they'd ask me for a short story or an essay I had written for a present.'[58] She has written many, many stories since then, with 24 books to her name at last count.[59] Her personal history (or herstory) is well known, with many journalists having interviewed her. I will thus omit details that are already in the public realm. It is also beyond the remit of this exercise to detail all of her many trips, which are already recounted in her books. Any short piece is bound to be incomplete, so I will focus upon those aspects of her character that illustrate her active cosmopolitanism.

It was from Lismore that she set out for her first major trip in January 1963, to cycle to India. The word 'major' means that it was her first trip outside of Europe and the first one she wrote about. She had taken several cycling trips throughout Europe before that, during the years in which she was caring for her elderly parents. After their demise, she set off. She has said that the feeling of liberty she experienced then ran through her body like an electric shock. This is a woman 'to whom freedom of the spirit is as vital as physical freedom.'[60] That winter was a historically cold and snowy one that made cycling next to impossible in places, but nothing could stop this woman. It was a trip that was to take six months, followed by a six-month stint volunteering in an orphanage.

The book of this journey, *Full Tilt*, is often as alarming as it is entertaining. She famously carried a loaded .25 automatic pistol with her, which she had to use to shoot two wolves that threatened to maul her in Eastern Europe. The European leg of this journey comprises only the introduction to this book, with the 'proper trip' starting in Iran. In this first section, we see a near fatal car crash, the aforementioned wolves incident and an attempted rape by a policeman in some godforsaken border outpost. She loved the landscape and people of Afghanistan, with one of the highlights being the giant, 120-foot-high statues of Buddha at Bamian. She must have been horrified and heart-broken when the Taliban blew them up in 2001, particularly as she feels some affinity with the values of Buddhism. Though still fresh, the occasional, amusingly-dated phrase reminds us of the fact that it was written almost fifty years ago: a goat is described as 'nigger-brown', a town is 'very gay', and she felt she needed a 'ciné-camera' to record her trip. When she finished writing *Full Tilt* she hand-delivered the manuscript to her London publisher, having cycled there from her home in Lismore.

Her travels have taken her across land to India, Nepal, Tibet, the Himalayas, Cuba, Siberia, the Russian Far East, the Balkans, Transylvania, Laos, Rwanda, South Africa, Kenya, Zimbabwe, Cameroon, Ethiopia, Madagascar and Peru. It is obviously impossible to recount details of all of these trips here. Suffice it to say that they all have involved extreme physical endurance tests, through searing deserts and snow-covered mountain passes. She usually travels on her bicycle, but sometimes also on mules, as in Ethiopia and in Peru. She took her daughter, Rachel, with her on some of her trips, against the advice of friends. She takes enormous risks with her personal safety that most of us would never dream of. She is incredibly positive, brave and fearless, tackling the world with gusto. However, she denies this characterisation vehemently, saying that fear is for 'when something *actually* happens' rather than 'being afraid that something *might* happen. That's the difference.'[61]

One of the rare occasions that she admitted to feeling fearful was in her own country – in Belfast in the 1970s. She was, quite sensibly, afraid to cycle through the Antrim Road area at 1.30 a.m. Journalists often ask her what her scariest moment has been on her travels, and she always answers that it was when Shiftas (bandits) in Ethiopia robbed her. They could have drowned her in a river, but they just took everything and left her behind.[62] She deals with crises and disasters with rock-solid common sense and jaunty good humour. She has endured illnesses like hepatitis and dysentery and injuries like broken ribs and scorpion bites. Taking a picture once in Rwanda led her to receive a smack around the head from a random passerby that left her neck sore and her ears ringing.

Her books always also describe the physical environment of each place, the relevant elements of societies and cultures, and are peppered with stories of hazardous journeys on every form of transport imaginable, but most of the time on her trusty bicycle. She always researches the social, historical and political context of the countries to which she goes, evidenced in the substantial bibliographies her books contain.

She has also published books on places closer to home, in Ireland and England. Her book on Northern Ireland, *A Place Apart*, attempts to get under the skin of a region that was disowned by most of those who lived south of the Border at the height of the Troubles. One of her books that I found most interesting was in fact *Tales From Two Cities*, in which she deals with race relations in northern English cities. She stayed in flats in Manningham in Bradford and Handsworth in Birmingham for about three months each. Research of this magnitude could easily earn her a PhD if she was so inclined. Indeed, lots of academics have built careers on a lot less. The former area is predominantly South Asian and the latter predominantly black. She tiptoes lightly between ethnography, sociology and journalism in this work, but she just says that she is interested in people's perceptions, how they feel and why. She is unhampered by academic disciplinary divides and is blissfully unconcerned with what academics and critics think of her work. This book is interesting because she chose to apply her cultural competence and cosmopolitan values in an area close to home, to try to understand what causes trouble in these areas between people of different ethnicities. In both areas, she spoke to everyone who would speak to her, drinking in local bars and visiting people's homes. She faithfully recounts the details of these conversations, or 'chat-shows', as she calls them. In a Birmingham pub, she was seriously harassed by Rastafarian youths who were suspicious of her motives. She refused to back down from their intimidation, however. She won their favour by producing a copy of her book on Ethiopia, which showed a picture of her with Haile Selassie's granddaughter. Her connection with their god had a serious impact. She was also caught up in riots in this area during her time there in 1985.

The website set up on Dervla by her current publisher, Eland, runs a tagline on its front page saying that she is 'that rare traveller who can make the world seem both wider and more intimate.' This apparent intimacy arises out of her strong sense of empathy with her fellow women and men. In her dealings with people, she is openhearted, sympathetic and completely unconcerned with social status. She sees straight through to the essence of the person, whether a mother, a miner or a maharaja. She apparently has an enormous talent for listening. A South African friend commented, 'when Dervla listens to you, you open up about aspects of your world that nobody else even thinks to enquire about.'[63] She is always tuned into life as seen through local women's eyes. In Afghanistan in the early 1960s, she observed, 'two women were travelling on the roof [of the bus] amidst everyone's goods and chattels – very symbolic!'

She is not shy to have opinions that might be unpopular in some circles. She noted, for example, how Cuba was generous in sending medical aid to New Orleans after Hurricane Katrina, in the very same country that has maintained a punishing embargo against it for so long. Also, she noted how women had much more freedom in Afghanistan under the Soviets and in Iraq under Saddam than in any subsequent regimes.[64] She also visited Three Mile Island in Pennsylvania, the site of a power plant that had a partial nuclear meltdown in 1979, after which she wrote a book about the dangers of nuclear power. Home in Ireland, she has published her opinions on Northern Irish politics and the Peace Process as well. She also visited Rwanda not long after the horrible genocide of 1994. At the end of this trip, she said, 'Rwanda has been a scary experience. Not because of the tiresome security problems but because it forces one to confront the evil inherent in us all, as human beings – however humane and compassionate we may seem as *untested* individuals … nothing done by humans is inhuman.'[65] [Emphasis added.]

Dervla's most recent book is on Palestine and Gaza.[66] She lived in Balata Camp, a refugee camp near the city of Nablus in the West Bank, for three months in 2009, as well as spending time in Israel. Remember, she did this at the age of 78. She took several trips to the region, staying in Gaza for a month at one point, in summer 2011. She says of Gaza:

I found the conditions are unbelievable – 27 miles by 8 miles of land to accommodate 1.5 million people. It is an open-air prison. These people have no freedom, no work, no possibility of setting up industry because they are not allowed to export.[67]

In February 2012, she wrote an open letter to the Irish President, Michael D. Higgins, which was published in *The Irish*

Examiner. In it, she beseeches him not to make an official visit to Israel, because 'you would be signalling to all the world that this country approves of a truly vicious regime.' In the letter she also quotes historian Tony Judt, some of whose family had been killed in Auschwitz, who said, before his own premature death, 'Europe can't live indefinitely on the credit of someone else's crimes to justify a state that creates and commits its own crimes … Israel should not be special because it is Jewish.'[68]

One of her constant bugbears is how young travellers these days are constantly in touch with loved ones at home via social media, staring into computer screens in Internet cafés for longer than they actually participate in local life. Over-reliance on this connection means that one is never truly *away*, alone with oneself, *testing* oneself out there in the world. Eschewing these links is just one of the pieces of advice she gives in a piece in *The Guardian* in 2009. These are her top ten tips to travellers:[69]

1. Choose your country, use guidebooks to identify the areas most frequented by foreigners – and then go in the opposite direction.
2. Mug up on history.
3. Travel alone, or with just one prepubescent child.
4. Don't overplan.
5. Be self-propelling: walk or cycle.
6. If assisted by a pack animal, take detailed local advice about the terrain ahead.
7. Cyberspace intercourse vitiates genuine escapism.
8. Don't be inhibited by the language barrier.
9. Be cautious – cautious as distinct from timid.
10. Invest in the best-available maps.

Now over 80 years of age, she shows no sign of stopping travelling and writing any time soon. She says that the major disadvantage of ageing is that she can no longer carry a rucksack and has to resort to what she sees as a very uncool wheelie suitcase. However, this, she feels, is offset by the major advantage of needing so much less sleep, which thereby adds several hours to her day.[70]

Dervla Murphy has achieved phenomenal things throughout her life, but she is famously straightforward, modest and self-deprecating. It appears that what drives her on is her active cosmopolitanism. She has always been globalised – this is nothing new to her. She is not, to my knowledge, a polyglot at home in many language fields. However, she doesn't let this stop her going wherever she pleases. She is insatiably curious about the world she lives in and wants to contribute to people's understanding of each other. She has a nose for injustice too, as we see in her recent public affinity with the cause of the Palestinians. She is, however, always willing to listen to different perspectives, to grasp the complexities of social life. She is empathetic enough to walk a mile in someone else's shoes, to try to see how they see the world. She says, 'if I am to be remembered, I'd like to be remembered as someone who was interested in the ordinary people of whatever country I was in.'[71]

Conclusion

The above discussion of cosmopolitanism and glimpses into the lives of some of the world's most inspiring active cosmopolitans serves to illustrate one worthwhile way of engaging with the world around us. There is currently a palpable sense among people that social life is beyond their control and that popular culture is undermining their sense of distinctiveness.

If one cultivates an active cosmopolitan outlook, however, this is a means of taking the reins, retaining control over our own life experiences. A crucial point is that the active cosmopolitan *seeks out* the distinctiveness of local cultures, so local cultural guardians perform a huge service in working at maintaining these. This is to say that 'there can be no cosmopolitans without locals.'[72] In this way, we can be very aware of what is unique in each place, in the light of comparison with others. This includes one's *own* place. We can also be comfortable with social change if we adopt what Doreen Massey terms 'an extroverted notion of the identity of place, an internationalist constitution of the local place and its particularity.'[73] We can thereby really appreciate and actually celebrate the similarities and differences between disparate groups of people. When we sneak backstage in other people's lives, it gives us a great sense of perspective on the value of cultural uniqueness. This also means that we can make learning a life-long process, rather than something associated with limited formal schooling.

Conclusion

On St. Patrick's weekend, in March 2012, the dead body of a 62-year-old English man was found in his house on a busy main street in the centre of Wexford town. He had been dead since the previous Christmas, a period of almost three months. A woman walking by noticed the fairy lights on the Christmas tree still flashing and thought something might be wrong. This incident has led to speculation as to how this could happen with people walking past his door all the time. It would, perhaps, be less surprising if he were living in an isolated rural location. Ironically, his house was across the street from a Franciscan friary.

Was it because he was a 'blow-in' to the area that nobody cared about him? After the discovery of his body, statements were issued from agencies dealing with elderly and vulnerable people: 'This sad incident must act as a wake up call for every community,' Age Action spokesman Eamon Timmins said. He continued:

> With more than a quarter of older people in Ireland living alone, and loneliness being one of the greatest problems facing many older people, communities have to be vigilant, they have to make special efforts to involve older people in community activities and to remain in regular contact with them.[1]

Seán Moynihan, CEO of ALONE, commented, 'we urge the public to ensure that they check on older people in the community at all times of year, not just during cold weather or Christmas time.' He added, 'We are very aware of the isolation of older persons as a continuing problem for our society … every week our Befriending Service volunteers visit 200 older people who would otherwise have little or no regular social contact.'[2]

The sad incident of this man's death has led people to wonder: has our sense of community become so degraded that nobody thought to check on this man for almost three months? It makes us wonder if it could happen in the places where we live and whether we would be the one to notice the disappearance of a neighbour. It is reminiscent of stories we used to hear in the 1970s and 1980s about big cities like London and New York, where there was alleged to be no sense of community or connection with other people. The irony of being found in such a state on the weekend that people are literally parading their Irishness hardly needs to be raised.

This case has taught us quite a bit about ourselves: we are reluctant to get involved in the lives of strangers, and we often live lives that are primarily focussed upon ourselves and a narrow circle of family and friends. Life has become more atomised and regulated than it was in the past – less random and more organised. This is not exactly the same as saying that there has been a decline in community values – I do not really believe this to be the case in any simple way. Firstly, I think that we always romanticise the past, just like people always say that the summers were better when they were young. It seems that we only remember the good ones. We also narrowly associate an idealised construction of community with rural life, which we assume to be undermined by urbanisation. As I have already discussed in Chapter 2, I feel this to be mistaken and wrong-headed.

Secondly, I think that we designate community functions more formally now. If we see somebody who is in trouble, we would be more likely to contact the police or the relevant voluntary organisation, rather than to take it on ourselves. We may fear the implications of our actions, with potential negative consequences of litigation or even violence. For example, if a woman is grieving after her husband dies, she is perhaps more likely to gain solace from a bereavement counselling group, rather than from neighbours popping in for a chat. Or if we want to find a good plumber, we are more likely to Google the request rather than ask the barman in the local pub.

As stated, the functions that we associate with a romantic vision of community are often now delegated to formal organisational structures, whether voluntary groups or state agencies. This might sound negative, but at least these bodies exist now, whereas they didn't in the past. And, realistically, people might actually get better quality help from such bodies than they would from a sympathetic neighbour, because these bodies know exactly what they are doing.

Our attachments to people and places need to be demystified and thought out carefully. We live complex lives, where the reality of community life often does not match the ideal in our heads. Our attempts to feel content and 'at home' are often challenging. We need to try to be comfortable with change, difference and impermanence. This 'does not equal the footloose cosmopolitan dream – it is the daily reality of an ever-growing group of grounded people living their home feelings "lightly".'[3] This is why I feel that an active cosmopolitan stance can strengthen our position. It can enable us to connect as human beings with relative strangers. It can help us forge a sense of empathy with the life experiences of people who might look very different to ourselves. When we adopt an open-minded attitude, we can explore cultural differences honestly and imagine what life is really like for those others. The fact that I was born a white-skinned English speaker was nothing more than an accident of birth. I could just as easily be brown or black, from Cuba or Cameroon. The actions we take are but coping strategies to make the most of the hand we are dealt. Adopting this empathetic approach helps us to understand people's actions that we might see as illogical or perhaps immoral. It helps us to create the best self we can when we walk a mile in someone else's shoes. It also undermines the foundations of dangerous racist ideologies, expressed, for example, in such extreme form in the mass murder of so many innocent people in Norway in July 2011.

The active cosmopolitan stance is also helpful in broadening our perspectives on the places in which we live. Each place 'is always and continuously being produced.'[4] This ongoing process is sometimes subject to conflict, which is an inevitable, permanent feature of social life. There will always be conflicting views as to the best future for particular areas, with representatives of different sets of knowledge challenging each other for dominance. In managing these negotiations, it helps to keep in mind that a 'large component of the identity of that place called home derived precisely from the fact that it had always in one way or another been open; constructed out of movement, communication, social relations which always stretched beyond it.'[5] No place has an essential identity that defines it forever. Many people live lives that are characterised by what Ulrich Beck terms 'place polygamy', living in many places at once and with global processes entering their personal lives.[6] This does not mean, however, that people do not need a sense of place, which, I feel, gives people a grounding, an orientation, a set of co-ordinates to negotiate their niche in a complex world. However, the mentality behind that sense of place needs to be an open, positive one, rather than closed and exclusive.

To say that one is place-based is not the same as being place-bound. When we adopt an active cosmopolitan attitude, we are more aware of cultural difference, as well as social inequality. We need 'places that provide healthy living environments and also nourish the soul-distinctive places worthy of our loyalty and commitment, places where we feel at home, places that inspire and uplift and stimulate us and provide social and environmental sustenance.'[7] Those of us who can make homes for ourselves within the comfort zone of such places are the lucky ones. It is important to remember that to live like this would be viewed as an unobtainable luxury for most of the world's population, who still have to struggle with the dire effects of poverty, war and environmental degradation.

Endnotes

Introduction

1   P. Iyer, *The Global Soul: Jet-Lag, Shopping Malls and the Search for Home* (London 2001) 12.
2   J. Tomlinson, *Globalization and Culture*, (Cambridge 1999) 27.

Chapter 1

1   J.W. Duyvendak, *The Politics of Home: Belonging and Nostalgia in Western Europe and the United States* (Basingstoke 2011) 27.
2   *Ibid.* 37.
3   This 'dramaturgical' analytical framework originated in Erving Goffman's classic *The Presentation of Self in Everyday Life* (Harmondsworth 1959).
4   F. O'Toole, 'The Home Place', *The Irish Times*, 21 April 2012.
5   One of the effects of information technology and the Internet is, ironically, blurring the boundaries between work and home once again.
6   The powerful and influential concept of public and private spheres came from Marxist feminism. For a manageable introduction to the idea, see M. Humm (ed.), *Feminisms: A Reader* (Hemel Hempstead 1992).
7   S. Scott, *Making Sense of Everyday Life* (Cambridge 2009) 54.
8   D. Murphy, 'Swept Away On My Own River of Life', *The Irish Times*, 8 August 2011.
9   N. Ní Dhomhnaill, 'When I am Far Away, It is Home', *The Irish Times*, 10 August 2011.
10 B. Keenan, *Four Quarters of Light: A Journey Through Alaska* (London 2005) 112.
11 M. Russell, *Journeys of a Lifetime* (London 2002) 105.

12 M. Ignatieff, *The Needs of Strangers* (London 1990) 141.
13 T. Turner, 'Homeworld', *New Internationalist*, November 1997, 28–30.
14 D. Harvey, *The Condition of Postmodernity* (Cambridge, MA 1989) 292.
15 See U. Beck, *Risk Society* (London 1992).
16 P. Iyer, *The Global Soul: Jet-Lag, Shopping Malls and the Search for Home* (London 2001) 13.
17 J. O'Connor, 'Introduction', *New Irish Short Stories* (London 2011) xiii.
18 William Smyth in *The Home Place*, RTÉ 1, 10/11 May 2011.
19 Willie Nolan in *The Home Place*, RTÉ 1, 10/11 May 2011.
20 Harry and Henry O'Grady in *The Home Place*, RTÉ 1, 10/11 May 2011.
21 G. Mak, *An Island in Time: The Biography of a Village* (London 2010) 37.
22 E. Hynes, *Knock: The Virgin's Apparition in Nineteenth Century Ireland* (Cork 2008).
23 B. Kingsolver, *Animal, Vegetable, Miracle: One Year of Seasonal Eating* (London 2007) 131.
24 G.W. Creed and B. Ching, 'Recognising Rusticity: Identity and the Power of Place' in B. Ching and G.W. Creed (eds.), *Knowing Your Place: Rural Identity and Cultural Hierarchy* (New York 1997) 17.
25 For an in-depth sociological analysis of the Rural Environment Protection Scheme, see E. Crowley *Land Matters* (Dublin 2006).
26 J. Waters, *Jiving at the Crossroads* (Belfast 1991) 66.
27 D. Cotter, *Wild Garlic, Gooseberries... and Me* (London 2010) 84.
28 D. McWilliams, *The Pope's Children* (Dublin 2006) 258.
29 O. James, *They F*** You Up: How to Survive Family Life* (London 2007).
30 M. Clifford, 'Simple Pleasures Ward Off Seclusion Threat', *The Irish Examiner*, 25 November 2011.
31 L. Tolstoy, *Anna Karenina* (London 1912).
32 C. Moran, *How To Be a Woman* (London 2011) 73.
33 Available from the Constitution Society's website: <http://www.constitution.org/cons/ireland/constitution_ireland-en.pdf>, accessed 10 April 2013.
34 C. Coulter, *The Hidden Tradition: Feminism, Women and Nationalism* (Cork 1993) 26–7.
35 See www.irishhistorian.com.
36 P. Crawley, 'The Keane Edge', *The Irish Times*, 19 November 2011.
37 T. Fahey, 'Family and Household in Ireland' in P. Clancy, S. Drudy, K. Lynch and L. O'Dowd (eds.), *Irish Society: Sociological Perspectives* (Dublin 1995) 205–34.

38 The Central Statistics Office (CSO) website (www.cso.ie) is the best source for these statistics, particularly *The Statistical Yearbook* for each year and also the annual report entitled *Women and Men in Ireland*.

39 U. Beck and E. Beck-Gernsheim, *The Normal Chaos of Love* (Cambridge 1995) 5.

40 M. Castells, *The Power of Identity* (Malden, MA 1997) 242.

41 A.D. Rees, *Life in a Welsh Countryside* (Cardiff 1950) 54, quoted in R. Frankenburg, *Communities in Britain* (Harmondsworth 1966) 101.

42 G. Mak, *An Island in Time: The Biography of a Village* (London 2010) 181.

43 C.W. Mills, *The Sociological Imagination* (Oxford 1959) 14.

Chapter 2

1 M. Ignatieff, *The Needs of Strangers* (London 1990) 138.

2 R. Jenkins, *Social Identity* (3rd ed.) (London 2008) 133.

3 A. Mason, *Community, Solidarity and Belonging* (Cambridge 2000) 17.

4 The two major classical theorists who defined this debate were German sociologist Ferdinand Tönnies (1855–1936) and French sociologist Émile Durkheim (1858–1917). Tönnies distinguished between *Gemeinschaft* (community) and *Gesellschaft* (society), and Durkheim defined the difference between mechanical solidarity and organic solidarity. Any introductory sociology text will provide details on their work. I recommend in particular A. Giddens, *Sociology* (Cambridge 2006).

5 M. Young and P. Wilmott, *Family and Kinship in East London* (London 1957).

6 See my section on rural housing in E. Crowley, *Land Matters: Power Struggles in Rural Ireland* (Dublin 2006) 154–65.

7 F. McDonald and J. Nix, *Chaos at the Crossroads* (Cork 2005) 71. This book is the single best source on recent planning issues in Ireland.

8 K. Keohane and C. Kuhling, *Collision Culture* (Dublin 2004) 57.

9 See K.C. Kearns, *Dublin's Lost Heroines: Mammies and Grannies in a Vanished City* (Dublin 2004).

10 Introduction to C.M. Arensberg and S.T. Kimball, *Family and Community in Ireland* (Ennis, County Clare 2001) [first published 1940 by Harvard College] XLI.

11 H. Brody, *Inishkillane: Change and Decline in the West of Ireland* (London 1973).

12 C. Eipper, *The Ruling Trinity: A Community Study of Church, State and Business in Ireland* (Aldershot 1986).

13 The most recent example of such Irish urban research is N. Hourigan (ed.), *Understanding Limerick: Social Exclusion and Change* (Cork 2011).

14 G. Delanty, *Community* (London 2003) 194.

15 A.P. Cohen, *The Symbolic Construction of Community* (London 2000) 15.

16 *Ibid.* 118.

17 A.P. Cohen, 'A Sense of Time, A Sense of Place: The Meaning of Close Social Association in Whalsay, Scotland' in A.P. Cohen (ed.), *Belonging: Identity and Social Organisation in British Rural Cultures* (Manchester 1982) 21.

18 G. Delanty, *Community* (London 2003) 189.

19 H. Tovey and P. Share, *A Sociology of Ireland* (Dublin 2003) 354.

20 L. Delaney and T. Fahey, *Social and Economic Value of Sport in Ireland* (Dublin 2005) 35.

21 T. Inglis, *Global Ireland: Same Difference* (New York 2008) 138.

22 A.P. Cohen, 'Blockade: A Case Study of Local Consciousness in an Extra-Local Event' in A.P. Cohen (ed.), *Belonging: Identity and Social Organisation in British Rural Cultures* (Manchester 1982) 307.

23 G. Mak, *An Island in Time: The Biography of a Village* (London 2010) 24.

24 A.P. Cohen, *The Symbolic Construction of Community* (London 2000) 28.

25 H. Tovey and P. Share *A Sociology of Ireland* (Dublin 2003) 406.

26 RTÉ News, 'Enda Kenny Speech on Cloyne Report', 20 July 2011, *rte.ie*, available from: <www.rte.ie/news/2011/0720/cloyne1.html>, accessed 12 March 2012.

27 Department of Health and Children, 'Strategic Taskforce on Alcohol – Interim Report' (Dublin 2002), quoted in H. Tovey and P. Share, *A Sociology of Ireland* (Dublin 2003) 372.

28 T. Inglis, *Global Ireland: Same Difference* (New York 2008) 66.

29 P. Cullen, 'Last Orders', *The Irish Times*, 30 December 2006.

30 R. Frankenburg, *Communities in Britain* (Harmondsworth 1966) 17.

31 See www.irishrurallink.ie.

32 C. Ketch, 'Community Outrage at Garda Station Closures', *The Irish Examiner: County Supplement*, 13 December 2011.

33 *Ibid.*

34 M. Clifford, 'Fighting the Fear of Living Alone in the Country', *The Irish Examiner*, 24 November 2011.

35 See U. Beck and E. Beck-Gernsheim, *Individualization: Institutionalized Individualism and its Social and Political Consequences* (London 2002) and A. Giddens, *The Transformation of Intimacy* (Cambridge 1992).
36 A. Etzioni, *The Spirit of Community: Rights, Responsibilities and the Communitarian Agenda* (London 1995) 247.
37 H. Tovey and P. Share, *A Sociology of Ireland* (Dublin 2003) 354.
38 P. Hoggett, 'Contested Communities' in P. Hoggett (ed.), *Contested Communities: Experiences, Struggles, Policies* (Bristol 1997).
39 R.D. Putnam, *Bowling Alone: The Collapse and Revival of American Community* (New York 2000) 19, 28.
40 *Ibid.*
41 K. Sheridan, 'Ten Years in the Park', *The Irish Times*, 3 November 2007.
42 Mary Davis, Chairperson of Task Force on Active Citizenship, interview with the author, Dublin, 17 November 2006.
43 *Ibid.*
44 *Ibid.*
45 A. Williams, 'Who Needs Community Anyway?' in D. Clements, A. Donald, M. Earnshaw and A. Williams (eds.), *The Future of Community: Reports of a Death Greatly Exaggerated* (London 2008) 5.
46 M. Clifford, 'Simple Pleasures Ward Off Seclusion Threat', *The Irish Examiner*, 24 November 2011.
47 M. Albrow, J. Eade, N. Washbourne and J. Durrschmidt, 'The Impact of Globalization on Sociological Concepts: Community, Culture and Milieu' in J. Eade (ed.), *Living the Global City: Globalization as a Local Process* (London 1997) 24.
48 A. Donald, 'A Death Greatly Exaggerated' in D. Clements, A. Donald, M. arnshaw and A. Williams (eds.), *The Future of Community: Reports of a Death Greatly Exaggerated* (London 2008) 184.
49 M. Farrar, *The Struggle for 'Community' in a British Multi-ethnic Inner City Area: Paradise in the Making* (Lampeter 2001) 343.
50 F. Barth, 'Boundaries and Connections' in A.P. Cohen (ed.), *Signifying Identities* (London 2000) 31.

Chapter 3

1 M. Castells, *The Informational City* (Oxford 1991) 349.
2 P. Gilroy, *Small Acts: Thoughts on the Politics of Black Cultures* (London 1993) 121.

3   G. Rose, 'Place and Identity: A Sense of Place' in D. Massey and P. Jess (eds.), *A Place in the World? Places, Cultures and Globalisation* (Oxford 1995) 99.

4   C. Creedon, 'The Cure', *Second City Trilogy* (Cork 2007) 5.

5   P. Mills, *Hymns to the Silence: Inside the Words and Music of Van Morrison* (London 2010) 272.

6   *Ibid.* 274.

7   *Ibid.* 273.

8   J. Tomlinson, *Globalization and Culture* (Cambridge 1999) 2.

9   M. Ignatieff, *The Needs of Strangers* (London 1990) 139.

10   A. Dirlik, 'The Global in the Local' in R. Wilson, and W. Dissanayake (eds.), *Global/Local: Cultural Production and the Transnational Imaginary* (Durham 1996) 31.

11   F. O'Toole, 'Brand Leader', *Granta* 53 (London 1996) 47, quoted in J. MacLaughlin 'The Devaluation of Nation as Home and the Depoliticisation of Recent Irish Emigration' in J. MacLaughlin (ed.), *Location and Dislocation in Contemporary Irish Society: Emigration and Irish Identities* (Cork 1997).

12   N. Chomsky, *Rogue States: The Rule of Force in World Affairs* (London 2000).

13   See E. Bircham and J. Charlton, *Anti-Capitalism: A Guide to the Movement* (London 2001).

14   M. McLuhan, *Understanding Media* (New York 1964).

15   A. Giddens, *The Consequences of Modernity* (Cambridge 1990).

16   U. Beck, A. Giddens and S. Lash, *Reflexive Modernisation: Politics, Traditions, and Aesthetics in the Modern Social Order* (Cambridge 1994) 174.

17   L. Sklair, 'Capitalism and Development in Global Perspective' in L. Sklair (ed.), *Capitalism and Development* (London 1994).

18   J. Tomlinson, *Globalization and Culture* (Cambridge 1999) 7.

19   S. Tharoor, *The Elephant, the Tiger and the Cellphone: Reflections on India in the Twenty-First Century* (New Delhi 2007) 6.

20   P. McMichael, *Development and Social Change: A Global Perspective* (4th ed.) (Los Angeles 2008) 285.

21   K. Allen, *The Corporate Takeover of Ireland* (Dublin 2007) 250.

22   See N. Klein, *No Logo* (London 2000).

23   R. Strassoldo, 'Globalism and Localism: Theoretical Reflections and Some Evidence' in Z. Mlinar (ed.), *Globalisation and Territorial Identities* (Aldershot 1992) 46.

24 T. Liebes and E. Katz, *The Export of Meaning: Cross-Cultural Readings of Dallas* (2nd ed.) (Cambridge 1993).

25 H. Mackay, 'The Globalization of Culture?' in D. Held (ed.), *A Globalizing World? Culture, Economics, Politics* (2nd ed.) (London 2004) 78.

26 J. Nye, *The Paradox of American Power* (Oxford 2002).

27 S. Tharoor, *The Elephant, The Tiger and The Cellphone: Reflections on India in the Twenty-First Century* (New Delhi 2007) 25.

28 R. Robertson, 'Glocalization: Time-Space and Homogeneity-Heterogeneity' in M. Featherstone, S. Lash and R. Robertson (eds.), *Global Modernities* (London 1995).

29 E. Crowley, 'Where Women are Told to be "Pale and Lovely"', *The Irish Examiner*, 15 June 2010.

30 Fair Trade clothing items can be bought from People Tree at www.peopletree.co.uk.

31 S. Hall, 'The Question of Cultural Identity' in S. Hall, D. Held & A. McGrew (eds.), *Modernity and Its Futures* (Cambridge 1993) 304.

32 J. Tomlinson, *Globalization and Culture* (Cambridge 1999) 6.

33 D. Massey, *Space, Place and Gender* (Cambridge 1994) 160.

34 A. Appadurai, 'Disjuncture and Difference in the Global Cultural Economy' in M. Featherstone (ed.), *Global Culture* (London 1990) 296–7.

35 *Ibid.* 297.

36 J. Tomlinson, *Globalization and Culture* (Cambridge 1999) 9.

37 A. Appadurai, 'Disjuncture and Difference in the Global Cultural Economy' in M. Featherstone (ed.), *Global Culture* (London 1990) 297.

38 P. Iyer 'Swap Deadlines for Lifelines', *The Irish Times Magazine*, 7 January 2012.

39 A. Appadurai, 'Disjuncture and Difference in the Global Cultural Economy' in M. Featherstone (ed.), *Global Culture* (London 1990) 297–8.

40 *Ibid.* 298.

41 T. Inglis, *Global Ireland: Same Difference* (New York 2008) 56.

42 J. MacLaughlin, 'The Devaluation of Nation as Home and the Depoliticisation of Recent Irish Emigration' in J. Mac Laughlin (ed.), *Location and Dislocation in Contemporary Irish Society: Emigration and Irish Identities* (Cork 1997) 193.

43 K. Allen, *The Celtic Tiger: The Myth of Social Partnership in Ireland* (Manchester 2000) 27.

44   A. Appadurai, 'Disjuncture and Difference in the Global Cultural Economy' in M. Featherstone (ed.), *Global Culture* (London 1990) 298–9.

45   *Ibid.* 300.

46   M. Albrow, 'Travelling Beyond Local Cultures: Socioscapes in a Global City' in J. Eade (ed.), *Living the Global City: Globalization as a Local Process* (London 1997) 38.

47   *Ibid.* 51.

48   *Ibid.* 53.

49   M. Glenny, *McMafia: Crime Without Frontiers* (London 2008) 6.

50   UNICEF, *Judicial Handbook on Combatting Trafficking of Women and Children for Commercial Sexual Exploitation* (Geneva 2006) 2.

51   A. Cockburn, '21st Century Slaves', *National Geographic*, September 2003, 10.

52   P. McMichael, *Development and Social Change: A Global Perspective* (4th ed.) (Los Angeles 2008) 207.

53   E. Crowley, *Daring to Dream* (Cork 2010) 121. This publication can be found on the following website: www.hopefoundation.ie.

54   E. Morgan, 'The Best Place to Live in Ireland', *The Irish Times*, 31 March 2012.

55   K. Sheridan, 'What We Can Learn From Ireland's Best Place', *The Irish Times*, 30 June 2012.

56   E. Carter, J. Donald and J. Squires, *Space and Place: Theories of Identity and Location* (London 1993) xii.

57   D. Massey, 'The Conceptualisation of Place' in D. Massey and P. Jess (eds.), *A Place in the World? Places, Cultures and Globalisation* (Oxford 1995) 61.

58   D. Kalb, 'Localizing Flows: Power, Paths, Institutions and Networks' in D. Kalb, M. van der Land, R. Staring, B. van Steenbergen and N. Wilterdink (eds.), *The Ends of Globalization: Bringing Society Back In* (Lanham 2000) 7.

59   E. Crowley, *Land Matters: Power Struggles in Rural Ireland* (Dublin 2006) 176.

60   D. Massey, 'Double Articulation: A Place in the World' in A. Bammer (ed.), *Displacements: Cultural Identities in Question* (Bloomington, IN 1995) 114.

61   *Ibid.* 116.

62   D. Massey, *Space, Place and Gender* (Cambridge 1994) 171.

63   *Ibid.* 155–6.

64   D. Massey, *For Space* (London 2007) 100.

65   D. Massey, *Spatial Divisions of Labour* (London 1984) 117–8.

66   D. Massey, *Space, Place and Gender* (Cambridge 1994) 136.

67   *Ibid.* 138.

68   M. McDonagh, 'Injecting Jobs Into Ireland: What Botox and Viagra Have Done For Us', *The Irish Times*, 14 January 2012.

69   *Ibid.*

70   www.allergan.com.

71   M. McDonagh, 'Injecting Jobs Into Ireland: What Botox and Viagra Have Done For Us', *The Irish Times*, 14 January 2012.

72   M. Albrow, 'Travelling Beyond Local Cultures: Socioscapes in a Global City' in J. Eade (ed.), *Living the Global City: Globalization as a Local Process* (London 1997) 53.

73   S. Mooney and T. McKenna, '21st Century Activists', *The Irish Times Magazine*, 12 January 2008.

74   See the campaign's website, www.shelltosea.com.

75   A. Dirlik, 'The Global in the Local' in R. Wilson and W. Dissanayake (eds.), *Global/Local: Cultural Production and the Transnational Imaginary* (Durham 1996) 31.

76   L. Browne, 'The Shrinking World', *The Irish Times Magazine*, 17 March 2007.

77   A. Dirlik, 'The Global in the Local' in R. Wilson and W. Dissanayake (eds.), *Global/Local: Cultural Production and the Transnational Imaginary* (Durham 1996) 35.

78   A. Arce and N. Long, 'Re-Positioning Knowledge in the Study of Rural Development' in D. Symes and A.J. Jansen (eds.), *Agricultural Restructuring and Rural Change in Europe* (Wageningen 1994) 81.

79   N. Long, 'Conclusion' in N. Long and A. Long (eds.), *Battlefields of Knowledge: The Interlocking of Theory and Practice in Social Research and Development* (London 1992) 274.

80   A. Arce and N. Long, 'Re-Positioning Knowledge in the Study of Rural Development' in D. Symes and A.J. Jansen (eds.), *Agricultural Restructuring and Rural Change in Europe* (Wageningen 1994) 77.

81   N. Long, 'From Paradigm Lost to Paradigm Regained? The Case for an Actor-oriented Sociology of Development' in N. Long and A. Long (eds.), *Battlefields of Knowledge: The Interlocking of Theory and Practice in Social Research and Development* (London 1992) 27.

82   A. Melucci, 'The Process of Collective Identity' in H. Johnston and B. Klandermans (eds.), *Social Movements and Culture* (London 1995) 62.

83   J. McGahern, 'The Local and the Universal' in S. van der Ziel (ed.), *Love of the World: Essays by John McGahern* (London 2009).

84   D. Massey, *Space, Place and Gender* (Cambridge 1994) 142.

85   A. Marwick, *The Sixties: Cultural Revolution in Britain, France, Italy and the Unites States* (Oxford 1998) 215.

86   *The Guardian*, 21 April 2012.

87   See their website, www.ezln.org.mx.

88   P. McMichael, *Development and Social Change: A Global Perspective* (4th ed.) (Los Angeles 2008) 262.

89   *Ibid.* 263.

90   H. Rangan, 'From Chipko to Uttaranchal' in R. Peet and M. Watts (eds.), *Liberation Ecologies: Environment, Development, Social Movements* (London 1996) 215.

91   D. Massey, *Space, Place and Gender* (Cambridge 1994) 132.

92   J. Tomlinson, *Globalization and Culture* (Cambridge 1999) 198.

93   D. O'Byrne, 'Working Class Culture: Local Community and Global Conditions' in J. Eade (ed.), *Living the Global City: Globalization as a Local Process* (London 1997) 80.

94   *Ibid.* 84.

95   This is especially true in the case of illegal activities, when knowing who's who and keeping quiet could be a matter of life and death. The rule of *omertà* among the Mafia is the ultimate formalisation of this, where there are very serious consequences to breaking their code of silence. For a fascinating sociological insight into Chicago gang culture and its connection with localism, see S. Venkatesh, *Gang Leader for a Day* (London 2008).

96   R.D. Putnam, *Bowling Alone: The Collapse and Revival of American Community* (New York 2000) 22–3.

97   U. Hannerz, *Transnational Connections: Cultures, People, Places* (London 1996) 9.

98   *Ibid.* 27.

Chapter 4

1   M. Castells, *The Power of Identity* (Malden, MA 1997) 7.

2   S. Hall, 'The Question of Cultural Identity' in S. Hall, A. Held and A. McGrew (eds.), *Modernity and Its Futures* (Cambridge 1993) 276.

3   G.H. Mead, *Mind, Self and Society* (Chicago 1934) 140.

4   R. Jenkins, *Social Identity* (3rd ed.) (London 2008) 5–6.

5   See E. Goffman, *Interaction Ritual* (New York 1955).
6   S. Hall, 'The Question of Cultural Identity' in S. Hall, A. Held and A. McGrew (eds.), *Modernity and Its Futures* (Cambridge 1993) 277.
7   G. Delanty, *Community* (London 2003) 187.
8   *Ibid.* 193.
9   A. Giddens, *Modernity and Self-Identity* (Cambridge 1991) 32.
10   U. Beck, A. Giddens and S. Lash, *Reflexive Modernization* (Cambridge 1994) 15.
11   R. Jenkins, *Social Identity* (3rd ed.) (London 2008) 34.
12   C. Kuhling and K. Keohane, *Cosmopolitan Ireland: Globalisation and Quality of Life* (London 2007) 24.
13   P. Bourdieu, *Distinction: A Social Critique of the Judgement of Taste* (London, 1984) 471. Pierre Bourdieu's theoretical approach is a major background influence on this work.
14   A. Giddens, *The Transformation of Intimacy* (Cambridge 1992) 174.
15   *Ibid.* 15.
16   D. Ferriter, *Occasions of Sin: Sex and Society in Modern Ireland* (London 2009) 546.
17   M. Luddy, *Prostitution and Irish Society 1800–1940* (Cambridge 2007) 205.
18   N. McCafferty, 'Ireland(s): Coping with the Womb and the Border' in R. Morgan (ed.), *Sisterhood is Global* (Harmondsworth 1984) 352.
19   Press release on the publication by P. Ryan, *Asking Angela MacNamara: An Intimate History of Irish Lives* (Dublin 2011), available from: <http://communications.nuim.ie/press/25112011.shtml>, accessed 13 April 2012.
20   M. O'Connell, *Changed Utterly: Ireland and the New Irish Psyche* (Dublin 2001) 77.
21   *Durex Global Sex Survey 2005*, available from: <http://www.data360.org/pdf/20070416064139.Global%20Sex%20Survey.pdf>, accessed 4 April 2013.
22   T. Inglis, *Global Ireland: Same Difference* (New York 2008) 185.
23   O'Connor, Annmarie, 'The Killer Heel Rises', *The Irish Examiner Weekend*, 16 September 2012.
24   H. McGee, *The SAVI Report: Sexual Abuse and Violence in Ireland* (Dublin 2002) xxxiii–v.
25   F. Gartland, 'Rape Crisis Centre Warns Against Cuts', *The Irish Times*, 23 November 2011, available from: <www.irishtimes.com/newspaper/ireland/2011/1123/122408000205.html>, accessed 14 April 2012.

26 T. Inglis, *Lessons in Irish Sexuality* (Dublin 1998) 170.
27 D. Ferriter, *Occasions of Sin: Sex and Society in Modern Ireland* (London 2009) 293.
28 M. Luddy, *Prostitution and Irish Society 1800–1940* (Cambridge 2007) 239.
29 D. Ferriter, *Occasions of Sin: Sex and Society in Modern Ireland* (London 2009) 328, 16.
30 *The Irish Examiner*, 'Full Text of Enda Kenny's Apology to the Magdalene Laundries Survivors', 19 February 2013, available from: <http://www.irishexaminer.com/breakingnews/ireland/full-text-of-enda-kennys-apology-to-the-magdalene-laundries-survivors-585372.html>, accessed 6 March 2013.
31 This is a lyric from Damien Dempsey's song 'Industrial School' from his album *Seize the Day*.
32 T. Garvin, *Preventing the Future: Why Was Ireland So Poor for So Long?* (Dublin 2004) 190.
33 D. Ferriter, *Occasions of Sin: Sex and Society in Modern Ireland* (London 2009) 546. Serious debate is even now occurring as to whether the confessional seal, sacrosanct under canon law and upheld by civil law, should maintain its status.
34 T. Inglis, *Global Ireland: Same Difference* (New York 2008) 25.
35 However, dear reader, if you wish to read further on this, see H. Tovey and P. Share, *A Sociology of Ireland* (2nd ed.) (Dublin 2003) 402–12.
36 M. Slattery, *Key Ideas in Sociology* (Cheltenham 2003) 183.
37 www.glenstal.org/hospitality/god-pods, accessed 5 March 2013.
38 S. Kennedy, 'Irish Women and the Celtic Tiger Economy' in C. Coulter and S. Coleman (eds.), *The End of Irish History? Critical Reflections on the Celtic Tiger* (Manchester 2003) 107.
39 See www.Ruhama.ie.
40 E. Mahon, C. Conlon and L. Dillon, *Women and Crisis Pregnancy* (Dublin 1998).
41 S. Kennedy, 'Irish Women and the Celtic Tiger Economy' in C. Coulter and S. Coleman (eds.), *The End of Irish History? Critical Reflections on the Celtic Tiger* (Manchester 2003) 99. Kennedy provides a good synopsis of Irish law on abortion and the detail surrounding the X case in 1992.
42 F. O'Toole, 'Campaign Against Abortion a Phoney War', *The Irish Times*, 28 August 2012, 14.
43 See www.mariestopes.org.uk.

44 E. Mahon, C. Conlon and L. Dillon, *Women and Crisis Pregnancy* (Dublin 1998).

45 K. Sheridan, 'The Case That Convulsed a Nation', *The Irish Times*, 4 February 2012.

46 J. McEnroe, 'Coalition Set to Reject Abortion Legislation', *The Irish Examiner*, 19 April 2012.

47 C. Pope, 'Close to Home', *The Irish Times Magazine*, 29 December 2012, 13.

48 G. Kennedy, 'Valuable Debate Complete with Medical Facts, Figures', *The Irish Times*, 12 January 2013, 13.

49 F. O'Toole, 'Campaign Against Abortion a Phoney War', *The Irish Times*, 28 August 2012, 14.

50 *Ibid.*

51 See E. Mahon, C. Conlon and L. Dillon, *Women and Crisis Pregnancy* (Dublin 1998) and M. Ruane, *The Irish Journey: Women's Stories of Abortion* (Dublin 2000).

52 K. Sheridan, 'Stories of Abortion By People Who Have Been Through It', *The Irish Times*, 24 March 2012.

53 C. Moran, *How To Be a Woman* (London 2011) 282.

54 See D. Ferriter, *Occasions of Sin: Sex and Society in Modern Ireland* (London 2009). The section from pp. 475–517 is a forensically-researched and highly-readable account of social and legal changes for gay people in Ireland, north and south. See also Í. O'Carroll and E. Collins (eds.), *Lesbian and Gay Visions of Ireland* (London 1995) and L. Connolly and N. Hourigan (eds.), *Social Movements and Ireland* (Manchester 2006).

55 D. Ferriter, *Occasions of Sin: Sex and Society in Modern Ireland* (London 2009) 506–7.

56 *Ibid.* 508.

57 L. Petitt, 'A Construction Site Queered: "Gay" Images in New Irish Cinema', *Cineaste*, 24(2/3) (1999), 61–3, quoted in H. Tovey and P. Share, *Sociology of Ireland* (Dublin 2003) 264.

58 C. Crimmins, 'Still Not Easy to be Gay in Ireland', *The Irish Examiner*, 29 December 2011, available from: <http://www.irishexaminer.com/ireland/still-not-easy-to-be-gay-in-ireland-178450.html>, accessed 12 February 2012.

59 K. Donnelly, 'Gay GAA Star Stands Up to Bullies', *Irish Independent*, 3 March 2012, available from: <http://www.independent.ie/

national-news/gay-gaa-star-stands-up-to-bullies-3038465.html>, accessed 12 February 2012.

60   K. Sweeney, 'Love is in the Airwaves as "Delighted" RTÉ Star Ties the Knot', *Irish Independent*, 15 June 2011, available from: <http://www. independent.ie/national-news/love-is-in-the-airwaves-as-delighted-rte-star-ties-knot-2675016.html>, accessed 12 February 2012.

61   B. Barnes, 'I Do, I Do, I Do, I Do, I Do...', *The New York Times: Sunday Styles*, 22 July 2012, 9.

62   D. Ferriter, *Occasions of Sin: Sex and Society in Modern Ireland* (London 2009) 511.

Chapter 5

1   D. Massey, *Space, Place and Gender* (Cambridge 1994) 149.

2   CSO, *Population and Migration Estimates: April 2011*, available from: <http://www.cso.ie/en/media/csoie/releasespublications/documents/ latestheadlinefigures/popmig_2012.pdf>, accessed 23 April 2012.

3   H. Fagan, 'Globalised Ireland, or, Contemporary Transformations of National Identity?' in C. Coulter and S. Coleman (eds.), *The End of Irish History? Critical Reflections on the Celtic Tiger* (Manchester 2003) 119.

4   H. McGee, 'Noonan Criticised for Remarks about Young Emigrants', *The Irish Times*, 20 January 2012, available from: <www.irishtimes. com/newspaper/ireland/2012/0120/1224310517506.html>, accessed 22 April 2012.

5   J. MacLaughlin, *Ireland: The Emigrant Nursery and the World Economy* (Cork 1994) 60.

6   P. Iyer, *The Global Soul: Jet-Lag, Shopping Malls and the Search for Home* (London 2001) 27.

7   C. Tóibín, *The South* (London 1990) 100–1.

8   S. Rushdie, *Imaginary Homelands: Essays and Criticism 1981–1991* (London 1991) 12.

9   P. Iyer, *The Global Soul: Jet-Lag, Shopping Malls and the Search for Home* (London 2001) 33.

10   F. McCann, 'There's No Fantasy Place Like Home', *The Irish Times*, 14 March 2009.

11   P. Iyer, *The Global Soul: Jet-Lag, Shopping Malls and the Search for Home* (London 2001) 18.

12   E. Carter, J. Donald and J. Squires, *Space and Place: Theories of Identity and Location* (London 1993) vii.

13   S. Rushdie, *Imaginary Homelands: Essays and Criticism 1981–1991* (London 1991) 125.

14   D. McWilliams, *The Pope's Children: Ireland's New Elite* (Dublin 2006) 229.

15   *Ibid.* 230.

16   *The Irish Times*, 'Humour, the Angelus and Mammy: What Irish Emigrants Miss', 3 December 2011.

17   H. Fagan, 'Globalised Ireland, or, Contemporary Transformations of National Identity?' in C. Coulter and S. Coleman (eds.), *The End of Irish History? Critical Reflections on the Celtic Tiger* (Manchester 2003) 117.

18   *The Irish Times*, 'Highlights from Census 2011', 29 March 2012, available from: <http://www.irishtimes.com/newspaper/breaking/2012/0329/breaking30.html>, accessed 23 April 2012.

19   C. O'Brien, 'Time to Clean Up Migrant's Rights', *The Irish Times*, 18 December 2004.

20   See K. Allen, *The Corporate Takeover of Ireland* (Dublin 2007) 94–9.

21   C. Kuhling and K. Keohane, *Cosmopolitan Ireland: Globalisation and Quality of Life* (London 2007) 191.

22   *The Irish Times*, 'Man Accused of Murdering Two Polish Men Pleads Guilty to Assault', 5 May 2010, available from: <http://www.irishtimes.com/newspaper/ireland/2010/0506/1224269792206.html>, accessed 24 April 2012.

23   *The Irish Times*, 'Dublin Man Convicted of Murder', 15 March 2012, available from: <http://www.irishtimes.com/newspaper/breaking/2012/0315/breaking179.html>, accessed 24 April 2012.

24   Central Statistics Office (CSO), *Population and Migration Estimates: April 2011*, available from: <http://www.cso.ie/en/media/csoie/releasespublications/documents/latestheadlinefigures/popmig_2012.pdf>, accessed 21 April 2012.

25   Central Statistics Office (CSO), *Foreign Nationals: PPSN Allocations, Employment and Social Welfare Activity, 2009*, available from: <http://www.cso.ie/en/media/csoie/releasespublications/documents/labourmarket/2011/ppsn_2011.pdf>, accessed 21 April 2012.

26   C. Eipper, *The Ruling Trinity: A Community Study of Church, State and Business in Ireland* (Aldershot 1986) 134.

27   D. Forsythe, 'Urban Incomers and Rural Change: The Impact of Migrants from the City on Life in an Orkney Community', *Sociologia Ruralis*, 20(4) (1980) 287.

28   H. Hegarty, 'Counter-Urbanisation in West Cork' in U. Kockel (ed.), *Landscape, Heritage and Identity: Case Studies in Irish Ethnography* (Liverpool 1995) 179–96.

29   E. Crowley, 'Towards Sustainable Agriculture? A Sociological Analysis of The Rural Environment Protection Scheme (REPS) in the South-West of Ireland' (Unpublished PhD dissertation, NUI Cork, 2000).

30   J.H. Gilligan, 'Visitors, Tourists, and Outsiders in a Cornish Town' in M. Bouquet and M. Winter (eds.), *Who From Their Labours Rest? Conflict and Practice in Rural Tourism* (Aldershot 1987) 78.

31   R.E. Pahl, *Whose City? And Further Essays on Urban Society* (Harmondsworth 1975).

32   G. Crow and G. Allan, *Community Life: An Introduction to Local Social Relations* (New York 1994) 84.

33   H. Hegarty, 'Counter-Urbanisation in West Cork' in U. Kockel (ed.), *Landscape, Heritage and Identity: Case Studies in Irish Ethnography* (Liverpool 1995) 193.

34   G. Rose, 'Place and Identity: A Sense of Place' in D. Massey and P. Jess (eds.), *A Place in the World? Places, Cultures and Globalisation* (Oxford 1995) 116.

35   A. Peace, '"A Different Place Altogether": Diversity, Unity, and Boundary in an Irish Village' in A.P. Cohen (ed.), *Symbolising Boundaries: Identity and Diversity in British Cultures* (Manchester 1986) 114.

36   W.M. Williams, *The Sociology of an English Village: Gosforth* (London 1956), quoted in R. Frankenburg, *Communities in Britain* (Harmondsworth 1966) 76.

37   G. Mak, *An Island in Time: The Biography of a Village* (London 2010) 19.

38   S.K. Phillips, 'Natives and Incomers: The Symbolism of Belonging in Muker Parish, North Yorkshire' in A.P. Cohen (ed.), *Symbolising Boundaries: Identity and Diversity in British Cultures* (Manchester 1986).

39   H. Hegarty, 'Counter-Urbanisation in West Cork' in U. Kockel (ed.), *Landscape, Heritage and Identity: Case Studies in Irish Ethnography* (Liverpool 1995) 186.

40   *Ibid.* 187.

41   M. Maffesoli, *The Time of the Tribes* (Cambridge 1996) 6. Also see E. Crowley, 'Local Exchange Trading Systems: Globalising Rural Communities', IIIS Discussion Paper No. 37, Institute for International Integration Studies (IIIS), (Trinity College Dublin 2004), available from: <http://ssrn.com/abstract=739064>, accessed 15 March 2012.

42 J. Tomlinson, *Globalization and Culture* (Cambridge 1999) 28–9.
43 S. McKay, 'Welcome to Our World', *The Irish Times Magazine*, 25 May 2008.
44 S. Rushdie, *Imaginary Homelands: Essays and Criticism 1981–1991* (London 1991) 210.
45 D. Morley and K. Robins, 'No Place Like Heimat: Images of Home(land) in European Culture' in E. Carter, J. Donald and J. Squires, *Space and Place: Theories of Identity and Location* (London 1993) 27.
46 P. Gilroy, *Black Atlantic* (London 1993) 4.
47 *Ibid.* 15.
48 *Ibid.* 31.
49 Sleeve notes to music CD, *The Rough Guide to Bhangra* (London 2011).
50 J. Nederveen Pieterse, 'Globalization as Hybridization' in M. Featherstone, S. Lash and R. Robertson (eds.), *Global Modernities* (London 1995) 64.
51 *Ibid.* 53.
52 P. Ó Conghaile, 'Language Lesson', *The Irish Examiner*, 27 October 2005.
53 See www.gaelchultur.com, accessed 7 March 2013.
54 See: <http://irishdancinginfo.co.uk/EuropeandRussia.aspx>, accessed 23 April 2012.
55 This reminds one of the Atlantean thesis put forward by film-maker and writer Bob Quinn, who argues that there is a strong Arab influence on ancient Irish culture due to trade links across the millennia. See his *The Atlantean Irish: Ireland's Oriental and Maritime Heritage* (Dublin 2004).
56 For a longer discussion, see F. Vallely's various works, including his *Companion to Irish Traditional Music* (Cork 2011); J. Waters, *Race of Angels: Ireland and the Genesis of U2* (Belfast 1994); and P. Mills, *Hymns to the Silence: Inside the Words and Music of Van Morrison* (New York 2010).
57 S. Campbell, *Irish Blood, English Heart: Second-Generation Irish Musicians in England* (Cork 2011) 1.
58 J. Mac Laughlin, '"Pestilence on Their Backs, Famine in Their Stomachs": The Racial Construction of Irishness and the Irish in Victorian Britain' in C. Graham, and R. Kirkland (eds.), *Ireland and Cultural Theory: The Mechanics of Authenticity* (London 1999) 57.

59   S. Campbell, *Irish Blood, English Heart: Second-Generation Irish Musicians in England* (Cork 2011) 6–7.

60   B. Walter, 'Contemporary Irish Settlement in London: Women's Worlds, Men's Worlds' in J. Mac Laughlin (ed.), *Location and Dislocation in Contemporary Irish Society: Emigration and Irish Identities* (Cork 1997) 88.

61   S. Campbell, *Irish Blood, English Heart: Second-Generation Irish Musicians in England* (Cork 2011) 7.

62   J. Nederveen Pieterse, 'Globalization as Hybridization' in M. Featherstone, S. Lash and R. Robertson (eds.), *Global Modernities* (London 1995) 56.

63   S. Campbell, *Irish Blood, English Heart: Second-Generation Irish Musicians in England* (Cork 2011) 9.

64   *Ibid.*

65   *Ibid.* 71–2.

66   Quoted in S. Campbell, *Irish Blood, English Heart: Second-Generation Irish Musicians in England* (Cork 2011) 76.

67   Quoted in S. Campbell, *Irish Blood, English Heart: Second-Generation Irish Musicians in England* (Cork 2011) 79. This was an unfortunate choice of language, seeing as abortions in London were usually literal rather than metaphorical ones.

68   K. Keohane, 'Traditionalism and Homelessness in Contemporary Irish Music' in J. Mac Laughlin (ed.), *Location and Dislocation in Contemporary Irish Society: Emigration and Irish Identities* (Cork 1997) 295.

69   *Ibid.*

70   J. Cleary, 'A Fairytale Steeped in Truth', *The Irish Times*, 16 December 2006.

71   K. Keohane, 'Traditionalism and Homelessness in Contemporary Irish Music' in J. Mac Laughlin (ed.), *Location and Dislocation in Contemporary Irish Society: Emigration and Irish Identities* (Cork 1997) 300.

72   J. Cleary, 'A Fairytale Steeped in Truth', *The Irish Times*, 16 December 2006.

73   E. Said, *Culture and Imperialism* (London 1993) 15.

74   A. Hussey, *Paris: The Secret History* (London 2007) 433.

75   J.W. Duyvendak *The Politics of Home* (London 2011) 75.

76   P. Linebaugh, *The London Hanged: Crime and Civil Society in the Eighteenth Century* (London 1991) 358.

77   R. Lichtenstein, *On Brick Lane* (London 2007) 317.

78 O. Kelly, '"Oriental Enclave" Recommended for Dublin', *The Irish Times*, 13 October 2011, available from: <www.irishtimes.com/newspaper/ireland/2011/1013/1224305705635.html>, accessed 25 April 2012.

79 Central Statistics Office (CSO) *Census 2006: Non-Irish Nationals Living in Ireland* (Dublin 2008).

80 S. Dean, 'Rio on Galway: Immigration and Ireland' in D. Clements, A. Donald, M. Earnshaw and A. Williams (eds.), *The Future of Community: Reports of a Death Greatly Exaggerated* (London 2008) 138.

81 C. Healy, 'Carnaval do Galway: The Brazilian Community in Gort, 1999–2006', *Irish Migration Studies in Latin America*, available from: <www.irlandeses.org/healy_gort.htm>, accessed 24 April 2012.

82 S. Dean, 'Rio on Galway: Immigration and Ireland' in D. Clements, A. Donald, M. Earnshaw and A. Williams (eds.), *The Future of Community: Reports of a Death Greatly Exaggerated* (London 2008) 143.

83 R. MacCormaic, 'Brazilian Thoughts Turn to Home', *The Irish Times*, 28 April 2008.

84 E. Crowley, 'Selling Regional Identity: The Case of Fuchsia Brands' in M. Peillon and M. Corcoran (eds.), *Place and Non-Place: The Reconfiguration of Ireland* (Dublin 2004) 131–41.

85 Interview with the author, December 2002.

86 Central Statistics Office (CSO), *Census 2006: Non-Irish Nationals Living in Ireland* (Dublin 2008).

87 A. Hopkin, 'Coming Down the Mountain', *The Irish Times Magazine*, 30 November 2002.

88 A. Blunt and R. Dowling, *Home* (London 2006) 199.

89 D. Massey, *Space, Place and Gender* (Cambridge 1994) 171.

Chapter 6

1 D. Held, *Cosmopolitanism: Ideals and Realities* (Cambridge 2010) 40.

2 *Ibid.* 41–3.

3 *Ibid.* 44–7.

4 This is a paraphrase of the famous first line of Simone De Beauvoir's *The Second Sex* (London 2009) [first published 1949].

5 U. Hannerz, 'Cosmopolitans and Locals in World Culture' in M. Featherstone (ed.), *Global Culture: Nationalism, Globalization and Modernity* (London 1990) 239.

6   D. Kalb, 'Localizing Flows: Power, Paths, Institutions and Networks' in D. Kalb, M. van der Land, R. Staring, B. van Steenbergen and N. Wilterdink (eds.), *The Ends of Globalization: Bringing Society Back In* (Lanham 2000) 13.

7   J. Tomlinson, *Globalization and Culture* (Cambridge 1999) 185.

8   J. Urry, *Consuming Places* (London 1995) 166.

9   J. Tomlinson, *Globalization and Culture* (Cambridge 1999) 6.

10   U. Beck, *Cosmopolitan Visions* (Cambridge 2006) 41–3.

11   J. Tomlinson, *Globalization and Culture* (Cambridge 1999) 204.

12   C. Kuhling and K. Keohane, *Cosmopolitan Ireland: Globalisation and Quality of Life* (London 2007) 63–4.

13   J. Tomlinson, *Globalization and Culture* (Cambridge 1999) 189. See also C. Kuhling and K. Keohane, *Cosmopolitan Ireland: Globalisation and Quality of Life* (London 2007) 2.

14   U. Hannerz, 'Cosmopolitans and Locals in World Culture' in M. Featherstone (ed.), *Global Culture: Nationalism, Globalization and Modernity* (London 1990) 241.

15   *Ibid.* 238.

16   See the longer discussion of exile and migration in Chapter 5.

17   T. Inglis, *Global Ireland: Same Difference* (New York 2008) 64.

18   U. Hannerz, 'Cosmopolitans and Locals in World Culture' in M. Featherstone (ed.), *Global Culture: Nationalism, Globalization and Modernity* (London 1990) 241.

19   M. Russell, *Journeys of a Lifetime* (London 2002) 105.

20   J. Tomlinson, *Globalization and Culture* (Cambridge 1999) 195.

21   U. Hannerz, 'Cosmopolitans and Locals in World Culture' in M. Featherstone (ed.), *Global Culture: Nationalism, Globalization and Modernity* (London 1990) 248.

22   P. Iyer, *The Global Soul: Jet-Lag, Shopping Malls and the Search for Home* (London 2001) 22.

23   T. Inglis, *Global Ireland: Same Difference* (New York 2008) 64.

24   *Ibid.*

25   U. Beck, *Cosmopolitan Visions* (Cambridge 2006) 11.

26   K. Appiah, 'Cosmopolitan Patriots' in P. Cheah and B. Robbins (eds.), *Cosmopolitics: Thinking and Feeling Beyond the Nation* (Minneapolis 1998) 91.

27   C. Kuhling and K. Keohane, *Cosmopolitan Ireland: Globalisation and Quality of Life* (London 2007) 211.

28   J. Tomlinson, *Globalization and Culture* (Cambridge 1999) 195.

29 C. Reilly, 'The Dunnes Stores Staff who Stood Up to Apartheid', *Metro Eireann*, 30 July 2009, available from: <http://metroeireann.com/article/the-dunnes-stores-staff-who-stood,2019>, accessed 30 March 2012. See also, T. Lodge, 'An "Boks Amach": The Irish Anti-Apartheid Movement', *History Ireland*, July/August 2006, available from: <http://www.historyireland.com/volumes/volume14/issue4/features/?id=330>, accessed 29 March 2012.

30 U. Beck, *Cosmopolitan Visions* (Cambridge 2006) 5.

31 See www.fairtrade.ie.

32 For example, www.peopletree.co.uk and www.belleetik.com.

33 P. McMichael, *Development and Social Change: A Global Perspective* (4th ed.) (Thousand Oaks, CA 2008) 260.

34 W. Sachs, 'One World' in W. Sachs (ed.), *The Development Dictionary* (London 1992) 113.

35 A. Seager, 'Starbucks Stirred by Fair Trade Film', *The Guardian*, 29 January 2007.

36 S. Ortiz, 'Reflections on the Concept of "Peasant Culture" and Peasant "Cognitive Systems"' in Shanin, T. (ed.), *Peasants and Peasant Societies* (Harmondsworth 1984) 333.

37 B. O'Neill, 'How Fair is Fairtrade?', *BBC News*, available from: <http://news.bbc.co.uk/2/hi/uk_news/magazine/6426417.stm>, accessed 21 March 2013.

38 P. McMichael, *Development and Social Change: A Global Perspective* (4th ed.) (Thousand Oaks, CA 2008) 270.

39 J. Tomlinson, *Globalization and Culture* (Cambridge1999) 207.

40 The book is called *Daring to Dream: The Work of the Hope Foundation in India* (Cork 2010). Read more about their work at www.hopefoundation.ie.

41 U. Beck, *Cosmopolitan Visions* (Cambridge 2006) 3.

42 D. Massey, *Space, Place and Gender* (Cambridge 1994) 156.

43 J. Tomlinson, *Globalization and Culture* (Cambridge1999) 194.

44 D. Held, *Cosmopolitanism: Ideals and Realities* (Cambridge 2010) 76.

45 C. Kuhling and K. Keohane, *Cosmopolitan Ireland: Globalisation and Quality of Life* (London 2007) 4.

46 Interestingly, Lenihan's father before him, Brian Lenihan, was probably denied the Irish Presidency in the 1990 election by sexist comments made by his fellow party member, Pádraig Flynn, about Mary Robinson's personal life as a woman. It was widely thought to have swung the female vote in Robinson's favour.

47   U. Beck, *Cosmopolitan Visions* (Cambridge 2006) 23.

48   *Ibid.* 36.

49   D. Held, *Cosmopolitanism: Ideals and Realities* (Cambridge 2010) 50.

50   All information for this section was gained from an interview with the author in 2009.

51   A. Sen, *Development as Freedom* (New Delhi 2000) 44.

52   All information for this section was gained from C. Moorehead, *Martha Gellhorn: A Life* (London 2004) and M. Gellhorn, *The Face of War* (London 1993).

53   She scorned this association in later life, stressing that she was, after all, only with him for five of her eighty-nine years.

54   A portion of international volunteers also joined Franco's nationalist side of the conflict.

55   All information for this section was gained from J. Szwed, *The Man Who Recorded the World: A Biography of Alan Lomax* (London 2011).

56   Seeger was only 19 years old then, and is still going strong now.

57   H. Thomson, 'Dervla Murphy Interview: Around the World in 80 Years', *The Telegraph*, 1 July 2010, available from: <http://www.telegraph. co.uk/travel/artsandculture/travelbooks/7865817/Dervla-Murphy-interview-Around-the-world-in-80-years.html>, accessed 12 May 2012.

58   N. Wroe, 'Free Wheeler', *The Guardian*, 15 April 2006, available from: <http://www.guardian.co.uk/books/2006/apr/15/featuresreviews. guardianreview11>, accessed 12 May 2012.

59   See www.dervlamurphy.com.

60   M. Russell, *The Blessings of a Good Thick Skirt: Women Travellers and their World* (London 1994) 139–40.

61   H. Bradt, 'Dervla Murphy at 80: Living at Full Tilt', *Wanderlust*, November 2011, available from: <http://www.wanderlust.co.uk/magazine/ articles/interviews/dervla-murphy-80th-birthday?page=all>, accessed 13 May 2012.

62   *The Irish Times*, 'True Characters', 26 November 2011, available from: <http://www.irishtimes.com/newspaper/magazine/2011/1126/ 1224307986148.html>, accessed 14 May 2012.

63   H. Bradt, 'Dervla Murphy at 80: Living at Full Tilt' *Wanderlust*, November 2011, available from: <http://www.wanderlust.co.uk/magazine/ articles/interviews/dervla-murphy-80th-birthday?page=all>, accessed 12 May 2012.

64   H. Thomson, 'Dervla Murphy Interview: Around the World in 80 Years', *The Telegraph*, 1 July 2010, available from: <http://www.telegraph.co.uk/travel/artsandculture/travelbooks/7865817/Dervla-Murphy-interview-Around-the-world-in-80-years.html>, accessed 13 May 2012.

65   D. Murphy, *Visiting Rwanda* (Dublin 1998).

66   D. Murphy, *A Month by the Sea: Encounters in Gaza* (London, 2013).

67   *The Irish Times*, 'True Characters', 26 November 2011, available from: <http://www.irishtimes.com/newspaper/magazine/2011/1126/1224307986148.html>, accessed 15 May 2012.

68   D. Murphy, 'Michael, Reject this Invitation', *The Irish Examiner*, 9 February 2012, available from: <http://www.irishexaminer.com/news/michael-reject-this-invitation-183133.html>, accessed 16 May 2012.

69   D. Murphy, 'First, Buy Your Pack Animal', *The Guardian*, 3 January 2009, available from: <http://www.guardian.co.uk/travel/2009/jan/03/dervla-murphy-travel-tips>, accessed 12 May 2012. She goes into detail on each of the items on this list, mixing solid advice with entertainment – very Dervla!

70   H. Bradt, 'Dervla Murphy at 80: Living at Full Tilt', *Wanderlust*, November 2011, available from: <http://www.wanderlust.co.uk/magazine/articles/interviews/dervla-murphy-80th-birthday?page=all>, accessed 12 May 2012.

71   C. Sheridan, 'Travelling A Different Path', *The Irish Examiner*, 26 November 2011, available from: <http://www.irishexaminer.com/weekend/travelling-a-different-path-174952.html>, accessed 13 May 2012.

72   U. Hannerz, 'Cosmopolitans and Locals in World Culture' in M. Featherstone (ed.), *Global Culture: Nationalism, Globalization and Modernity* (London 1990) 250.

73   D. Massey, 'Double Articulation: A Place in the World' in A. Bammer (ed.), *Displacements: Cultural Identities in Question* (Bloomington, IN 1994) 117.

Conclusion

1   Age Action Ireland, 'Wexford Death a Wake Up Call for All Communities', *ageaction.ie*, 20 March 2012, available from: <http://www.ageaction.ie/wexford-death-wake-call-all-communities>, accessed 22 March 2012.

2 ALONE, 'Tragic Undiscovered Death of Older Man in Wexford: ALONE Statement', *alone.ie*, available from: <http://alone.ie/press-releases/tragic-undiscovered-death-of-older-man-in-wexford-alone-statement/>, accessed 22 March 2012.

3 J.W. Duyvendak, *The Politics of Home* (London 2011) 124.

4 D. Massey, *Space, Place and Gender* (Cambridge 1994) 171.

5 *Ibid.*

6 U. Beck, *What is Globalization?* (Cambridge 2002) 72.

7 T. Beatley, *Native to Nowhere: Sustaining Home and Community in a Global Age* (Washington DC 2004) 2–3.

Further Reading

This is a list of books consulted by the author that contain relevant material on the various themes raised in this book. Some of them are monographs and others are edited collections that contain relevant chapters, to which specific reference has been made in the endnotes. They range across the genres, from classical and contemporary sociological theory and contemporary Irish sociological commentary to online sources, travelogues, journalism and fiction.

Allen, K., *The Celtic Tiger: The Myth of Social Partnership in Ireland* (Manchester 2000).

Allen, K., *The Corporate Takeover of Ireland* (Dublin 2007).

Arensberg, C.M. and S.T. Kimball, *Family and Community in Ireland* (Ennis, County Clare 2001) [first published 1940 by Harvard College].

Bammer, A. (ed.), *Displacements: Cultural Identities in Question* (Bloomington, IN 1995).

Beatley, T., *Native to Nowhere: Sustaining Home and Community in a Global Age* (Washington DC 2004).

Beck, U., *Risk Society* (London 1992).

Beck, U., *What is Globalization?* (Cambridge 2002).

Beck, U., *Cosmopolitan Visions* (Cambridge 2006).

Beck, U., A. Giddens and S. Lash, *Reflexive Modernisation: Politics, Traditions, and Aesthetics in the Modern Social Order* (Cambridge 1994).

Beck, U. and E. Beck-Gernsheim, *The Normal Chaos of Love* (Cambridge 1995).

Beck, U. and E. Beck-Gernsheim, *Individualization: Institutionalized Individualism and its Social and Political Consequences* (London 2002).

Bircham, E. and J. Charlton, *Anti-Capitalism: A Guide to the Movement* (London 2001).

Blunt, A. and R. Dowling, *Home* (London 2006).

Bourdieu, P., *Distinction: A Social Critique of the Judgement of Taste* (London, 1984).

Brody, H., *Inishkillane: Change and Decline in the West of Ireland* (London 1973).

Campbell, S., *Irish Blood, English Heart: Second-Generation Irish Musicians in England* (Cork 2011).

Carter, E., J. Donald and J. Squires, *Space and Place: Theories of Identity and Location* (London 1993).

Castells, M., *The Informational City* (Oxford 1991).

Castells, M., *The Power of Identity* (Malden, MA 1997).

Central Statistics Office (CSO), *Population and Migration Estimates: April 2011*, available from: <http://www.cso.ie/en/media/csoie/releasespublications/documents/latestheadlinefigures/popmig_2012.pdf >, accessed 21 March 2013.

Central Statistics Office (CSO), *Foreign Nationals: PPSN Allocations, Employment and Social Welfare Activity, 2010–2011*, available from: <http://www.cso.ie/en/media/csoie/releasespublications/documents/labourmarket/2011/ppsn_2011.pdf>, accessed 21 March 2013.

Cheah, P. and B. Robbins (eds.), *Cosmopolitics: Thinking and Feeling Beyond the Nation* (Minneapolis 1998).

Ching, B. and G.W. Creed (eds.), *Knowing Your Place: Rural Identity and Cultural Hierarchy* (New York 1997).

Chomsky, N., *Rogue States: The Rule of Force in World Affairs* (London, 2000).

Clancy, P., S. Drudy, K. Lynch and L. O'Dowd (eds.), *Irish Society: Sociological Perspectives* (Dublin 1995).

Clements, D., D. Alastair, M. Earnshaw and A. Williams (eds.), *The Future of Community: Reports of a Death Greatly Exaggerated* (London 2008).

Cohen, A.P., *The Symbolic Construction of Community* (London 2000).

Cohen, A.P. (ed.), *Belonging: Identity and Social Organisation in British Rural Cultures* (Manchester 1982).

Cohen, A.P. (ed.), *Signifying Identities* (London 2000).

Connolly, L. and N. Hourigan (eds.), *Social Movements and Ireland* (Manchester 2006).

Cotter, D., *Wild Garlic, Gooseberries... and Me* (London 2010).

Coulter, C., *The Hidden Tradition: Feminism, Women and Nationalism* (Cork 1993).

Coulter, C. and S. Coleman (eds.), *The End of Irish History? Critical Reflections on the Celtic Tiger* (Manchester 2003).

Creedon, C., 'The Cure', *Second City Trilogy* (Cork 2007).

Crow, G. and G. Allan, *Community Life: An Introduction to Local Social Relations* (New York 1994).

Crowley, E., 'Towards Sustainable Agriculture? A Sociological Analysis of The Rural Environment Protection Scheme (REPS) in the South-West of Ireland' (Unpublished PhD dissertation, NUI Cork, 2000).

Crowley, E., 'Local Exchange Trading Systems: Globalising Rural Communities', *IIIS Discussion Paper No. 37*, Institute for International Integration Studies (IIIS), (Trinity College Dublin 2004), available from SSRN: <http://ssrn.com/abstract=739064>, accessed 10 May 2012.

Crowley, E., *Land Matters: Power Struggles in Rural Ireland* (Dublin 2006).

Crowley, E., *Daring to Dream: The Work of the Hope Foundation in India* (Cork 2010), available via www.hopefoundation.ie.

Delanty, G., *Community* (London 2003).

Duyvendak, J.W., *The Politics of Home: Belonging and Nostalgia in Western Europe and the United States* (Basingstoke 2011).

Eade, J. (ed.), *Living the Global City: Globalization as a Local Process* (London 1997).

Eipper, C., *The Ruling Trinity: A Community Study of Church, State and Business in Ireland* (Aldershot 1986).

Etzioni, A., *The Spirit of Community: Rights, Responsibilities and the Communitarian Agenda* (London 1995).

Farrar, M., *The Struggle for 'Community' in a British Multi-ethnic Inner City Area: Paradise in the Making* (Lampeter 2001).

Featherstone, M. (ed.), *Global Culture: Nationalism, Globalization and Modernity* (London 1990).

Featherstone, M., S. Lash and R. Robertson (eds.), *Global Modernities* (London 1995).

Ferriter, D., *Occasions of Sin: Sex and Society in Modern Ireland* (London 2009).

Frankenburg, R., *Communities in Britain* (Harmondsworth 1966).

Garvin, T., *Preventing the Future: Why Was Ireland So Poor for So Long?* (Dublin 2004).

Gellhorn, M., *The Face of War* (London 1993).

Giddens, A., *The Consequences of Modernity* (Cambridge 1990).

Giddens, A., *Modernity and Self-Identity* (Cambridge 1991).

Giddens, A., *The Transformation of Intimacy* (Cambridge 1992).

Gilroy, P., *Black Atlantic* (London 1993).

Gilroy, P., *Small Acts: Thoughts on the Politics of Black Cultures* (London 1993).

Glenny, M., *McMafia: Crime Without Frontiers* (London 2008).

Goffman, E., *Interaction Ritual* (New York 1955).

Graham, C. and R. Kirkland (eds.), *Ireland and Cultural Theory: The Mechanics of Authenticity* (London 1999).

Hall, S., D. Held & A. McGrew (eds.), *Modernity and Its Futures* (Cambridge 1993).

Hannerz, U., *Transnational Connections: Cultures, People, Places* (London 1996).

Harvey, D., *The Condition of Postmodernity* (Cambridge, MA 1989).

Held, D. (ed.), *A Globalizing World? Culture, Economics, Politics* (2nd ed.) (London 2004).

Held, D., *Cosmopolitanism: Ideals and Realities* (Cambridge 2010).

Hoggett, P. (ed.), *Contested Communities: Experiences, Struggles, Policies* (Bristol 1997).

Hourigan, N. (ed.), *Understanding Limerick: Social Exclusion and Change* (Cork 2011).

Hussey, A., *Paris: The Secret History* (London 2007).

Hynes, E., *Knock: The Virgin's Apparition in Nineteenth Century Ireland* (Cork 2008).

Ignatieff, M., *The Needs of Strangers* (London 1990).

Inglis, T., *Lessons in Irish Sexuality* (Dublin 1998).

Inglis, T., *Global Ireland: Same Difference* (New York 2008).

Iyer, P., *The Global Soul: Jet-Lag, Shopping Malls and the Search for Home* (London 2001).

James, O., *They F*** You Up: How to Survive Family Life* (London 2007).

Jenkins, R., *Social Identity* (3rd ed.) (London 2008).

Johnston, H. and B. Klandermans (eds.), *Social Movements and Culture* (London 1995).

Kalb, D., M. van der Land, R. Staring, B. van Steenbergen and N. Wilterdink (eds.), *The Ends of Globalization: Bringing Society Back In* (Lanham, 2000).

Kearns, K.C., *Dublin's Lost Heroines: Mammies and Grannies in a Vanished City* (Dublin 2004).

Keenan, B., *Four Quarters of Light: A Journey Through Alaska* (London 2005).

Keohane, K. and C. Kuhling, *Collision Culture* (Dublin 2004).

Kingsolver, B., *Animal, Vegetable, Miracle: One Year of Seasonal Eating* (London 2007).

Klein, N., *No Logo* (London 2000).

Kockel, U. (ed.), *Landscape, Heritage and Identity: Case Studies in Irish Ethnography* (Liverpool 1995).

Kuhling, C. and K. Keohane, *Cosmopolitan Ireland: Globalisation and Quality of Life* (London 2007).

Lichtenstein, R., *On Brick Lane* (London 2007).

Liebes, T. and E. Katz, *The Export of Meaning: Cross-Cultural Readings of Dallas* (2nd ed.) (Cambridge 1993).

Long, N. and A. Long (eds.), *Battlefields of Knowledge: The Interlocking of Theory and Practice in Social Research and Development* (London 1992).

Luddy, M., *Prostitution and Irish Society 1800–1940* (Cambridge 2007).

MacLaughlin, J., *Ireland: The Emigrant Nursery and the World Economy* (Cork 1994).

Mac Laughlin, J. (ed.), *Location and Dislocation in Contemporary Irish Society: Emigration and Irish Identities* (Cork 1997).

Maffesoli, M., *The Time of the Tribes* (Cambridge 1996).

Mahon, E., C. Conlon and L. Dillon, *Women and Crisis Pregnancy* (Dublin 1998).

Mak, G., *An Island in Time: The Biography of a Village* (London 2010).

Marwick, A., *The Sixties: Cultural Revolution in Britain, France, Italy and the United States* (Oxford 1998).

Mason, A., *Community, Solidarity and Belonging* (Cambridge 2000).

Massey, D., *Spatial Divisions of Labour* (London 1984).

Massey, D., *Space, Place and Gender* (Cambridge 1994).

Massey, D., *For Space* (London 2007).

Massey, D. and P. Jess (eds.), *A Place in the World? Places, Cultures and Globalisation* (Oxford 1995).

McDonald, F. and J. Nix, *Chaos at the Crossroads* (Cork 2005).

McGee, H., *The SAVI Report: Sexual Abuse and Violence in Ireland* (Dublin 2002).

McLuhan, M., *Understanding Media* (New York 1964).

McMichael, P., *Development and Social Change: A Global Perspective* (4th ed.) (Los Angeles 2008).

McWilliams, D., *The Pope's Children* (Dublin 2006).

Mead, G.H., *Mind, Self and Society* (Chicago 1934).

Mills, C.W., *The Sociological Imagination* (Oxford 1959).

Mills, P., *Hymns to the Silence: Inside the Words and Music of Van Morrison* (London 2010).

Mlinar, Z. (ed.), *Globalisation and Territorial Identities* (Aldershot 1992).

Moorehead, C. *Martha Gellhorn: A Life* (London 2004).

Moran, C., *How To Be a Woman* (London 2011).

Murphy, D., *Visiting Rwanda* (Dublin 1998).

Nye, J., *The Paradox of American Power* (Oxford 2002).

O'Carroll, Í. and E. Collins (eds.), *Lesbian and Gay Visions of Ireland* (London 1995).

O'Connell, M., *Changed Utterly: Ireland and the New Irish Psyche* (Dublin 2001).

Pahl, R.E., *Whose City? And Further Essays on Urban Society* (Harmondsworth 1975).

Peet, R. and M. Watts (eds.), *Liberation Ecologies: Environment, Development, Social Movements* (London 1996).

Peillon, M. and M. Corcoran (eds.), *Place and Non-Place: The Reconfiguration of Ireland* (Dublin 2004).

Putnam, R.D., *Bowling Alone: The Collapse and Revival of American Community* (New York 2000).

Quinn, B., *The Atlantean Irish: Ireland's Oriental and Maritime Heritage* (Dublin 2004).

Ruane, M., *The Irish Journey: Women's Stories of Abortion* (Dublin 2000).

Rushdie, S., *Imaginary Homelands: Essays and Criticism 1981–1991* (London 1991).

Russell, M., *The Blessings of a Good Thick Skirt: Women Travellers and their World* (London 1994).

Russell, M., *Journeys of a Lifetime* (London 2002).

Ryan, P., *Asking Angela MacNamara: An Intimate History of Irish Lives* (Dublin 2011).

Sachs, W. (ed.), *The Development Dictionary* (London 1992).

Said, E., *Culture and Imperialism* (London 1993).

Scott, S., *Making Sense of Everyday Life* (Cambridge 2009).

Sen, A., *Development as Freedom* (New Delhi 2000).

Sklair, L. (ed.), *Capitalism and Development* (London 1994).

Slattery, M., *Key Ideas in Sociology* (Cheltenham 2003).

Symes, D. and A.J. Jansen (eds.), *Agricultural Restructuring and Rural Change in Europe* (Wageningen 1994).

Szwed, J., *The Man Who Recorded the World: A Biography of Alan Lomax* (London 2011).

Tharoor, S. *The Elephant, the Tiger and the Cellphone: Reflections on India in the Twenty-First Century* (New Delhi 2007).

Tóibín, C., *The South* (London 1990).

Tolstoy, L., *Anna Karenina* (London 1912).

Tomlinson, J., *Globalization and Culture* (Cambridge 1999).

Tovey, H. and P. Share, *A Sociology of Ireland* (Dublin 2003).

UNICEF, *Judicial Handbook on Combating Trafficking of Women and Children for Commercial Sexual Exploitation* (Geneva 2006).

Urry, J., *Consuming Places* (London 1995).

Vallely, F., *Companion to Irish Traditional Music* (Cork 2011).

van der Ziel, S. (ed.), *Love of the World: Essays by John McGahern* (London 2009).

Venkatesh, S., *Gang Leader for a Day* (London 2008).

Waters, J., *Jiving at the Crossroads* (Belfast 1991).

Waters, J., *Race of Angels: Ireland and the Genesis of U2* (Belfast 1994).

Wilson, R. and W. Dissanayake (eds.), *Global/Local: Cultural Production and the Transnational Imaginary* (Durham 1996).

Young, M. and P. Wilmott, *Family and Kinship in East London* (London 1957).